Handbook of Energy Policy for Local Governments

Handbook of Energy Policy for Local Governments

Edward H. Allen
Utah State University

Lexington Books
D. C. Heath and Company
Lexington, Massachusetts
Toronto   London

Library of Congress Cataloging in Publication Data

Allen, Edward H
Handbook of energy policy for local governments.

Bibliography: p.
Includes index.
1. Energy policy—United States—Handbooks, manuals, etc. I. Title.
HD9502.U52A4   352′.94′232   74-25074
ISBN 0-669-97386-6

Copyright © 1975 by D. C. Heath and Company

Published simultaneously in Canada

Printed in the United States of America

International Standard Book Number: 0-669-97386-6

Library of Congress Catalog Card Number: 74-25074

Contents

List of Figures

List of Tables

Preface

This handbook is designed to help local governments improve energy management, particularly in these times of shortage and crisis. It is aimed at the small municipal corporation, but contains information that will be helpful to counties and large cities as well. It offers detailed, step-by-step practical suggestions on how to handle commonly encountered energy supply problems. It also contains information on who to call at the state and federal offices to get more petroleum, propane, or other fuels, and on responses to energy emergencies and how to avoid them. There is a series of model energy management ordinances, and there is discussion of the legal problems of energy management. Aside from this introduction and its sequel (a general discussion of the role of local government in energy policy), this handbook is designed to cover three topics: the energy policy administrations at the federal and at the state levels, the energy policy alternatives of local government, and some basic information on managing energy emergencies and supply disruptions. An encyclopedic index offers a comprehensive guide to this handbook and a glossary of energy policy and related terms.

The information contained in this handbook is not intended as a final solution to any energy problem that may arise; nor is it a substitute for sound legal and consulting services. Our experience with managing energy shortages is too sparse to provide anything but broad guidelines. Rather, the suggestions presented here are but a synthesis of two years of national experience in energy policy; they are intended to provide the beginnings of an energy policy for local government and to stimulate some planning for energy crisis problems.

An earlier version of this handbook was prepared as part of a project to carry energy policy advice to local governments in western states. The project was funded by a grant from the Extension Service of the US Department of Agriculture. The goals of that project were:

To build the capability of local governments to manage the energy economy under their jurisdiction in accordance with the principles of public welfare protection and the preservation of the free market. The general aims of this management include: (1) minimize the possibility of a severe local crisis, (2) minimize the damages from energy emergencies over which the local government has no control (e.g., national emergencies, natural disasters, etc.), and (3) facilitate the constant flow of adequate stocks [of fuels] from the regular private and public suppliers during low risk periods.

The team assembled for this earlier project included: Edward H. Allen, project leader; Joe A. Green, research assistant; Virginia Ream, editorial and production assistant; H. Preston Thomas, legal consultant; and Calvin W. Hiibner, public administration consultant. This team worked under the able administration of the Extension Service, including: Charles W. McDougall, acting administrator; William V. Neely, project manager for this project; Clark Ballard, director of Extension Service, Utah State University.

While this handbook has been designed to provide accurate and authoritative information, the publisher is not engaged in rendering legal, accounting, or other professional service. If legal or other expert advice is required, the services of a competent professional should be sought.

Handbook of Energy Policy for Local Governments

1

How to Use this Handbook

There are three circumstances in which this handbook will prove of immediate use: in the event that an energy source or fuel supply is unexpectedly shut off, and emergency action is required; in the event that the near term (the immediate six-month period) is expected to bring shortages or curtailments, and preparation for a possible crisis is advisable; or in the event that potentially troublesome shortages are expected in the midterm (five to ten years), and programmatic action appears prudent.

Energy Emergencies

An energy emergency is a sudden, unexpected disruption of the balance between supply and demand that requires immediate action. Moreover, the cause of the disruption usually takes a secondary position to the need to redress the balance. Energy emergencies can result from interruptions in the normal flow of supply (electrical blackouts, petroleum shortfalls, ets.) or sudden fluctuations in demand (severe weather, changes in bulk power transmission arrangements, etc.). Responses to such emergencies require, first, that everything be done to ameliorate hardship and to reduce risks of additional damage, and second, that efforts be made to restore normal supply flows, replace interrupted supplies, relocate affected individuals or goods to uninterrupted areas, or impose conservation measures. Often extraordinary powers, such as martial law, are invoked by governments charged with managing such emergencies.

Chapter 10 of this handbook is devoted to the management of emergencies, particularly reducing hardship and further risks of damage. Two kinds of information are provided to help in emergencies: suggested executive actions to be carried out in any energy emergency, and actions suggested only for specific crisis: natural gas interruptions, electrical blackouts, etc.

If an emergency is unexpected, begin by reading the relevant pages in the appendix to chapter 10; follow that with a quick reading of the chapter itself, which provides basic instructions on setting up a crisis-management team. Finally, phone your state office of emergency services for advice and support.

If an emergency seems likely in a few days, seek advice on emergency management from your state office of emergency services and start reading this handbook with chapter 10. Following that chapter, then, set up a management team and charge them with the responsibility of elaborating a plan; they might want to read the relevant pages in the handbook for suggestions.

If an emergency is anticipated by more than a few days, consider some prophylactic measures. (Begin by reading chapters 6 and 7.) Moreover, if there is a possibility that the emergency will last more than a few days, some demand reduction (conservation) or reallocation measures might be considered. (Begin by reading chapters 7 and 9.)

In some cases escape from emergency conditions will require action to restore the normal flow of supplies, which may require federal or state help. (Read chapters 4 and 5.)

Anticipated Near-Term Crisis.

A number of events can cause you to anticipate a crisis six or more months in advance. The most common is notification by suppliers that they will not be able to fill their customary orders. A second important source of foreknowledge is a group of US government publications, particularly the *Monthly Energy Review,* published by the Federal Energy Administration's National Energy Information Center. Write to the center for a subscription at Washington, D.C., 20461; additional information on this valuable publication appears in chapter 8. Some larger jurisdictions may assign staff to periodic investigation of supply adequacy and discover an impeding crisis that way. Even the smaller communities may invite local suppliers to a meeting to discuss near-term adequacy.

If a crisis is expected in the near term, a range of alternatives is open. The Federal Energy Administration representative in your state could provide advice. Perhaps the crisis can be muted by federal or state aid or intervention. (Begin by reading chapter 3 and continue on to chapters 4 and 5 if appropriate.) Perhaps some local action, such as a conservation or a rationing program, a stockpiling effort, etc., would help minimize the dangers. (Begin with chapter 7, although some help may be provided by chapter 6 as well.)

Troubles in the Midterm

A series of midterm crises allows a greater flexibility of response, but at the same time, you face a sluggish and disinterested federal and state bureaucracy distracted by shorter-term problems. The essential objective is to improve the tools you have for dealing with energy emergencies or near-term crises. Particularly important will be long-term conservation programs (read chapter 9), providing for adequate energy storage facilities (read chapter 7), and setting up a good mechanism for monitoring energy flows in the jurisdiction (read chapter 8).

Problem Solving

This handbook contains a special "encyclopedic index" designed to provide answers to a range of specific energy administration and policy problems as well as to key you into the portion of the handbook that deals with that problem in greater depth. For example, if you need additional heating fuel oil, look in the index under "petroleum allocation, residential users," where you will find a short statement on how to proceed; entries under "heating emergency problems," "fuel oil emergency problems," and so forth also refer you to the same statement.

2

Energy and Public Policy: The Local Government Perspective

This chapter introduces the concept of local government energy policy and discusses the duties of local government in energy-policy matters, particularly as they relate to local responsibility for energy sensitive areas like health, welfare, employment, and economic growth. An appendix to this chapter provides an introduction to the energy industry and outlines some aspects of energy industry structure relevant to local-level policy.

Powers and Duties of Local Government in Energy Policy Matters

Local governments fall into two broad categories: those that are created in order to simplify the administration of state government powers, such as counties, and those that are an immediate reflection of a body politic and have been created, not primarily for the administrative convenience of the state, but rather for the delegation of local self-government powers to that body politic, such as the municipal corporation. This handbook is aimed largely at the municipal corporation, the powers of which tend to be somewhat broader than those of other types of local governmental units.

> A municipal corporation is a body politic created by organizing the inhabitants of a prescribed area, under the authority of the legislature, into a corporation with all the usual attributes of a corporate entity, but endowed with a public character by virtue of having been invested by the legislature with subordinate legislative powers to administer local and internal affairs of the community, and by virtue of its creation as a branch or agency of the state government to assist in the administration of the government of the state.[1]

The municipal corporation has powers and duties relevant to energy policy in both its corporate and municipal aspects.

In its corporate or proprietary character, a municipal corporation may own a constellation of facilities critical to the energy economy of its inhabitants. These properties may include energy supply facilities, such as

5

fuel yards, gas and electrical utilities, etc., and big energy consumers like water utilities, street lights, trash collection, and various emergency services, as well as other energy-related items. Managing these facilities has great impact on the adequacy of energy flow to all users in the jurisdiction, as well as those beyond it if, as is often the case, facilities or services are contractually provided to adjacent areas.

In its corporate character, the municipality must operate under the law governing all corporations and, with certain limitations based on its public character, enjoys all the rights of corporate personalities. As such, the municipal corporation may sue and be sued and, in a proper case, even be found criminally liable. In the energy area this means that any service guarantees, either express or implied, whether accepted by contract or imputed by tradition, are actionable under law; the corporation is not legally immune. For example, public utilities delivering electricity or gas are obligated to provide adequate, continuous service and, in general, are liable for damages resulting from service interruptions; municipally owned and operated utilities share that liability. In another case, the municipality must take reasonable care not to operate its energy facilities in a negligent manner. In a proper instance, failure to adopt and pursue a reasonable energy policy may constitute actionable negligence. For example, failure to acquire sufficient gasoline stocks to run the usual snow-removal program may in some instances be deemed negligent.

In its public character, a municipal corporation has a responsibility to execute in its jurisdiction the policies dictated by organic law and the state legislature, as well as a reasonable responsibility to protect the health, the safety, the morals, and the welfare of its inhabitants and provide for their comfort, convenience, and prosperity.

With regard to its ministerial administration of state policy and organic law, it can be said that municipal corporations are generally (but not always legally) responsible for the application of federal energy policy and programs within their jurisdictions. This is so because the states have been delegated certain duties and powers under federal energy legislation and thus have adopted as part of state energy policy these components of federal policy (chapter 5).

An increasing number of states are adopting energy policy statutes and programs of their own in addition to the federally inspired policies. The main impact of these policies appears to be the erosion of some of the powers traditionally exercised by local units. For example, California's legislation includes provisions that centralize power plant site licensing in one state agency; this may, in effect, limit the discretion of local governments with regard to zoning and certain licensing functions.

The "general welfare clause" controlling most municipal corporations confers both powers and duties upon the corporation to protect the health, safety, morals, and general welfare of its inhabitants. The scope of the powers conferred greatly exceeds that of the duties; thus, the corporation is not normally required to provide street lighting under the welfare clause, but the clause enables it to do so if it desires. In some cases state legislatures have statutorily required certain duties, such as providing police protection, and, in general, the courts have tended to view certain functions as logically imperative. Thus, a municipal corporation may, in a proper case, be found negligent if it does not provide for police, sanitation, and certain other basic services. It follows that the more closely an aspect of energy policy is tied to such imperatives, the more necessary it becomes. Thus, it seems clear that policies designed to provide gasoline for patrol cars, heat and light for city hospitals, and power for water and sewer systems may be viewed as compelling duties of the corporation.

Less legally compelling than these duties, but central to the concept of responsible government, is the commitment of a municipal corporation to promote the prosperity of its inhabitants. As recent experience demonstrates, energy supply interruptions may have a deleterious impact on employment and wage levels, may be a strong inflationary force, and may have other serious effects.

Local Energy Policy and Economic Health

A major difficulty with energy policy at any level of government is tied to the close relationship between energy availability and economic growth. Energy conservation policies are widely believed to have a dampening effect on economic growth. Certain analysts, however, have argued that conservation may not affect economic growth deleteriously if it is pursued through increases in efficiency rather than cutbacks in consumption; improving the efficiency of air conditioners, for example, may have as great an impact on energy consumption as restricting their use and would have a greatly reduced impact on the economy and on personal habits. Also qualifying as efficiency improvements would be actions to substitute energy-diffuse techniques for energy-intensive ones. For example, aluminum industry spokesmen recently announced a new process that may cut electricity use in the industry in half; wearing warm clothes in a cool room rather than light garments in a highly heated room is another example.

The social and economic impacts of several kinds of energy policies were recently examined by Ford Foundation researchers. Basically, Ford's researchers

constructed three different versions of possible energy futures for the United States through the year 2000.

The second scenario, *Technical Fix,* differs little from *Historical Growth,* [the first scenario involving no energy conservation measures] in its mix of goods and services. The rate of economic growth is very slightly slower, so that by 2000 the real GNP is nearly 4 percent less than in *Historical Growth* (but still more than twice as high as in 1973). This scenario reflects a conscious national effort to use energy more efficiently through engineering know-how—that is, by putting to use the practical, economical, energy-saving technology that is either available now or soon will be . . . if we were to apply these tech-

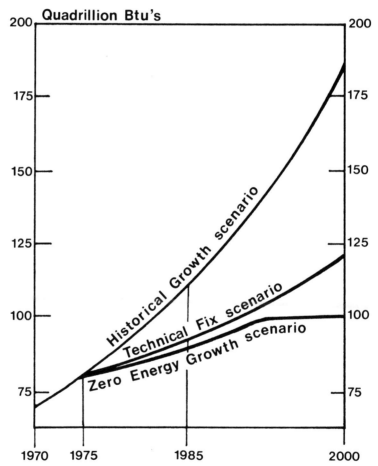

Source: Adapted from The Energy Policy Project of the Ford Foundation, "Exploring Energy Choices: A Preliminary Report," The Ford Foundation, © 1974, p. 40

Figure 2-1. Future Energy Consumption in the US: Three scenarios Developed by the Ford Foundation Researchers

niques consistently, an energy growth rate of 1.9 percent annually would be adequate to satisfy our national needs. This is little more than half the rate of *Historial Growth. Technical Fix* would use about 124 quadrillion Btu's.

Our *Zero Energy Growth* (ZEG) scenario represents a modest departure from that track. It would not require austerity, nor would it preclude economic growth. The real GNP in this scenario is approximately the same as in *Technical Fix,* and it actually provides more jobs. It includes all the energy-saving devices of *Technical Fix,* plus extra emphasis on efficiency. Its main difference lies in a small but distinct redirection of economic growth, away from energy-intensive industries toward economic activities that require less energy. An energy excise tax, by making energy more expensive, would encourage the shift. Compared with the other energy futures, a ZEG future would have less emphasis on making things and more on offering services— better bus systems, more parks, better health care. About 2 percent of GNP would be diverted through the higher energy taxes to these public purposes—purposes designed to enhance the quality of life, as defined in the scenario.[2]

The emphasis on efficiency is probably a good one at the local level as well. For example, in the long term an energy policy that focuses on management of gasoline stocks will not be as viable as one aiming to substitute mass transportation for private automobiles in commuting.

Appendix 2A: Industry Structure

Formulation of an energy policy requires some knowledge of the character of the energy industry. The following outline covers only the most basic elements. For a deeper knowledge turn to the materials listed in the bibliography that immediately follows this outline.

US Energy Consumption

Gross energy consumption in the United States was 75.6 quads (75.6 x 10^{15} Btu) in 1973 (table 2-1). This represented slightly more than 29 percent of world consumption. It is estimated that about 18 percent of the US total is used (by electrical utilities, for example) before it gets into the consuming sectors of the economy—leaving a "net energy input" to the US consumer of 62.2 quads. Consumption breakdowns by major sectors are shown in table 2-1.

US Energy Production

The United States produced only 62 quads (82 percent) of the 75.6 quads consumed in 1973. Domestic energy production reached a plateau in 1970 and has not increased since. While the US imported only 18 percent of its total energy consumption in 1973, most of that 18 percent was petroleum—the critical element in the transportation sector. More than one third of our oil is imported, of which about 22 percent comes from Canada, 20 percent from Venezuela, 9 percent from the Netherlands Antilles, 7 percent from Saudi Arabia, 7 percent from Nigeria, 6 percent from the Virgin Islands, and the remainder from a host of smaller areas.

Primary and Secondary Fuels

Primary energy sources, in distinction to secondary sources or "products," consist of raw fuels, such as coal, crude petroleum, natural gas, hydropower, nuclear power, etc. Secondary sources include fossil-fuel-generated electricity, refined oils, some synthetic gases, coke, etc. Primary sources would also include proposed solar heating and solar electric conversion schemes as well as geothermal power, kerogen (the crude product from oil-shale mining), and the like; secondary sources now under development

Table 2-1

US Gross Consumption of Energy Resources by Major Sources and Consuming Sectors (Trillion Btu).[a]

Consuming sectors	Anthracite	Bituminous coal and lignite	Natural gas dry[b]	Petroleum[c]	Hydropower[d]
Household and Commercial:					
1972............	75	312	7,642	6,667	—
1973 (preliminary)........	75	295	8,001	7,024	—
Industrial:					
1972.........	35	4,232	10,591	5,668	35
1973 (preliminary).......	29	4,425	10,825	6,043	35
Transportation:[g]					
1972............	—	4	790	17,264	—
1973 (preliminary).......	—	5	814	17,927	—
Electricity Generation, utilities:[d]					
1972............	40	7,797	4,102	3,134	2,911
1973 (preliminary)........	36	8,655	3,918	3,435	2,906
Miscellaneous and unaccount for:					
1972...........	—	—	—	233	—
1973 (preliminary)........	—	—	—	260	—
Total energy inputs:					
1972............	150	12,345	23,125	32,966	2,946
1973 (preliminary)........	140	13,380	23,558	34,689	2,941

Table 2-1 (continued)

Consuming Sectors	Nuclear Power [d]	Total gross energy inputs [e]	Utility electricity distributed [f]	Total net energy inputs	Percentage change from 1972
Household and commercial;					
1972	—	14,696	3,478	18,174	
1973 (preliminary)	—	15,395	3,727	19,122	+5.2
Industrial:					
1972	—	20,561	2,493	23,054	
1973 (preliminary)	—	21,357	2,671	24,028	+4.2
Transportation: [g]					
1972	—	18,058	17	18,075	
1973 (preliminary)	—	18,746	18	18,764	+3.8
Electricity generation, utilities: [d]					
1972	576	233	5,988		
1973 (preliminary)	853	260	6,416		+6.7
Miscellaneous and unaccounted for:					
1972	—	—		233	
1973 (preliminary)	—	—		260	
Total energy inputs:					
1972	576	72,108		59,536	
1973 (preliminary)	853	75,561		62,174	+4.8

[a] Gross energy is the total of inputs into the economy of the primary fuels (petroleum, natural gas, and coal, including imports) or their derivatives, plus the generation of hydro and nuclear power converted to equivalent energy inputs.

[b] Excludes natural gas liquids.

[c] Petroleum products including still gas, liquefied refinery gas, and natural gas liquids.

[d] Outputs of hydropower (adjusted for net imports or net exports) are converted to theoretical energy inputs calculated from national average heat rates for fossil-fueled steam-electric plants provided by the Federal Power Commission using 10,379 Btu per net kilowatt-hour. Energy inputs for nuclear power are converted at an average heat rate of 10,660 Btu per net kilowatt-hour based on information from the Atomic Energy Commission. Excludes inputs for power generated by nonutility plants, which are included within the other consuming sectors.

[e] Gross energy resource inputs with electricity generation shown as separate consuming sectors.

[f] Utility electricity generated and imported, distributed to the other consuming sectors as energy resource inputs. Distribution to sectors is based on sales reported in the Edison Electric Institute "Statistical Year Book of the Electric Utility Industry for 1972." Conversion of electricity to energy equivalent by sector was made at the value of contained energy corresponding to 100 percent thermal efficiency using a theoretical rate of 3412 Btu/kwhr.

[g] Includes bunkers and military transportation.

Source: Division of Fossil Fuels-Minerals Supply, Bureau of Mines, US Department of the Interior.

include a wide range of schemes for producing liquid and gaseous fuels from coal, developing the energy potential in organic wastes, and so forth.

Coal

Coal is classified by rank and by grade. The rank is a function of the heat content (Btu per pound) and the percentage of fixed carbon (versus moisture and volatile matter; see figure 2A-1). The grade of coal is a measure of its quality independent of rank; grade is determined on the basis of the content of ash, sulphur, various trace elements, and other impurities (table 2A-1). Total US coal production in 1973 was 569

Table 2A-1

Grades of Coal, Distribution, in Percent, or Identified United States Coal Resources According to Rank and Sulfur Content

| Rank | Sulfur Content (in percent) | | |
	Low 0-1	Medium 1.1-3.0	High 3
Anthracite	97.1	2.9	—
Bituminous coal	29.8	26.8	43.4
Subbituminous coal	99.6	.4	—
Lignite	90.7	9.3	—
All Ranks	65.0	15.0	20.0

million short tons (about 13.5 quads). Of the US coal resources (all ranks and grades), Paul Averit of the US Geological Survey concludes: "On a uniform Btu basis, US coal resources are larger than the combined domestic resources of petroleum, natural gas, oil shale, and bituminous sandstone." [3]

In 1971 there were some 5576 active coal-mining operations in the United States. These coal firms tend to fall into three categories: those that mine coal for general distribution, those that mine coal only for metallurgical use (largely for the steel industry), and those that mine only for use in the thermal-electric utility industry. Firms in these last two categories tend to be owned and operated by the utilities or companies they supply (the "captive industry model"). Most high-grade (low sulfur content) coal from eastern and midwestern mines is owned by metallurgical interests; western fields will be supplying more and more of the

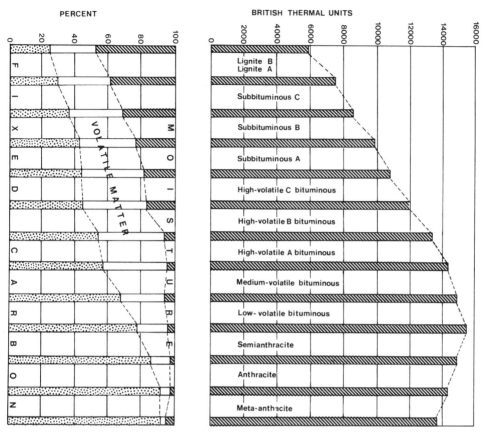

Source: Paul Averitt, "Coal"; in D.A. Brobst and W.P. Pratt, Editors. *United States Mineral Resources;* Geological Survey Professional paper 820. Washington, D.C. US Government Printing Office, 1973, p. 135.

Figure 2A-1: Comparison of Heat Values and Proximate Analysis of Coal of Various Ranks.

needs of the nation's electrical utilities, which currently burn about two-thirds of the US production.

Coal prices averaged $7.07 per ton (all ranks and qualities) in 1971; however, real prices may have tripled by 1974 and are expected to continue increasing. Three pressures are forcing prices upward: efforts by the reformed United Mine Workers Union to increase substantially the wages and benefits of UMW members, efforts to develop and market less easily accessible coal deposits, and additional quality requirements, such as EPA regulations, technical requirements of some of the new uses, etc., which prohibit the development of certain coal deposits. Indirect pressures on price include cost of transportation, financing costs, and a shortage of miners.

Under the authority of the Defense Production Act and the Federal Energy Administration Act, the FEA has the authority to set up and administer a coal allocation program. The first steps toward such a program were taken during the summer and fall of 1974. Other federal agencies that play an important role in the coal industry are the Department of the Interior, the Environmental Protection Agency, the Federal Power Commission, the Tennessee Valley Authority, and the Energy Resource and Development Administration (chapter 4).

Petroleum

US consumption of petroleum products for all uses in 1973 was 6.295 billion barrels, the equivalent of 34.7 quads. About 10 percent of this use was for other than fuel and power purposes, (asphalt, road oil, etc.). Some 35 percent of our petroleum came from abroad in 1973 and that percentage is growing. A handful of Mid Eastern countries dominate the world oil market by means of a cartel organization, the Organization or Petroleum Exporting Countries (OPEC). They have 60 percent of world reserves and produce 70 percent of the world's export oil. The effectiveness of this cartel is demonstrated by its ability to maintain world oil prices at artificially high levels, about three times that of US crude.

The petroleum industry in the United States consists of four sectors: crude exploration and production, refining, transportation, and marketing. Some of the biggest firms engage in all four operations (the majors), while others engage in only one or two of the operations, usually including refining (the independents). In the refinery sector, the majors appear to process about 83 percent of US refinery feedstocks, the independents handling the rest.

Crude production in the US has been declining since its 1970 peak of about 12 million barrels/day, and the big finds on the north slope of Alaska are only expected to reverse that trend temporarily. There are about 500,000 operating wells in the US. There is some question about the quantity of petroleum reserves remaining in the US and its continental shelf. Recent estimates by the Geological Survey and by Dr. King M. Hubbert conclude that the US has adequate reserves for only twenty-six-to-forty-five years and ten-to-eighteen years more of production respectively.[4] Even though great tax and other incentives exist for drilling exploratory wells, the number drilled has been declining. Some efforts have been made to render additional production from nearly depleted wells more attractive by allowing additional price increases on oil from these "stripper wells."

Crude prices are still largely government controlled (chapter 4), even though other price controls have been lifted. A two-tier pricing system, one price for domestically produced crude, another for imported crude, has emerged. Because this price differential acts as a disincentive to investment in domestic crude and related industries, the FEA is formulating an equalization program. In the long run, many observers argue that the price of domestic crude can be expected to rise somewhat, while international prices should fall off a bit.

As of 1971 the refining sector in the US was composed of some 247 refineries (operated by 129 companies) with an aggregate capacity of slightly less than 14 million barrels per day. Thus, with US refineries operating at capacity, we would have needed to import about 1.5 million barrels per day of refined products. Refining capacity is inadequate, and new capacity is slow in being added. There is some contention over why this is so. The Federal Trade Commission, arguing that the sluggish response is intentional, has filed an antitrust suit against a number of majors.[5] A typical refinery produces 45 percent gasoline, 22 percent distillate fuel oils, 8 percent jet fuel, 7 percent residual fuel oil, 3 percent kerosene, 2 percent lubricants; and a quantity of residue.

Refineries are subject to federal regulation and monitoring, notably by the FEA, which is empowered to determine output products mix and price. Equally important is the fact that most refining capacity is held by the major integrated oil companies, and thus the corporate decisions governing them tend to reflect a broad range of issues including the international competitiveness of the refinery in question.

Most refineries receive crude feedstock via pipeline, and most pipeline mileage is owned by the major integrated oil companies and is regulated as a common carrier by the Interstate Commerce Commission. It is estimated that about 27 percent of refinery product is carried by pipeline to depots where it is stored for transshipment by truck or rail.[6]

Natural Gas

Natural gas is produced in the US from wells, often in association with petroleum. In 1973 the US consumed some 23.6 quads of natural gas.

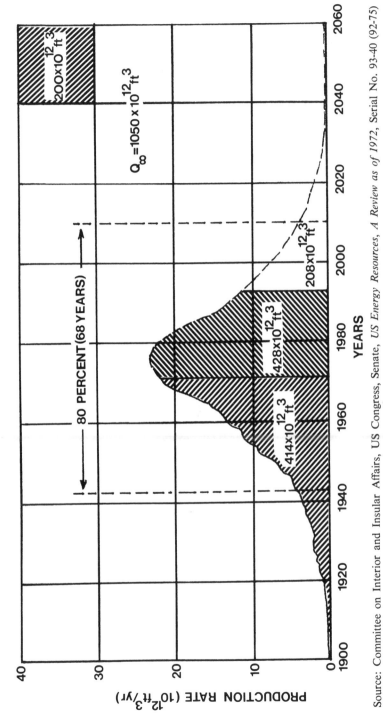

Figure 2A-2: Natural Gas Production Cycle
(Estimate as of 1972 of Complete Cycle of Natural-Gas Production in Coterminous United States.

Source: Committee on Interior and Insular Affairs, US Congress, Senate, *US Energy Resources, A Review as of 1972*, Serial No. 93-40 (92-75) Washington, D.C., US Government Printing Office, 1974, p. 148.

Proved reserves have been falling off in recent years, and production has just begun falling as well. Natural gas is the only important fossil fuel that is near exhaustion (figure 2A-2). Plans and construction are now underway to replace failing reserves with supplies manufactured from coal and other hydrocarbons. Imports of natural gas (almost exclusively from Canada) amounted to some 5 percent of consumption in 1974 but are expected to shrink due to new restrictions imposed by Canada.

The natural gas industry, unlike the petroleum industry, is not extensively integrated among the three chief sectors handling production, long-distance transmission, and marketing. The most salient characteristic of the industry is the restrictive complex of regulatory agencies overlaying it. The Federal Power Commission regulates the interstate commerce in natural gas, and state public utility commissions regulate the marketing. A diversity of regulative policies has resulted in a three-tier price system; in 1973 the price of FPC regulated gas was roughly 20 cents per thousand cubic feet, average intrastate gas price was about 50 cents, and imports in cryogenic tankers were running at about $1 per thousand CF. Shortage problems, however, have led to vigorous efforts toward better integration of the regulation system. The major such proposal currently under discussion involves the deregulation of natural gas prices; a freer price structure, it is argued, would result in a more efficient industry and might, in fact, revise the rather gloomy reserve picture as industry profit growth revitalizes exploratory activity. The FPC apparently blunted deregulation proposals recently by a succession of price increases.

An equally salient aspect of the natural gas industry is the traditional discrimination among classes of users, particularly the contractual distinction between "firm" and "interruptible" customers. Gas suppliers are legally obligated to provide continuous and adequate service to firm customers or pay damages. Interruptible customers, however, may be cut off (or have their service "curtailed") during periods of shortage; for putting up with this possible inconvenience they pay a lower price. Most interruptibles have capability to burn alternative fuels; in many areas residential users are enjoined by law from entering into interruptible contracts. In 1973 the FPC revised their regulations to the effect that no one using natural gas as a boiler fuel could enter into a firm contract.

Since 1970 supply deficiencies have been growing. Deficiencies during the winter of 1974 were estimated to be 80 percent greater than 1973 curtailments. The bulk of curtailed customers are electrical utilities and industrial users.

Appendix 2B: Bibliography on Industry Structure

National Policy Aims and Issues

Arthur D. Little, Inc. *Energy Policy Issues for the United States During the Seventies.* Arlington, Va.: National Energy Forum, 1971.

Berlin, Edward, Charles J. Cicchetti, William J. Gillen. *Perspective on Power.* Cambridge, Mass.: Ballinger Publishing Company, 1974.

Committee on Interior and Insular Affairs, U.S. Congress, House. *Selected Readings on the Fuels and Energy Crisis.* Washington: U.S. Govt. Print. Off., 1972.

Committee on Interior and Insular Affairs, U.S. Congress, Senate. *Energy Policy Papers,* Serial No. 93-43 (92-78). Washington: U.S. Govt. Print. Off., 1974.

Davis, P. H. *Energy Politics.* New York: St. Martin's Press, 1974.

DeGolyer and MacNaughton. *Report on National Energy Policy.* Washington: Office of Naval Petroleum and Shale Reserves, 1971.

Denton, Jesse C. *An Assessment of the National Energy Problem.* Washington: National Science Foundation, 1971.

Fabricant, Neil and Robert M. Hallmen. *Toward a Rational Power Policy.* New York: George Braziller, 1971.

Federal Energy Administration. *Executive Summary, Project Independence.* November 1974. Other Project Independence reports on various topics are available also.

Ford Foundation. *A Time to Choose.* Cambridge, Mass.: Ballinger Publishing Company.

Freeman, S. David. *Energy—The New Era.* New York: Walker and Company, 1974.

Holdren, John and Phillip Herrera. *Energy.* San Francisco: Sierra Club, 1971.

Intertechnology Corporation. *The U.S. Energy Problem.* Washington: National Science Foundation, 1971.

Lawrence, R. M., N. I. Wengert et al. *The Energy Crisis: Reality or Myth.* The Annals of the American Academy of Political and Social Science. Philadelphia: 1973.

Mitre Corporation. *Energy, Resources and the Environment—Major U.S. Policy Issues.* Washington, 1972.

Morrison, David L., Donald E. Erb, and William T. Reid. *Energy in the Urban Environment.* New York: American Institute of Aeronautics and Astronautics, 1971. (American Institute of Aeronautics and Astronautics. Paper No. 71-526).

21

National Economic Research Associates, Inc. *Energy Consumption and Gross National Product in the United States: An Examination of a Recent Change in the Relationship.* Washington, 1971.

National Rural Electric Cooperative Association. Research Division. *Dimensions of the National Power Crisis; Basic Information in Question-and-Answer Form for the Consumer-Owners, Officers, Directors and Staffs of Rural Electric Utility Systems.* Washington, 1971. Research Paper No. 71-3. 16 p.

Pikl, I. James, Jr. *Public Policy and the Future of the Petroleum Industry.* Laramie: University of Wyoming, 1970.

Starr, Chauncey. "Energy and Power." *Scientific American.* September 1971.

Symposium on Coal and Public Policies, Knoxville, Tenn., 1971. *Proceedings.* Oak Ridge, Tenn.: Oak Ridge National Laboratory, 1971.

U.S. Department of the Interior. *U.S. Energy—A Summary Review.* Washington. 1971.

Utton, Albert E. *National Petroleum Policy: A Critical Review.* Albuquerque: University of New Mexico Press, 1970.

Projections of Future Demand and Supply

American Gas Association. Dept. of Statistics. *Gas Utility and Pipeline Industry Projections: 1969-1973, 1975, 1980, 1985, and 1990.* New York, 1969.

———. *The Natural Gas Supply Problem.* New York, 1971.

Colorado School of Mines. *Future Natural Gas Resources Will Be Expensive to Find.* Golden, Col., 1971.

Cornell Department of Agricultural Economics. *Predicting the Past and Future in Electricity Demand.* February 1972.

Culberson, O. L. *The Consumption of Electricity in the United States.* Oak Ridge, Tenn.: Oak Ridge National Laboratory, 1971. (Oak Ridge National Laboratory. Publication ODNL-NSF-EP-55).

Federal Energy Administration. *Petroleum Supply and Demand in the Non-Communist World.* Washington, 1974.

Federal Power Commission. *The Gas Supplies of Interstate Natural Gas Pipeline Companies.* Washington, 1970.

Hittman Associates. *Electric Power Supply and Demand Forecasts for the U.S. through 2050.* Washington. U.S. Govt. Print. Off., 1971.

Mooz, W. E. *Some Facts on the Supply of Energy.* Washington: National Science Foundation, 1970.

National Academy of Engineering. *U.S. Energy Prospects: An Engineer-Viewpoint.* Washington, 1974.

National Petroleum Council. *U.S. Energy Outlook.* 1625 K Street, N.W., Washington, D.C., 20006, 1971.

Rand Corporation. *The Growing Demand for Energy,* 1971.

Stanford Research Institute. *Patterns of Energy Consumption in the United States,* 1972.

University of Denver Research Institute. *Future Gas Consumption in the United States.* Denver, Col. 1973.

U.S. Atomic Energy Commission. *Forecast of Growth of Nuclear Power.* Washington, 1971.

U.S. Bureau of Natural Gas. *National Gas Supply and Demand, 1971-1990.* Washington, 1972.

U.S. Bureau of Mines. *Analysis of the Availability of Bituminous Coal in the Appalachian Region.* Washington, 1971.

Resources and Their Management

Altman, Manfred, Maria Telkes, and Martin Wolf. *The Energy Resources and Electric Power Situation in the United States.* Philadelphia: University of Pennsylvania Press, 1971.

Braymer, Daniel T. *The Controlled Energy Growth Concept: The National Economy and Prospects for Power.* New York: National Electrical Manufacturers Association, 1971.

Committee on Interior and Insular Affairs, U.S. Congress, Senate. *U.S. Energy Resources: A Review as of 1972,* Serial No. 93-40 (92-7). Washington: U.S. Govt. Print. Off., 1974.

Committee on Science and Astronautics, U.S. Congress, House. Subcommittee on Science, Research, and Development. Task Force on Energy. *Energy—The Ultimate Resource.* Washington: U.S. Govt. Print. Off., 1971. (Serial J).

Department of the Interior, Bureau of Mines. *Commodity Data Summaries.* January 1972.

———. Mineral Industry Surveys. *Bituminous Coal and Lignite Distribution,* quarterly.

———. Mineral Industry Surveys. *Petroleum Statement,* monthly.

Department of Interior. *Energy Fact Sheets by States and Regions.* Washington, 1973.

Department of the Interior, U.S. Geological Survey. Professional papers (various titles and authors) compiled in *United States Mineral Resources,* published annually. Washington.

Federal Energy Administration. *Petroleum Situation Report.* Washington: National Energy Information Center.

Federal Power Commission. *National Power Survey.* Various years.

————. *Natural Gas Supply and Demand 1971-1990*. February 1972.

Hottel, H. C. and J. B. Howard. *New Energy Technology, Some Facts and Assessments*. Cambridge, Mass.: M.I.T. Press, 1971.

Hubbert, M. K. "The Energy Resources of the Earth." *Scientific American* 225 (1971): 60.

Hudson Institute. *Energy and Energy Fuels,* 1972.

Makhijani, A. B. and A. J. Lightenberg. *An Assessment of Energy and Materials Utilization in the U.S.A*. September 1971.

National Coal Association. *Bituminous Coal Facts—1970*. Washington, 1970.

Stanford Research Institute. *End Uses of Energy*. Menlo Park, Calif., 1971.

Utility Executive Conference. *Proceedings: Building the Power Systems of the Seventies*. Chicago, 1971.

Production

Department of the Interior, Bureau of Mines. *Progress in Coal Gasification*. Washington, November 1970.

Institute of Gas Technology. *Coal Gasification for Electric Power*. Washington, April 1972.

Miller, A. J. et al. *Use of Steam-Electric Power Plants to Provide Thermal Energy to Urban Areas*. Oak Ridge, Tenn.: Oak Ridge National Laboratory, 1971.

Walker, H. K. *Electric Power Reliability*. Oak Ridge, Tenn.: Oak Ridge National Laboratory, 1971.

Transportation

American Transit Association. *Transit Fact Book*. Washington, 1971.

Automobile Manufacturers Association. *Automobile Facts and Figures*. Detroit, annual.

Department of Transportation. *A Statement on National Transportation Policy*. 1971.

————, Federal Aviation Administration. *Statistical Handbook of Aviation,* 1970.

————, Federal Highway Administration. *Estimated Motor Vehicle Travel in the U.S. and Related Data,* 1971.

————. *Highway Statistics/1970,* 1971.

————. *Transportation Projections: 1970 and 1980,* 1971.

Fraize, W. E. and J. K. Dukowicz. *Transportation Energy and Environmental Issues.* Washington: Mitre Corporation, 1972.

Hirst, Eric. *Energy Consumption for Transportation in the U.S.* Oak Ridge, Tenn.: Oak Ridge National Laboratory, March 1972.

Transportation Association of America. *Transportation Facts and Trends,* 8th ed. Washington, 1971.

Conservation

Executive Office of the President. *Potential for Energy Conservation.* Washington: U.S. Govt. Print. Off.

McDonald, Stephen L. *Petroleum Conservation in the United States: An Economic Analysis.* Baltimore: Resources for the Future, Johns Hopkins Press, 1971.

National Power Survey. Technical Advisory Committee on Transmission. *The Transmission of Electric Power.* Washington: Federal Power Commission, 1970.

Environmental Impacts

Abrahamson, D. E. *Environmental Cost of Electric Power.* New York: Scientists' Institute for Public Information, 1970.

California Institute of Technology. Environmental Quality Laboratory. *People, Power, and Pollution.* Pasadena, 1971.

Cornell Workshop on Energy and the Environment, Ithaca, New York, 1972. *Summary Report.* Washington: U.S. Govt. Print. Off., 1972.

Council on Environmental Quality. *Environmental Quality.* Washington: U.S. Govt. Print. Off., Annual Reports.

Department of Commerce. *Automotive Fuels and Pollution.* Washington: U.S. Govt. Print. Off., March 1971.

Edison Electric Institute. Plant Siting Task Force." Major Electric Power Facilities and the Environment." New York: Edison Electric Institute, 1970.

Energy Policy Staff, Office of Science and Technology. *Electric Power and the Environment.* Washington: U.S. Govt. Print. Off., 1970.

Murdoch, William W. *Environment: Resources, Pollution and Society.* Stamford, Conn.: Sinauer Associates, 1971.

National Petroleum Council. *Environmental Conservation—The Oil and Gas Industries.* Washington, 1971-1972.

Odum, H. T. *Environment, Power and Society*. New York: Wiley-Interscience, 1971.

Schurr, S. H., ed. *Energy, Economic Growth, and the Environment*. Baltimore: Johns Hopkins Univ. Press, 1972.

U.S. Atomic Energy Commission. Division of Reactor Development and Technology. *Thermal Effects and U.S. Nuclear Power Stations*. Washington: U.S. Govt. Print. Off., 1971.

Regulatory Policy and Issues

American Public Power Association, and National Rural Electric Cooperative Association. *Artificial Restraints on Basic Energy Sources*. Washington, 1971.

Bryan, R. H., B. L. Nichols, and J. N. Ramsey. *Summary of Recent Legislative and Regulatory Activities Affecting the Environmental Quality of Nuclear Facilities*. Oak Ridge, Tenn.: Oak Ridge National Laboratory, 1971.

Committee on Interior and Insular Affairs, U.S. Congress, Senate. *Oversight—Mandatory Petroleum Allocation Program*. Washington: U.S. Govt. Print. Off., 1974.

Kahn, A. E. *The Economics of Regulation: Principles and Institutions*. New York: Wiley, 1970.

National Academy of Engineering. *Engineering for Resolution of the Energy-Environment Dilemma*. Washington, 1971.

Finance, Taxes, and Prices

Bowers, H. I. and M. L. Myers. *Estimated Capital Costs of Nuclear and Fossil Power Plants*. Oak Ridge, Tenn.: Oak Ridge National Laboratory, 1971.

Committee on Interior and Insular Affairs. *Financial Requirements of the Nation's Energy Industries*. Washington: U.S. Govt. Print. Off., 1973.

Olson, C. E. *Cost Considerations for Efficient Electricity Supply*. East Lansing: Michigan State University, 1970.

Sanders, Diana E. *The Inverted Rate Structure, an Appraisal*. Part I, *Residential Usage*. Albany: Department of Public Service, State of New York, 1972.

Sparling, R. C. et al. *Financial Analysis of the Petroleum Industry*. New York: Chase Manhattan Bank, 1971.

U.S. Atomic Energy Commission. *Updated Cost-Benefit Analysis: U.S. Breeder Reactor Program*. Washington: U.S. Govt. Print. Off., 1972.

U.S. Bureau of Mines. *Transportation Costs of Fossil Fuels*. Washington: U.S. Govt. Print. Off., 1971.

Institutional Structure and Industry Statistics

American Petroleum Institute. *Annual Statistical Review—U.S. Petroleum Industry Statistics*. Washington: U.S. Govt. Print. Off.

Atomic Energy Commission. *Annual Reports to Congress*. Washington: U.S. Govt. Print. Off., various years.

Edison Electric Institute. *Statistical Yearbook of the Electric Utility Industry,* annual.

Federal Energy Administration. *Monthly Energy Review*. Washington: U.S. Govt. Print. Off.

Federal Power Commission. *Annual Reports*. 1971.

Independent Petroleum Association of America. *The Oil Producing Industry in Your State*. Tulsa, Okla., annual.

Intertechnology Corporation. *The U.S. Energy Problem*. Vols. I and II, 1971.

Lapp, R. E. *A Citizen's Guide to Nuclear Power*. Washington: New Republic, 1971.

National L-P Gas Association. *L-P Gas Market Facts,* annual, West Monroe Street, Chicago, Illinois, 60603.

Netschert, B. C., A. Gerber, and I. Stelzer. *Competition in the Energy Markets*. Washington: National Economic Research Associates, 1970.

Office of Coal Research. *Annual Reports*. Washington: U.S. Govt., Print. Off., various years.

U.S. Department of the Interior, Bureau of Mines. *International Coal Trade*. Washington: U.S. Govt. Print. Off., monthly.

Vennard, E. *The Electric Power Business*. 2d ed. New York: McGraw-Hill, 1970.

3

Energy Administration in the United States

The responsibility for administration of energy policy in the United States is divided among a large group of federal, regional, and state agencies. County, municipal, and other local agencies also play important roles. A comprehensive effort to study and report on all phases of energy policy, administration, and problems has been undertaken by the Senate Committee on Interior and Insular Affairs, under Henry M. Jackson. The publications of this committee constitute the richest and most reliable source of information on energy questions. The Jackson committee's work was authorized by Senate Resolution 45, adopted May 3, 1971, which called for a "National Fuels and Energy Policy Study." Bibliographies of the committee's publication are available from the committee staff.

The committee found that because of dispersal of responsibility and programs, no unified national energy policy existed until the attempt to devise one under the aegis of Project Independence. (See Project Independence summary in the appendix to this chapter.) At the same time, Congress and the president have been working to develop mechanisms for administering a national policy. The emergence of the Federal Energy Administration (FEA) in June 1974, followed by the creation of the Energy Resources and Development Administration in October, were the culmination of these efforts. Both agencies are under the direct supervision of the president, who has in effect delegated that authority to Rogers C. B. Morton, secretary of the interior, who chairs the cabinet-level advisory group, the Energy Resources Council. Nonetheless, a handful of agencies with missions in areas other than energy have in the past indirectly affected the national and local energy situation, and still do. Currently, the other key agencies in the administration of energy policy at the federal level include: the Department of the Interior, the Environmental Protection Agency, and the Federal Power Commission. Lesser roles are given to the Department of Commerce, the Nuclear Regulatory Commission, the Department of State, and others.

Many federal agencies, however, have missions that bear upon some aspect of energy policy in a general sense. Missions that are particularly important to the energy situation include: management of fuel resources on public lands, federal water policy, economic regulation and development policy, tax policy, national security policy, health, safety, and environmental management policy, and research and development policy. These missions are assigned to a number of federal agencies, listed below.[1]

Agencies with Direct Impact on Energy Flows

Policy Formation: Planning and Forecasting

Executive Office of the President: Domestic Council; Office of Management and Budget, Natural Resources Division; Federal Council for Science and Technology; Oil policy Committee; Joint Board on Fuel Supply and Transport.
   Department of Commerce: Office of Energy Programs.
   Department of Defense: Army Corps of Engineers; Office of Naval Petroleum and Oil Shale Reserves.
   Department of Interior: Alaska Power Administration; Bonneville Power Administration; Bureau of Land Management; Bureau of Reclamation; Mining Enforcement and Safety Administration; Southeastern Power Administration; Southwestern Power Administration.
   Department of Justice: Anti-Trust Division.
   Department of the Treasury: General Council.
   Energy Research and Development Administration.
   Energy Resources Council.
   Environmental Protection Agency: Office of Air Quality and Planning Standards; Office of Radiation Programs; Office of Solid Waste Management Programs.
   Federal Energy Administration.
   Federal Power Commission.
   Tennessee Valley Authority.
   Water Resources Council

Policy Formation: Formulation of Standards, Rules, Regulations, and Rates

Executive Office of the President: Office of Management and Budget; Natural Resources Division; Oil Policy Committee.
   Department of Defense: Office of Naval Petroleum and Oil Shale Reserves.
   Department of Interior: Alaska Power Administration; Bonneville Power Administration; Bureau of Land Management; Bureau of Mines;

Bureau of Reclamation; Bureau of Sport Fisheries and Wildlife; Mining Enforcement and Safety Administration; Southeastern Power Administration; Southwestern Power Administration.

Department of State: Office of Fuels and Energy.

Environmental Protection Agency: Office of Air Quality and Planning Standards; Office of Radiation Programs.

Federal Energy Administration.

Federal Highway Administration.

Federal Maritime Commission.

Federal Power Commission.

General Services Administration: Federal Supply Service.

Nuclear Regulatory Commission: Office of Nuclear Reactor Regulation; Office of Nuclear Material Safety and Safeguards.

Securities and Exchange Commission.

Small Business Administration.

Tennessee Valley Authority.

Policy Formation: Preparation and Review of
Proposed Legislation

Executive Office of the President: Domestic Council; Office of Management and Budget, Natural Resources Division.

Department of Interior: Alaska Power Administration; Bonneville Power Administration; Bureau of Land Management; Bureau of Mines; Bureau of Reclamation; Geological Survey.

Department of Justice: Land and Natural Resources Division.

Environmental Protection Agency: Office of Air Quality and Planning Standards; Office of Radiation Programs.

Federal Power Commission.

Tennessee Valley Authority.

Policy Implementation: Operations of Energy Facilities
or Production or Marketing of Energy Resources

Department of Agriculture: Rural Electrification Administration.

Department of Defense: Army Corps of Engineers.

Department of the Interior: Alaska Power Administration; Bonneville Power Administration, Bureau of Land Management; Bureau of Mines; Bureau of Reclamation; Mining Enforcement and Safety Administration; Southeastern Power Administration; Southwestern Power Administration.

Department of Transportation: Office of the Secretary (grants-in-aid for natural gas pipeline safety).

Energy Research and Development Administration.

Environmental Protection Agency: Office of Solid Waste Management Programs.

Federal Energy Administration.

General Services Administration: Federal Supply Service.

Small Business Administration.

Tennessee Valley Authority.

Policy Implementation: Management of Energy Resources

Department of Agriculture: Forest Service.

Department of Defense: Army Corps of Engineers; Office of Naval Petroleum and Oil Shale Reserves.

Department of Interior: Alaska Power Administration; Bonneville Power Administration; Bureau of Land Management; Bureau of Mines; Bureau of Reclamation; Mining Enforcement and Safety Administration; Southeastern Power Administration; Southwestern Power Administration.

Energy Research and Development Administration.

Environmental Protection Agency: Office of Solid Waste Programs.

Tennessee Valley Authority.

Policy Implementation: Enforcement of Rules and Regulations

Executive Office of the President: Import Appeals Board.

Department of Defense: Army Corps of Engineers; Office of Naval Petroleum and Oil Shale.

Department of Interior: Bureau of Land Management; Bureau of Mines; Bureau of Reclamation; Bureau of Sport Fisheries and Wildlife; Mining Enforcement and Safety Administration.

Department of Justice: Land and Natural Resources Division.

Energy Research and Development Administration.

Environmental Protection Agency: Office of Radiation Programs.

Federal Energy Administration.

Federal Power Commission.

Federal Trade Commission.

General Services Administration: Federal Supply Service.

Oil Import Appeals Board.

Securities and Exchange Commission.

Tennessee Valley Authority.

Policy Implementation: Research and Development,
Data Collection, and Technical Assistance

Executive Office of the President: Federal Council on Science and Technology.

Department of Defense: Office of Naval Petroleum and Oil Reserves.

Department of the Interior: Alaska Power Administration; Bonneville Power Administration; Geological Survey; Office of Oil and Gas.

Department of State: Office of Fuels and Energy.

Energy Research and Development Administration: Solar Energy Coordination and Management Project.

Environmental Protection Agency: Office of Radiation Programs; Office of Solid Waste Management Programs.

Federal Energy Administration.

Federal Power Commission.

General Services Administration: Federal Supply Service.

National Aeronautics and Space Administration: Space and Power Program.

National Science Foundation.

Tennessee Valley Authority.

Water Resources Council.

Agencies with Indirect Impact on Energy Flows

Policy Formation: Planning and Forecasting.

Executive Office of the President: Council on Environmental Quality; Office of Management and Budget, Budget Review Division; President's Panel on Oil Spills; President's Task Force on Air Pollution.

Department of Transportation: Office of the Secretary, Transportation Planning Research and Development; Federal Highway Administration.

Environmental Protection Agency: Office of Water Programs.

Policy Formation: Formulation of Standards, Rules,
Regulations, and Rates

Executive Office of the President: Council on Environmental Quality; Office of Management and Budget, Budget Review Division.

Department of Transportation: Coast Guard (oil pollution).

Department of the Treasury: Internal Revenue Service.

Environmental Protection Agency: Office of Water Programs.
Interstate Commerce Commission.

Policy Formation: Preparation or Review of
Proposed Legislation

Executive Office of the President: Council on Environmental Quality;
Office of Management and Budget, Budget Review Division.
   Department of the Treasury: Internal Revenue Service.
   Department of Transportation: Federal Highway Administration.
   Environmental Protection Agency: Office of Water Programs.

Policy Implementation: Operation of Facilities of
Production of Resources having Unique
Impacts upon the Energy System

Department of Commerce: Federal Maritime Administration.
   Department of Defense: Defense Supply Agency, Central Supply and
Maintenance.
   Department of Transportation: Coast Guard (oil pollution); Federal
Highway Administration.
   Civil Aeronautics Board (subsidy of Air Service).

Policy Implementation: Management of Resources

Department of Defense: Defense Supply Agency, Central Supply and
Maintenance.
   Department of Transportation: Federal Highway Administration.
   Department of the Interior: Bureau of Indian Affairs.

Policy Implementation: Enforcement of Rules
and Regulations

Department of Transportation: Coast Guard (oil pollution).
   Department of Justice: Anti-Trust Division.
   Department of Treasury: Internal Revenue Service.
   Environmental Protection Agency: Office of Water Programs.
   Interstate Commerce Commission.

Policy Implementation: Research and Development, Data
Collection, and Technical Assistance

Department of Commerce: Bureau of the Census.

Department of Defense: Defense Supply Agency, Central Supply and Maintenance.

Department of Housing and Urban Development: Department participation in urban transportation research and development.

Department of Transportation: Office of the Secretary (transportation planning research and development); Coast Guard (oil pollution); Urban Mass Transportation Administration; Federal Highway Administration.

Environmental Protection Agency: Office of Water Programs.

National Aeronautics and Space Administration: Office of Applications.

Energy Policy Agencies

In 1974 energy policy administration was reformed by Congress, which created three new agencies: the Energy Resources Council, the Federal Energy Administration, and the Energy Research and Development Administration. The FEA has the overall federal responsibility for managing and mitigating the energy crisis; it is best known as the agency responsible for fuel allocation and pricing. It is the lead agency for all energy policy except R&D policy and the agency of greatest relevance to local governments in developing local policy to handle shortages and manage conservation programs. In other policy areas, such as energy resource development problems, the FEA competes for the lead with Interior, Agriculture, HUD, and others. A special section on the FEA is included in this part of the handbook; summaries of selected programs of other agencies follow:

Energy Resource and Development Administration

ERDA's responsibilities, though not yet fully worked out, are likely to be limited to finding long-term solutions to the energy crisis. Much of their work is expected to focus upon development of new kinds of energy sources and, therefore, may not be directly relevant to crisis policy at the local level. However, if they develop an effort in the conservation area, they may become relevant.

Bureau of Land Management (Department of the Interior)

The BLM issues leases and various permits under which oil, gas, coal, oil shale, tar sands, geothermal and various other energy resources are extracted from federal lands and the outer continental shelf. The BLM is forced to conduct its business systematically and openly by virtue of its responsibility to prepare and review environmental impact statements (EISs) on its actions. Local government can directly influence BLM decisions through the EIS preparation and review process.

Bureau of Reclamation (Department of the Interior)

The Bureau of Reclamation operates the majority of the federally owned hydroelectric plants in the seventeen contiguous western states. The bureau cooperates with other federal agencies to review environmental impact statements for projects involving disposition of waters.

Geological Survey (Department of the Interior)

In the energy area the USGS is best known for its annual inventory of US mineral resources. In addition, however, USGS cooperates with other agencies in formulating mineral-leasing policies, reviewing and supervising certain leases, and is expected to play a leading role in supervising the development of outer continental shelf resources.

Office of Energy Programs (Department of Commerce)

Of note for local government are the responsibilities of this agency in promoting voluntary conservation programs in industry and commerce; much useful material on conservation is available from this office.

Environmental Protection Agency

Because most aspects of the energy production cycle produce effluents, most energy industry activities fall within the regulatory authority of one or more of EPA's air and water pollution control programs. Additionally, the EPA cooperates in the review and preparation of environmental impact statements.

US Army Corps of Engineers (Department of Defense)

The Corps of Engineers regulates certain aspects of design and construction of overhead transmission lines, pipelines, and any structure, discharge, or water use impacting on navigable waters and water courses, including the outer continental shelf.

Federal Power Commission

This independent regulatory commission administers the federal authority over interstate commerce in the natural gas and electrical utilities. Of major interest to local governments are the FPC powers to influence local tariffs for gas and electricity by their powers over interstate rates, FPC's power to force the commencement or discontinuance of service, and its publications on the utilities.

Nuclear Regulatory Commission

The NRC was created to receive the regulatory functions relinquished by the disbanded Atomic Energy Commission. The NRC supervises the nuclear fuel cycle, including: license and regulation of commercial power reactors and regulation of the handling of radioactive materials.

Oil Policy Committee

This interagency committee advises the FEA's office of oil and gas on oil and gas import matters. Any action taken by the FEA under the oil import program may be appealed by the affected party to the Oil Import Appeals Board.

Office of Natural Resources and Energy (Department of the Treasury).

This office acts as liaison between the federal energy policy network and those sections of Treasury concerned with various economic policy issues: taxes, monetary policy, balance of payment problems, etc.

Congressional Committees

Among the most effective ways to approach the federal government is through your senator or congressman. In particular, several congressional committees deal directly with energy matters.

In the Senate, the Committee on Interior and Insular Affairs supervises the National Fuels and Energy Policy Study and is a likely place to begin with a request for new legislation or intervention with federal executives. Of occasional interest may be the Armed Services Committee (it has some interest in fossil fuel reserves and materials required for defense or preparedness) and the Finance Committee's Subcommittee on Energy.

In the House, three committees are of direct interest: Interstate and Foreign Commerce (includes electrical transmission and energy transportation generally), Interior and Insular Affairs (energy resource development and conservation), and Public Works, Subcommittee on Energy (hydropower, port facilities, etc.). The Science and Astronautics Committee may be of help in the area of energy R&D.

Finally, the Joint Committees on Economic Policy and on Atomic Energy may be of interest in their respective areas.

Appendix 3A: Excerpts from the Project Independence Summary (FEA Print, November 1974)

Introduction

—[This] report is an evaluation of the Nation's energy problem . . . [it] contrasts the broad strategic options available to the U.S.: increasing domestic supply, conserving and managing energy demand, establishing standby emergency programs. The strategies are evaluated in terms of their impact on: development of alternative energy sources, vulnerability to import disruptions, economic growth, inflation and unemployment, environmental effects, regional and social impacts.

Background

Domestic energy demand has been growing at 4-5 percent per year. The U.S. was self-sufficient in energy through about 1950, but our situation has deteriorated rapidly since then. Coal production is still at 1940's levels; crude oil production has been declining since 1970; natural gas consumption has been exceeding new discoveries since 1968; our dependence on foreign oil had grown to 35 percent of domestic petroleum consumption in 1973. The world oil market is dominated by several Middle East countries [with] 60 percent of world reserves [and producing] 70 percent of world oil exports. The 1973 embargo demonstrated our domestic vulnerability to insecure imports. The embargo affected 14 percent of U.S. petroleum consumption; its economic impact was a $10-20 billion drop in GNP; 400,000 additional people were unemployed at its peak.

Alternative Energy Strategies

U.S. options to reduce vulnerability fall into three distinct categories. While each has significant impact, a national energy policy will probably combine elements from each.

Accelerating Domestic Supply

Federal policies to lease the Atlantic OCS [outer continental shelf], re-open the Pacific OCS and tap the Naval Petroleum Reserves can dramatically increase domestic oil production. At $7 prices, domestic production by 1985 could rise from 8.9 MMBD to 12.8 MMBD. At $11 prices, production could reach as high as 17 MMBD, although less is needed to achieve zero imports. Shale oil production could reach one MMBD in 1985. Accelerating nuclear power plant construction does not reduce imports much; in general, it replaces new coal-fired power plants. Accelerating synthetic fuel production . . . may not be practical in the 1985 time frame.

Accelerating domestic energy production could be inhibited by several key constraints. In the short term, many shortages of materials, equipment, and labor will persist. By 1985, however, most critical shortages will be overcome sufficiently to meet the requirements of the accelerated supply scenario. Financial and regulatory problems in the utility and railroad industries could hamper their ability to purchase needed facilities and equipment. Water availability will be a problem in selected regions by 1985.

Energy Conservation and Demand Management

Energy conservation actions can reduce demand growth to about 2 percent per year between 1972 and 1985. To achieve reductions beyond those induced by price could require new standards on products and buildings, and/or subsidies and incentives. Major actions could include standards for more efficient new autos, incentives to reduce miles traveled, incentives for improved thermal efficiency in existing homes and offices and minimum thermal standards for new homes and offices. Petroleum demand could be reduced by 2.2 MMBD by 1985. Electricity consumption could be reduced from 12.3 quads to about 11.0 quads in 1985, compared with 5.4 in 1972.

Demand management can further reduce dependence on limited oil and gas supplies by actions that involve switching from petroleum and natural gas consumption to coal or coal-fired electric power.

Emergency Programs

Standby conservation or curtailment measures can reduce vulnerability. Depending on the level of demand in 1985, curtailment measures in response to an embargo can cut consumption by 1-3 MMBD. At higher world oil prices curtailment is less effective because there is less "fat" in energy consumption. [Curtailment measures] involve almost no cost when not needed and relatively small administrative costs and some economic impact when implemented; they can be instituted in 60-90 days.

Emergency storage is cost-effective in reducing the impact of an embargo. Storage to insure against a one MMBD cutoff for one year would cost $6.3 billion over ten years; one MMBD interruption of oil supply for one year during that period could cost the economy $30-40 billion. This cost effectiveness holds for any level of insecure imports and applies if there is a one-in-five chance of one disruption in ten years.

Comparison of Alternative Energy Strategies

Import Vulnerability

Domestic supply and demand actions can greatly reduce U.S. vulnerability to import disruptions by 1985. At $7 per barrel oil with all supply and demand actions implemented, 3 MMBD could still be subject to cutoff; at $11, either all the demand actions or only a portion of the supply strategy would completely eliminate our vulnerability. Domestic supply and demand strategies are cheaper in economic terms than imported oil or any other emergency option. At either $7 or $11, they have a lower present resource cost than imports, and reduce insecure imports.

After domestic actions, standby demand curtailment is most effective in reducing vulnerability. Demand curtailment and storage can be designed to buffer against large levels of insecure imports.

Economic and Regional Impacts

Accelerating domestic supply or reducing demand will mean lower energy costs for the Nation and, hence, higher economic growth. Reduced energy costs will benefit lower income groups. The economy can absorb the increased financial costs of reducing vulnerability.

Environmental Impacts

The conservation strategy has the lowest environmental impact. A demand management strategy which substitutes coal for oil and gas will result in the greatest increase in environmental impact over the base case. The accelerated supply strategy has mixed environmental impacts. Air pollution is lower due to more nuclear plants and increased oil and gas production. Solid waste is up dramatically due to increased shale oil production. Many virgin resource areas will be disturbed for the first time.

Major Uncertainties

If demand is much less sensitive to price than is assumed, we will be much more vulnerable in 1977 and in 1985 at higher world oil prices; mandatory energy conservation measures or diversification and acceleration of supply hedge against this uncertainty.

Literally all the new oil production forecast comes from frontier areas in Alaska and the Atlantic OCS, or from improved tertiary recovery techniques. If the frontier areas do not prove productive, 1985 domestic production could decline to 5 MMBD at $7 oil prices; and at $11, with accelerated supply actions, total production could still not exceed about 11 MMBD.

Policy Implications

Although $11 world oil prices make achievement of self-sufficiency easier, the United States is still better off economically with lower world oil prices. The implementation of a limited number of major supply or demand actions could make us self-sufficient. By 1985, we could be at zero imports at $11, and down to 5.6 MMBD of imports at $7 prices. Not all of these actions may be warranted, but they indicate we have significant flexibility when one considers: some projected imports in 1985 are from secure sources, some insecure imports can be insured against, and not all of the supply and demand actions must be implemented to achieve the desired result.

Accelerating domestic supply, while economic, has some important drawbacks. It will adversely affect environmentally clear areas. It requires massive regional development in areas which may not benefit from or need increased supply. It is a gamble on as yet unproved reserves of oil and gas. It may well be constrained by key materials and equipment shortages.

Implementing a conservation strategy has positive environmental effects and alleviates constraint problems, but it requires intervention and regulation in previously free market areas, and it results in increased nonmarket costs due to more limited individual choice and changed lifestyles.

While cost effective, there are several important ramifications to a storage program. It will take a few years to implement and our vulnerability will be greatest during that period. It requires more imports now, which will act to sustain cartel prices in the near term. We could suffer major capital losses—$4 billion for each one billion barrels stored if the world oil price drops from $11 to $7.

Our actions to increase domestic self-sufficiency could have an appreciable impact on world oil price. US reduction in imports can make even $7 hard for OPEC to maintain. World oil price reductions could jeopardize domestic energy investments and could require price guarantees or other supports.

Any domestic energy policy must be designed to resolve uncertainties and minimize the risk of not anticipating world oil prices correctly. Policy programs should include actions to reduce domestic uncertainty, such as exploring the frontier areas. Policies may be needed to avoid or defer major investments or actions if they involve significant costs of being wrong, until world uncertainty is reduced. A flexible and dynamic approach must be balanced against the need for a stable long-term policy which encourages domestic energy investment.

4

Federal Energy Policy Administration

The federal agencies with key responsibilities to see that the nation's immediate energy needs are met are: the Energy Resources Council, the Federal Energy Administration, the Federal Power Commission, the Department of Interior, and the Nuclear Regulatory Commission.

The Energy Resources Council

The Energy Reorganization Act states that the Energy Resources Council shall:

(1) insure communication and coordination among the agencies of the Federal Government which have responsibilities for the development and implementation of energy policy or for the management of energy resources;

(2) make recommendations to the President and to the Congress for measures to improve the implementation of Federal energy policies or the management of energy resources with particular emphasis upon policies and activities involving two or more Departments or independent agencies; and

(3) advise the President in the preparation of [further] reorganization recommendations.[1]

The council is currently operating as the nation's top federal energy policy-making body, with FEA. ERDA, and the others reporting to it (even though many of these agencies are statutorily required to report directly to the president). For local governments, the council may represent an appeals forum on some decisions made by FEA, Interior, etc.

As with much of the energy administration set up in the past two years, the Energy Resources Council and the hierarchical structure it imposes on the administration of federal energy policy are quite possibly temporary. The Energy Reorganization Act requires that the president provide Congress with additional reorganization proposals by June 30, 1975. Specifically, the Congress wants to consider three alternative reorganizational acts for energy administration: (1) the creation of a new cabinet-level

45

Department of Energy and Natural Resources, (2) the creation of an Energy Policy Council, or (3) "a consolidation in whole or in part of regulatory functions concerning energy." [2] These proposals are described in the appendix to this chapter.

The Federal Energy Administration

According to the Federal Energy Administration Act, the FEA was chartered to "conserve scarce energy supplies, to insure fair and efficient distribution of, and the maintenance of fair and reasonable consumer prices for, such supplies, to promote expansion of readily usable energy sources, and to assist in developing policies and plans to meet the energy needs of the Nation." [3]

The FEA is headed by an administrator, who is directly responsible for all actions taken to meet the nation's energy needs. He advises the president and the Congress on energy policy, assesses the adequacy of energy resources to meet demand, and develops plans for state and local government participation in resolving energy problems. He is also expected to promote stability in energy prices, assure energy programs are fair, develop and implement voluntary and mandatory energy conservation programs, and recommend policies on import and export of energy. The administrator must also insure that all actions and regulations are evaluated for their impact on the various sectors of the economy. This evaluation is to be made as much as possible in consultation with state and local governments. Responsibility for collecting and analyzing energy-related data is also given to the FEA, and the administrator is required to publish all information. FEA publications are distributed by their Office of Public Affairs (Office of Public Affairs; Federal Energy Administration; Washington, D.C., 20461).

Also of interest to local governments is the Office of Private Grievances and Redress. All appeals concerning regulations and actions go through this office (Washington, D.C., 20461).

To the FEA has fallen the administration of the Mandatory Petroleum Allocation Program, the Propane Allocation Program, the Priority Delivery of Coal Program, and several others.

Petroleum Allocation

Under the authority of the Emergency Petroleum Allocation Act of 1973, the administrator of the FEA set up allocation procedures for all petroleum products in the United States and its territories. The program is to be suspended during period of surplus, and authority for the program will expire June 30, 1975 unless extended by legislation. FEA as well as congressional spokesmen have privately stated that the allocation program is likely to remain with us for a decade or more. Court tests have largely affirmed the legitimacy of the program, though some important issues await resolution.

In an energy crisis, the Mandatory Petroleum Allocation Program provides a major means of procuring extra petroleum supplies. Thus, it is important for local officials to understand the fundamental character of the mandatory allocation regulations. The purposes of the mandatory program are to facilitate operations by small refiners, to see that refined petroleum products and liquefied petroleum gas are distributed equitably, and to provide a reserve of fuel for priority users. This is accomplished by requiring suppliers to use a system of formula allocations, reports, appeals, and application procedures. In effect the federal government has attempted to replace the oligarchic energy marketplace with a formal bureaucracy.

Because of their fluidity, it is impossible to include an up-to-date copy of the program's regulations in this handbook. However, some excerpts from the Emergency Petroleum Allocation Act which describe the program are included in the appendix. The FEA liaison officer in each state has the specific assignment of being up to date on all new aspects of the mandatory regulations.

Fundamentally, the rules of the mandatory program serve to divide up as fairly as possible the fuel available. To do this, a base period was established for each type of fuel, which then serves as the user's basic fuel entitlement. This basic entitlement may be adjusted by the supplier under certain conditions and may be further adjusted if the user applies for an increase in this allocation. The circumstances under which these adjustments are made are set forth in the FEA regulations. Every user entitled to an allocation is guaranteed a supplier. It should be noted that two users having the same volume of allocation but different suppliers may not receive the same actual volume of product. This is because prime suppliers may have different allocation fractions within a given state. Each supplier's allocation fraction is determined by dividing his supply obligation into the amount of product available in a given state; for instance, if a supplier had a supply obligation of 1,000,000 gallons of diesel fuel and only had 900,000 gallons of diesel fuel available for that month, his allocation fraction would be 90 percent. The rules do nothing to improve the supply situation; rather, they aim to prevent any one user from suffering any more than any other. For emergencies and other contingencies a percentage of the more commonly used petroleum stocks are "set aside"; this reserve stock is managed by state officials (the state

"Setaside"). The mandatory program enlists the supplier as the agent for equitable allocation. However, because of the potential for discrimination among users by suppliers, articles in the regulations protect the user. In particular, all suppliers are required to supply all of their wholesale purchasers of record as of the base period (1972 for motor gasoline, middle distillate, and aviation fuels; 1973 for residual fuel oil; and October 3, 1972 through April 30, 1973 for propane). Suppliers are not required to supply wholesale purchasers not serviced during the base period, unless assigned to do so by the FEA or under the state setaside program. All wholesale users and end-users (except civil air carriers, utilities, and space heating users) are entitled to buy a quantity of fuel based either on their purchases in the base year or, for certain essential public services and critical industries, a quantity based on their current requirements. Some other key provisions of the regulations are:

Adjustments. The regulations set forth procedures for adjustments between wholesale purchasers and suppliers, and between end-users and suppliers.

State Setaside. For each state in which they operate, refiners, importers, and prime suppliers are required to set aside a specific percentage of the fuel they supply each month. This applies to motor gasoline, distillate, propane, and residual fuel oils. This setaside is to be used by the state offices of petroleum allocation (the SOPAs) in meeting emergency and hardship needs. Such hardship needs will be handled at the direction of the state on a case-by-case basis. Any retail supplier who is ordered by the state to deliver fuel for such emergency needs will do so from working stocks and will have that amount of fuel replenished by his supplier.

Space Heating. Space-heating customers of distillate and residual oils have been required to turn down their thermostats by 6 degrees Fahrenheit in homes and schools, and 10 degrees in most other buildings. Fuel distributors are assigned the impossible task of monitoring their space-heating customers (by using degree-day formulas). Distributors must warn customers who do not cooperate that they will only receive enough fuel to maintain the lowered temperatures.

Utilities. Electric utilities receive FEA-ordered fuel oil cut-backs if necessary in a manner that provides an equal percentage reduction in power transmissions by all utilities.

Aviation. Civil air carriers and public aviation, except air taxi/commercial operators, are allocated fuel by the FEA National Office. All matters pertaining to the allocation of aviation fuels for general aviation, air taxi/commercial operators, public aviation, and nonflying users of aviation fuels are addressed to the appropriate supplier. These allocations will be calculated by suppliers based on either base period use or current requirements.

Retail Gasoline Stations. Retail gasoline stations are not required to keep detailed allocation records similar to other suppliers. These retail dealers are encouraged to attempt to fill the current requirements of known priority customers, and to attempt to distribute their stocks equitably among all other users.

Supplier's Sources. Each supplier who purchases products covered by the program is a wholesale purchaser in the eyes of his supplier. Therefore, his supplier must apply the same allocation rules covering all wholesale purchasers in determining his allocations to that supplier.

If a supplier or customer desires an increased amount of fuel, the regulations specify that he is to file form FEO-17, "Request for Assignment of Supplier or Adjustment of Base Period Supply Volume." Copies of this form can be acquired through the state Office of Petroleum Allocation or the state FEA Liaison Office.

Propane and Butane Allocation

The mandatory allocation regulations covering propane and propane/butane mixes were promulgated on January 15, 1974 and are similar to those for petroleum: allocations are made to priority users based upon current requirements or actual historical use during the base period October 3, 1972 through April 30, 1973.

Allocation levels are currently set as follows: 100 percent of current requirements for agricultural production, dispensing stations or resellers selling only bottled propane in quantities up to 15,000 gallons per year, emergency services, energy production, sanitation services, telecommunications services, passenger transportation services, and medical and nursing buildings; 95 percent of base-period volume for all residential use; 90 percent of base-period volume (with certain other limits) for commercial, industrial, other transportation, petrochemical, and school use; and limited quantities for peak shaving by gas utilities, based on amounts contracted for or purchased for delivery during the base period.

All other uses of propane are nonpriority uses. Priority users requesting amounts of propane in excess of the entitlement amounts cited above will have those excess amounts considered as for nonpriority uses.

Coal Allocation

The Priority Delivery of Coal Program is a contingency plan to force delivery of coal needed for national defense in the event of a coal shortage.

> Section 101 (a) of the Defense Production Act of 1950, as amended, authorizes the President "to require that performance under contracts or orders (other than contracts of employment) which he deems necessary or appropriate to promote the national defense shall take priority over performance under any other contract or order, and, for the purpose of assuring such priority, to require acceptance and performance of such contracts or orders in preference to other contracts or orders by any person he finds to be capable of their performance. . . ." Section 4 of the Executive Order No. 11790, dated June 25, 1974 (39 FR23185), delegates to the Administrator of the FEA the President's authority under the Act, "as it relates to the production, conservation, use, control, distribution, and allocation of energy. . . ." [4]

FEA has announced no other plans to allocate coal, although they do plan to provide oil to coal-users in shortfall areas, provided such users have oil-burning capability.

The Federal Power Commission

The Federal Power Commission is an independent regulatory agency empowered to license and regulate nonfederal hydroelectric installations, all electric utilities engaged in interstate commerce (nearly all utilities are), and the interstate transportation of natural gas.

Electricity Allocation

Under the Federal Power Act, the FPC has authority to allocate electrical power in emergencies. Rules for such allocations were proposed on August 30, 1974 (39 FR 31654). The relevant section of the Federal Power Act states:

> 202 (c) . . . whenever the Commission determines that an emergency exists by reason of a sudden increase in the demand for electric energy, or a shortage of electric energy or of facilities for the generation or transmission of electric energy, or of fuel or water for generating facili-

ties, or other causes, the Commission shall have authority, either upon its own motion or upon complaint, with or without notice, hearing, or report, to require by order such temporary connections of facilities and such generation, delivery, interchange, or transmission of electric energy as in its judgment will best meet the emergency and serve the public interest. If the parties affected by such order fail to agree upon the terms of any arrangement between them in carrying out such order, the Commission, after hearing held either before or after such order takes effect, may prescribe by supplemental order such terms as it finds to be just and reasonable, including the compensation or reimbursement which should be paid to or by any such party.[5]

Under FPC rules covering section 202 (c), any application for relief must show that the applicant has exhausted all other reasonable avenues to find additional power and that the shortage is potentially serious (greater than 10 percent normal load) and imminent (thirty days or less for coal, fifteen for petroleum-fired plants, 20 percent curtailment projected to last thirty days or more for gas-fired or hydroelectric facilities). Applications are to be filed with the Federal Power Commission, Washington, D.C., 20426. However, to meet the requirement that other possibilities be exhausted first, applicants should get in touch with the state public utility regulatory commission to work out a strategy.

In planning a strategy or in an actual emergency, some action under section 202 (d) of the Federal Power Act might be considered:

202 (d) During the continuance of any emergency requiring immediate action, any person engaged in the transmission or sale of electric energy and not otherwise subject to the jurisdiction of the Commission may make such temporary connections with any public utility subject to the jurisdiction of the Commission or may construct such temporary facilities for the transmission of electric energy in interstate commerce as may be necessary or appropriate to meet such emergency, and shall not become subject to the jurisdiction of the Commission by reasons of such temporary connection or temporary construction: *Provided,* that such temporary connection shall be discontinued or such temporary construction removed or otherwise disposed of upon the termination of such emergency: *Provided further,* that upon approval of the Commission permanent connections for emergency use only may be made hereunder.[6]

Before taking action under 202 (d), the FPC offices in Washington should be contacted.

Natural Gas Allocation

By virtue of the Natural Gas Act of 1938, as amended, the FPC has the power to allocate natural gas and to fix its price. Pursuant to that power and in view of the scarcity of natural gas, the FPC has made a policy statement on gas, followed by a series of orders.

In the statement of policy the FPC announces their intent to adjust natural gas curtailments so as to insure "the protection of deliveries for the residential and small volume consumers who cannot be safely curtailed on a daily basis" and to require instead "reduction in deliveries for large volume interruptible sales." They add:

> We are impelled to direct curtailment on the basis of end-use rather than on the basis of contract simply because contracts do not necessarily serve the public interest requirement of efficient allocation of this wasting resource. In time of shortage, performance of a firm contract to deliver gas for an inferior use, at the expense of reduced deliveries for priority uses, is not compatible with consumer protection. . . .
>
> Finally, if curtailment reaches beyond the level of interruptible service into firm contract service, we commit ourselves to the proposition that large volume boiler fuel usage is inferior and should be curtailed before other firm service.[7]

In their order 467, the commission promulgated this policy. In its substantive portion the order states:

> The national interests in the development and utilization of natural gas resources throughout the United States will be served by recognition and implementation of the following priority-of-service categories for use during periods of curtailed deliveries by jurisdictional pipeline companies:
>
> (1) Residential, small commercial (less than 50 Mcf on a peak day).
>
> (2) Large commercial requirements (50 Mcf or more on a peak day), firm industrial requirements for plant protection, feedstock and process needs, and pipeline customer storage injection requirements.
>
> (3) All industrial requirements not specified in (2), (4), (5), (6), (7), (8), or (9).
>
> (4) Firm industrial requirements for boiler fuel use at less than 4,000 Mcf per day, but more than 1,500 Mcf per day, where alternate fuel capabilities can meet such requirements.
>
> (5) Firm industrial requirements for large column (3,000 Mcf or

more per day) boiler fuel use where alternate fuel capabilities can meet such requirements.

(6) Interruptible requirements of more than 300 Mcf per day, but less than 1,500 Mcf per day, where alternate fuel capabilities can meet such requirements.

(7) Interruptible requirements of intermediate volumes (from 1,500 Mcf per day through 3,000 Mcf per day), where alternate fuel capabilities can meet such requirements.

(8) Interruptible requirements of more than 3,000 Mcf per day, but less than 10,000 Mcf per day, where alternate fuel capabilities can meet such requirements.

(9) Interruptible requirements of more than 10,000 Mcf per day, where alternate fuel capabilities can meet such requirements.

The priorities-of-deliveries set forth above will be applied to the deliveries of all jurisdictional pipeline companies during periods of curtailment on each company's system; except, however, that, upon a finding of extraordinary circumstances after hearing initiated by a petition filed under Section 1.7 (b) of the Commission's Rules of Practice and Procedure, exceptions to those priorities may be permitted.

The above list of priorities require the full curtailment of the lower priority category volumes to be accomplished before curtailment of any higher priority volumes is commenced. Additionally, the above list requires both the direct and indirect customers of the pipeline that use gas for similar purposes to be placed in the same category of priority.

The tariffs filed with this Commission should contain provisions that will reflect sufficient flexibility to permit pipeline companies to respond to emergency situations (including environmental emergencies) during periods of curtailment where supplemental deliveries are required to forestall irreparable injury to life or property.[8]

Additionally, proposals pending would free natural gas prices from government regulation. The purpose of these proposals is twofold: to achieve better allocation of natural gas through market mechanisms, and to improve the investment climate in the natural gas industry.

The Nuclear Regulatory Commission

The NRC is a regulatory commission whose five members serve at the pleasure of the president. The commission was created by the Energy Reorganization Act of 1974 (P.L. 93-438) which, in effect, transferred the regulatory and licensing functions of the Atomic Energy Commission (abolished by the same act) to the new commission. The NRC licenses and regulates commercial power reactors and the radioactive material associated with them. While the commission regulates the nuclear fuel cycle, it does not regulate the production, pricing, or distribution of the electricity the reactors generate; this is the responsibility of the FPC. Nonetheless, NRC decisions and practices have quite a strong indirect effect on the volume and price of nuclear electricity. NRC has direct allocative and pricing authority over all radioactive materials, including reactor fuels. The NRC's offices of Nuclear Reactor Regulation and of Nuclear Material Safety and Safeguards administer the commission's authority in these areas.

Energy Prices

The energy industry in the United States directly affects nearly every other sector of the economy; any economic disturbance there has very wide ripple effects almost immediately in such basic sectors as metals and finished durable goods. Thus, the Cost of Living Council began regulating energy prices during 1971. Currently, the FEA sets prices on petroleum products, while the FPC sets prices for electricity and natural gas. Coal prices are not now regulated by federal agents, although the FEA probably has the authority to do so. FEA sets prices on the basis of cost of production for crude producers, refiners, resellers and retailers; in addition, FEA regulates the price of real property used by gasoline retailers. In general, FEA posts a price allowable; under the regulations, no one is allowed to pay or charge a price above that. Price increases cannot be made without giving the FEA thirty days notice; FEA may at any time during that thirty-day period issue an order disapproving, modifying, suspending or deferring the proposed increase.

FPC sets the prices allowable for sale of natural gas or electricity in interstate commerce. Before approving any increase, FPC must hold a hearing, and each order issued by the FPC is subject to appeal.

Appendix 4A: Excerpts from *Federal Energy Organization, A Staff Analysis*

I. High Level Surveillance of Energy System and Provision for Policy Advice

The high-level surveillance of the energy system and provision for policy advice has been the subject of several major proposals: S. 3330 introduced by Senator Jackson, the "National Resources Planning and Policy Act of 1972"; H.R. 15752 introduced by Congressman Keith to create a Council on Energy Policy, which would advise the President and the Congress on energy policy and exercise leadership in formulating that policy; S. 3802 introduced by Senators Hollings and Magnuson to create a Council on Energy Policy, which would serve as a central point for collecting and analyzing energy statistics, coordinating all Federal energy activities, and preparing long-range plans related to energy; S. 3641 introduced by Senator Pearson to create a National Energy Advisory Board; and H.R. 258 introduced by Congressman Murphy to create a Commission on Fuels and Energy. . . .

II. Coordination and Augmentation of Federal Operating Programs

Two major proposals have emerged addressing the coordination and augmentation of Federal operating programs: the proposal of the Ash Council for creation of an Energy and Mineral Resources component in a proposed Department of Natural Resources and the President's subsequent, modified proposal to Congress. . . .

President's Proposal for a Department of Natural Resources

The proposed creation of a Department of Natural Resources (DNR) would combine policy making and operations for energy research and development. This department would be one of the four proposed super departments for Natural Resources, Community Development, Human

Printed for the Senate Committee on Interior and Insular Affairs, Serial No. 93-6 (92-41), Washington: Government Printing Office, 1973.

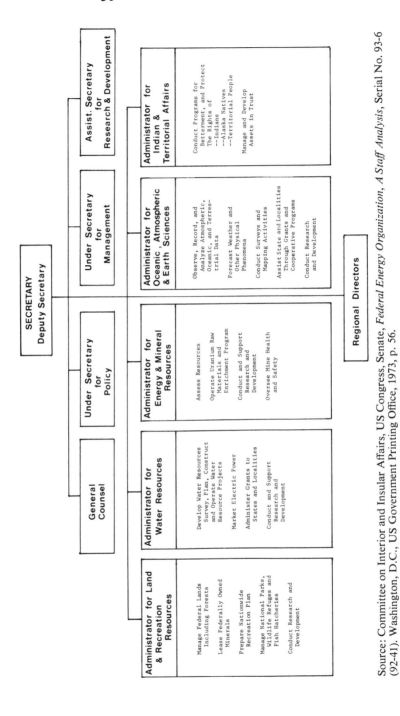

SECRETARY
Deputy Secretary

General Counsel

Under Secretary for Policy

Under Secretary for Management

Assist. Secretary for Research & Development

Administrator for Land & Recreation Resources

Manage Federal Lands Including Forests

Lease Federally Owned Minerals

Prepare Nationwide Recreation Plan

Manage National Parks, Wildlife Refuges and Fish Hatcheries

Conduct Research and Development

Administrator for Water Resources

Develop Water Resources Survey, Plan, Construct and Operate Water Resource Projects

Market Electric Power

Administer Grants to States and Localities

Conduct and Support Research and Development

Administrator for Energy & Mineral Resources

Assess Resources

Operate Uranium Raw Materials and Enrichment Program

Conduct and Support Research and Development

Oversee Mine Health and Safety

Administrator for Oceanic, Atmospheric & Earth Sciences

Observe, Record, and Analyze Atmospheric, Oceanic, and Terrestrial Data

Forecast Weather and Other Physical Phenomena

Conduct Surveys and Mapping Activities

Assist State and Localities Through Grants and Cooperative Programs

Conduct Research and Development

Administrator for Indian & Territorial Affairs

Conduct Programs for Betterment, and Protect The Rights of
--Indians
--Alaska Natives
--Territorial People

Manage and Develop Assets in Trust

Regional Directors

Source: Committee on Interior and Insular Affairs, US Congress, Senate, *Federal Energy Organization, A Staff Analysis*, Serial No. 93-6 (92-41). Washington, D.C., US Government Printing Office, 1973, p. 56.

Figure 4A-1. The Proposed Department of Natural Resources.

Resources, and Economic Affairs. The Department of Natural Resources would comprise five major administrations, one of which would be for energy and mineral resources. . . .

Energy Administration as Proposed by
the Ash Council

The President's Advisory Council on Executive Organization (Ash Council) in its November 1970 memoranda to the President entitled "Establishment of a Department of Natural Resources/Organization for Social and Economic Goals" recommended the creation of an Energy and Mineral Resources component in a proposed Department of Natural Resources.

IV. Coordination and Augmentation of Federal Regulatory Functions

Two major proposals which address the coordination and augmentation of Federal regulatory functions as they relate to fuels and energy are the Ash Council recommendations and a study by the Bar of the City of New York, "Electricity and the Environment."

Ash Council Report on Independent Regulatory Agencies

The President's Advisory Council on Executive Organization (the Ash Council) submitted its report on the independent regulatory agencies to the President on January 30, 1971. However, the recommendations were not submitted to the Congress.

The report made several far-ranging recommendations for restructuring the various commissions. Seven regulatory agencies were considered—the Interstate Commerce Commission, the Civil Aeronautics Board, the Federal Maritime Commission, the Securities and Exchange Commission, the Federal Power Commission, the Federal Trade Commission, and the Federal Communications Commission—and, with the exception of the Federal Communications Commission, the report recommended that the independent commissions be abolished and their functions be combined into five agencies—a Transportation Regulatory Agency, a Federal Trade Practices Agency, a Federal Antitrust Board, a Securities and Exchange Agency, and a Federal Power Agency—headed by a single Administrator appointed by and serving at the pleasure of the President, and confirmed by the Senate.

The report also recommended a streamlining of the adjudicative processes of the regulatory functions by restricting review of hearing examiner decisions so that "hearing examiners would enjoy the status of administrative judicial officers." Review by the Administrator would be limited to policy review within a 30 to 45 day period after the hearing examiner had rendered his decision.

Appeals from the transportation, securities, and power agencies' final judgment would be taken to a new Administrative Court composed of 15 judges serving 15 year terms with appeal only to the Supreme Court. At present, appeals from Commission decisions are taken to the Federal Courts of Appeal with the exception of ICC determinations which are reviewed by a three-judge Federal District Court.

Report of Special Committee on Electric Power and the Environment, New York City Bar

The Special Committee grew out of a joint project originated early in 1971 by four regular committees of the Association of the Bar of the City of New York—Administrative Law, Atomic Energy, Environmental Law, and Science and Law—dealing with electric plant-siting problems in the State of New York. The Special Committee transmitted its final report in August 1972, and although its focus was not on Federal reorganization, it made several recommendations for reform of the Federal regulatory framework.

The report recommends the creation of an Energy Commission which would be a regulatory body "consolidating the regulatory duties of the FPC, the AEC, and preferably, those parts of the Federal government which deal with energy forms other than electricity," and an Energy Agency which would be "a developmental body consolidating the research activities of the AEC, the Office of Coal Research, and all other administrative and executive offices concerned with energy R & D."

The Energy Commission would have the responsibility for studying the extent to which the demand for energy should be encouraged or discouraged and presenting its recommendations to Congress. The Commission would also have the responsibility to review the intermediate-range plans of utilities and regional reliability councils, and to conclude how much new capacity is actually needed and in what generalized locations such new capacity should be sited. The proposed Energy Agency is designed to be a one-stop regulatory framework for power plants, although the requirements of other agencies such as EPA would be unaffected.

Appendix 4B: Excerpts from the Emergency Petroleum Allocation Act of 1973 (P.L. 93-159)

Sec. 4. [T]he President shall promulgate a regulation providing for the mandatory allocation of crude oil, residual fuel oil, and each refined petroleum product, in amounts specified in (or determined in a manner prescribed by) and at prices specified in (or determined in a manner prescribed by) such regulation. . . .

The regulation, to the maximum extent practicable, shall provide for—

(A) protection of public health, safety, and welfare (including maintenance of residential heating, such as individual homes, apartments, and similar occupied dwelling units), and the national defense;

(B) maintenance of all public services (including facilities and services provided by municipally, cooperatively, or investor owned utilities or by any State or local government or authority, and including transportation facilities and services which serve the public at large);

(C) maintenance of agricultural operations, including farming, ranching, dairy, and fishing activities, and services directly related thereto;

(D) preservation of an economically sound and competitive petroleum industry; including the priority needs to restore and foster competition in the producing, refining, distribution, marketing, and petrochemical sectors of such industry, and to preserve the competitive viability of independent refiners, small refiners, nonbranded independent marketers, and branded independent marketers;

(E) the allocation of suitable types, grades, and quality of crude oil to refineries in the United States to permit such refineries to operate at full capacity;

(F) equitable distribution of crude oil, residual fuel oil, and refined petroleum products at equitable prices among all regions and areas of the United States and sectors of the petroleum industry, including independent refiners, small refiners, nonbranded independent marketers, branded independent marketers, and among all users;

(G) allocation of residual fuel oil and refined petroleum products in such amounts and in such manner as may be necessary for the maintenance of, exploration for, and production or extraction of, fuels, and for required transportation related thereto;

(H) economic efficiency; and

(I) minimization of economic distortion, inflexibility, and unnecessary interference with market mechanisms.

In specifying prices (or prescribing the manner for determining them), such regulation shall provide for—

(A) a dollar-for-dollar passthrough of net increases in the cost of crude oil, residual fuel oil, and refined petroleum products to all marketers or distributors at the retail level; and

(B) the use of the same date in the computation of markup, margin, and posted price for all marketers or distributors of crude oil, residual fuel oil and refined petroleum products at all levels of marketing and distribution.

The President in promulgating the regulation shall give consideration to allocating crude oil, residual fuel oil, and refined petroleum products in a manner which results in making available crude oil, residual fuel oil, or refined petroleum products to any person whose use of fuels other than crude oil, residual fuel oil, and refined petroleum products has been curtailed by, or pursuant to a plan filed in compliance with, a rule or order of a Federal or State agency, or where such person's supply of such other fuels is unobtainable by reason of an abandonment of service permitted or ordered by a Federal or State agency.

To the extent practicable the regulation shall be so structured as to result in the allocation in an amount not less than the amount sold or otherwise supplied to such marketer or refiner during the corresponding period of 1972, adjusted to provide—

(A) in the case of refined petroleum products, a pro rata reduction in the amount allocated to each person engaged in the marketing or distribution of a refined petroleum product if the aggregate amount of such product produced in and imported into the United States is less than the aggregate amount produced and imported in calendar year 1972; and

(B) in the case of crude oil, a pro rata reduction in the amount of crude oil allocated to each refiner if the aggregate amount produced in and imported into the United States is less than the aggregate amount produced and imported in calendar year 1972.

The provisions of the regulation shall specify (or prescribe a manner for determining) prices of crude oil at the producer level.

If at any time after the date of enactment of this Act the President finds that application of the regulation under subsection (a) to crude oil, residual fuel oil, or a refined petroleum product is not necessary to carry out this Act, that there is not shortage of such oil or product, and that exempting such oil or product from such regulation will not have an adverse impact on the supply of any other oil or refined petroleum products subject to this Act, he may prescribe an amendment to the regulation exempting such oil or product from such regulation for a period of not more than ninety days.

Appendix 4C: Excerpts from the Economic Stabilization Act of 1970 (P.L. 9l-379 as Amended

Sec. 202. Findings

It is hereby determined that in order to stabilize the economy, reduce inflation, minimize unemployment, improve the Nation's competitive position in world trade, and protect the purchasing power of the dollar, it is necessary to stabilize prices, rents, wages, salaries, dividends, and interest, and that in order to maintain and promote competition in the petroleum products to meet the essential needs of various section of the Nation, it is necessary to provide for the rational and equitable distribution of these products. The adjustments necessary to carry out this program require prompt judgments and actions by the executive branch of the Government. The President is in a position to implement promptly and effectively the program authorized by this title.

Sec. 203. Presidential Authority

(a) The President is authorized to issue such orders and regulations as he deems appropriate, accompanied by a statement of reasons for such orders and regulations, to—

(1) stabilize prices, rents, wages, and salaries. . . .
(2) stabilize interest rates and corporate dividends and similar transfers at levels consistent with orderly economic growth; and
(3) provide . . . for the establishment of priorities of use and for systematic allocation of supplies of petroleum products including crude oil in order to meet the essential needs of various sections of the Nation and to prevent anticompetitive effects resulting from shortages of such products.

Such orders and regulations shall provide for the making of such adjustments as may be necessary to prevent gross inequities. . . .
. . . the President shall issue standards to serve as a guide for determining levels of wages, salaries, prices, rents, interest rates, corporate dividends, and similar transfers which are consistent with the purposes of this title and orderly economic growth. Such standards shall—

(1) be generally fair and equitable;

(2) provide for the making of such general exceptions and variations as are necessary to foster orderly economic growth and to prevent gross inequities, hardships, serious market disruptions, domestic shortages of raw materials, localized shortages of labor, and windfall profits;

(3) take into account changes in productivity and the cost of living, as well as such other factors consistent with the purposes of this title as are appropriate;

(4) provide for the requiring of appropriate reductions in prices and rents whenever warranted after consideration of lower costs, labor shortages, and other pertinent factors; and

(5) call for generally comparable sacrifices by business and labor as well as other segments of the economy.

5

The State's Role in Energy Policy Administration

The past two years have demonstrated that states can play a major part in energy policy. At the same time it has been shown that most state governments have chosen to reduce their role to one of dependency upon federal initiative or, in the extreme, to merely that of executing federal directives. A wide range of legislative and administrative styles of solving energy policy problems has emerged among the states. Only three features are widely shared: the concept of the state office of petroleum allocation (the SOPA), the state/FEA liaison office, and certain federal inspired conservation legislation, such as the 55 miles per hour speed limit, the emergency daylight savings time plans, etc. Beyond these features little uniformity exists; some states have large, aggressive, and well-financed energy agencies (or energy offices within existing agencies) that are fully independent of the federal government (California, Michigan); others have put together energy study commissions with very little program responsibility or funding (Florida, Utah); still others responded to the crisis with legislation to elaborate civil emergency powers and services (Maine, Maryland); yet other states apparently did nothing beyond federal requirements (Nevada, Arizona).

The State Office of Petroleum Allocation

An important feature of the mandatory petroleum allocation program was the creation, on paper, of a stockpile of fuel in each state to meet emergency and hardship needs within the state. The disposition of these stocks, called the "state setaside," is under the guidance of the FEA. However, all states have applied to FEA to have the administrative authority over the setaside delegated to them under section 211.15 of the regulations. The regulations under which all SOPAs operate are reprinted in the appendix to this chapter.

Any end-user or supplier of propanes, gasoline, middle distillate, or residual oil may apply for quantities of state setaside for temporary relief, by submitting FEA form 20 (see appendix) to the SOPA. The state setaside can only be used for hardships and emergencies within the state. Other problems, such as assignment of suppliers to retailers and adjustments of assignments, are handled by the national or regional FEA offices. All necessary forms and information concerning these procedures go through FEA's liaison offices. Thus, if the SOPA is unable to meet needs, referral is made to the FEA liaison office in the state.

Federal-State FEA Liaison Office

The liaison office for each state is an appendage of the regional FEA office. The liaison officer is not empowered to make or enforce regulations, but rather is an information officer. The director of the state office provides advice and guidance on FEA rules, regulations, and programs to state and local officials and serves as the federal representative throughout the state for the Mandatory Petroleum Allocation Program. However, enforcement of the mandatory regulations is the responsibility of the Compliance and Enforcement Division of the FEA regional offices. In addition the liaison officer is responsible for providing technical advice and support to state and local energy offices, and representing the regional administrator at policy-level meetings of state and local officials. Excerpts from FEA act provisions governing the liaison function appears in the appendix to this chapter.

Federally Inspired State Programs

The federal government has asked the states to embark upon a series of energy conservation measures, including reduced speed limits, retail gasoline sales regulation, reduced energy consumption by state agencies, and others. A summary of state programs released by FEA's Office of Energy Conservation shows that every state has an energy conservation program or is planning one.

"In those 32 states where the program is mandatory for state facilities and employees, thermostats have been set at 68 degrees maximum; lighting, indoors and outdoors, has been reduced; state-owned vehicles are restricted to 50 miles per hour; and compact cars are being bought to replace older, larger energy users," stated John Gibbons, Director of the Office of Energy Conservation.[1]

The states have sought to solve several problems with retail gasoline sales regulation. First, some programs have been aimed at reducing consumption of gasoline by rationing, closing stations earlier and on holidays, restricting sales to cars with tanks less than half full, etc. Second, some programs have been aimed at holding gas prices down to reasonable levels (potentially even below federal ceilings); such programs have been deemed constitutional in federal court. Third, some programs have been aimed at maintaining order in the marketplace: even-odd day gas sales to reduce lines, regulation of dealer franchises, protection for independents, and the prohibition of various unfair and fraudulent practices.

State Programs to Solve Special Problems

Many states have given attention to some specific side effects of the energy crisis. The most common problem has been the impact of increased fuel costs on certain fixed budgets, particularly public works contracts and transportation budgets of schools and local governments. Thus, many states have approved modifications of contracts and special supplemental appropriations for various agencies. Connecticut passed legislation to the effect that artificially contrived energy shortages (supplier hoarding) are illegal.

Many states revised their emergency powers in an effort to be better prepared for energy shortages. Some states merely established a list of priority users of fuels to determine the order of cut off in the event of a shortage. Others revised the emergency powers of the governor so that they might be better tailored to energy crisis problems. Some states established emergency conservation programs and set up commissions to prepare contingency plans. Examples of enabling statutes for each of these three categories of emergency programs appears in an appendix to this chapter.

A few states have passed legislation to require the energy industry to disclose information regarding demand and supply for planning purposes. (The substance of one such law appears in an appendix to this chapter.)

State Energy Policy Programs

States have sought to increase supply, reduce demand, and reallocate supplies to priority users. The most common approach to improving supply in the states was to grant, or make provision to grant, temporary variances from air-quality standards. Variances permitted the burning of a wider range of fuels and thus increased apparent supply. Some states took additional steps aimed at encouraging production, particularly of clean energy, in their jurisdiction. California permitted rapid amortization of public utility facilities using geothermal resources; Indiana enacted tax incentives for the construction of solar energy systems. Many states established state research and development bodies charged with developing proposals for increasing supply.

Demand reduction or conservation strategies at the state level are more common than supply enhancement efforts. Certain federally inspired conservation measures have already been mentioned. In addition, some states reduced the number of required school days or otherwise modified the school year to reduce heating-oil consumption. Many states modified their building codes to impose stricter insulation and other energy-efficient regulations. To encourage conservation, some states are considering changes in public utility rate structures to eliminate discounts for volume purchases. Finally, several states have temporarily reduced or modified the work week (including, in some cases, retail sales hours) to reduce consumption. Other conservation programs include street and decorative lighting cutbacks, gasoline tax increases, and certain practices by public utility commissions, such as, permitting brownouts.

Reallocation of energy supplies to priority users has been considered by several states. Hawaii passed an amendment to their emergency powers statute enabling reallocation (see appendix). Several of the extant state gasoline allocation programs have the effect of reallocation; they provide for specific exceptions for such priority users as police, ambulances, and farming.

State Multipurpose Energy Agencies

More than twenty states have centralized some or all of their energy program authority into multipurpose energy agencies. The model legislation is probably California's Energy Conservation Act of 1974, because it is so extensive. The key provisions are:

1. inclusion of an energy impact section in environmental impact statements;
2. creation of a State Energy Resources Conservation and Development Commission to study energy problems and make recommendations to the governor and legislature, set energy standards for public facilities, and serve as state energy data center and information clearing house;
3. centralization of all state energy facility siting authority in the same Commission;
4. development of an Energy Shortage Contingency plan, again by the commission; and
5. financing by fees of the commission including a surcharge on consumer's electric bills.

Legal Problems with State Programs

The overriding problem facing state (and local) programs is the question of preemption by federal action. If Congress has acted in a specific area where its authority is valid (say, under the power to regulate interstate commerce) then, in general, state programs are limited to those actions that further the purposes of the federal program. For example, state and local air quality maintenance efforts in excess of federal requirements have operated in California under this provision. It is sometimes difficult to tell which programs do and which do not support federal efforts. For example, New York City ordinances requiring landlords to provide tenants with specific quantities of heat were deemed to be in concert with (and not in conflict with) the federal mandatory allocation program.

If Congress has not acted, the field is open for state and/or local entry, provided the actions do not have a disruptive effect on interstate commerce. Further discussion on the field available for local action appears in chapters 6 and 7 of this handbook.

Appendix 5A: Excerpts from FEA Regulations Governing the State Setaside and the State Office of Petroleum Allocation

Section 211.15 State Offices of Petroleum Allocation

(a) Any state may apply to the National Office of the FEO, to create a State Office of Petroleum Allocation within the State.

(b) Upon certification by the FEO such State Office of Petroleum Allocation will be delegated authority to administer the state set-aside program, to provide assistance in obtaining adjustments. . . .

Section 211.17 State Set-Aside

(a) A state set-aside system shall be established for propane, middle distillate, motor gasoline and residual fuel oil (except as used by utilities or as bunker fuel for maritime shipping). Authority may be delegated to a State office to administer the state set-aside for that State. The state set-aside shall be utilized by a State office to meet hardship and emergency requirements of all wholesale purchaser-consumers and end-users within that state from the state set-aside volumes, including wholesale purchaser-consumers and end-users which are part of any governmental organization. To facilitate relief of the hardship and emergency requirements of wholesale purchaser-consumers and end-users, the State office may direct that a wholesale purchaser-reseller be supplied from the state set-aside in order that the wholesale purchaser-reseller can supply the wholesale purchaser-consumers and end-users experiencing the hardship or emergency. . . .

(b) All hardship and emergency applications for assignment from the State set-aside system and appeals thereof shall be filed with and resolved by the appropriate State Office. . . . The final decision of a State Office . . . regarding an application for assignment due to hardship or emergency requirements shall be subject to judicial review. . . .

(c) Suppliers shall provide the assigned amount of an allocated product to an applicant when presented with an authorizing document. The authorizing document shall entitle the applicant to receive product from any convenient local distributor of the prime supplier from which the state set-aside assignment has been made. Wholesale purchaser-resellers of prime suppliers shall, as non-prime suppliers, honor such authorizing documents upon presentation, and shall not delay deliveries required by

69

the authorizing document while confirming such deliveries with the prime supplier. Any non-prime supplier which provides an allocated product pursuant to an authorizing document shall in turn receive from its supplier an equivalent volume of the allocated product which shall not be considered part of its allocation entitlement otherwise authorized. . . .

(d) (1) At any time during the month, the State office may order the release of part or all of a prime supplier's set-aside volume through the prime supplier's normal distribution system in the State.

(2) From time to time, the State office may designate certain geographical areas within the State as suffering from an intra-State supply imbalance. At any time during the month, the State office may order some or all of the prime suppliers with purchasers within such geographical areas to release part or all of their set-aside volume through their normal distribution systems to increase the allocations of all the supplier's purchasers located within such areas.

Appendix 5B: FEA Form 20: Application to State for Petroleum Product Supply Assistance

Who Should Submit?

(a) *For temporary hardship relief*—Any end-user or supplier of propane, gasoline, middle distillate (including kerosene, #2 heating oil, and diesel fuel), or residual oil.

(b) *For permanent supply adjustment*—End-users of any petroleum product who are not wholesale purchasers for assignment of a supplier or increased supply volume.

Form Approved OMB 042R-1685

FORM FEO-20 (Recommended for State Use)

FEDERAL ENERGY OFFICE
APPLICATION TO STATE FOR PETROLEUM PRODUCT
SUPPLY ASSISTANCE

(Do Not Write in This Space)

Case Number: _____
Received: _____
Reviewed: _____
Reply: _____

1. Name and address of applicant:

_____
_____
_____
_____ Telephone _____

2. Applicant is:

☐ End user requesting product for own use
☐ Supplier requesting product for customer(s)
☐ Other: _____

3. If you have filled out a Form FEO-17 check here ☐ and attach a copy of that form. If you have been assigned a case number in connection with your Form FEO-17 enter it here: _____

4. This application is for: ☐ Temporary hardship relief   ☐ Increased supply volume (permanent)
☐ Assignment of a supplier (permanent)   ☐ Other (explain) _____

5. Type of product requested: ☐ Propane   ☐ Motor Gasoline   ☐ Kerosene   ☐ #2 Heating Oil   ☐ Diesel Fuel
☐ Residual Fuel Oil (Specify Grade #: ___)   ☐ Other: _____

6. For temporary hardship applicants: a) Quantity requested: _____ gallons   b) Date(s) required: From _____ To _____

7. For permanent adjustments (new supplier or increased supply volume) show desired quantity by month for next twelve months (in gallons):

MONTH AND YEAR	QUANTITY	MONTH AND YEAR	QUANTITY	MONTH AND YEAR	QUANTITY

8. Supplier(s) name and address: (If you have no supplier, enter names and addresses of two potential suppliers you have contacted):

a) _____   b) _____
_____   _____

Person to contact: _____ Telephone _____   Person to contact: _____ Telephone _____
Check one: ☐ Existing Supplier ☐ Potential Supplier   Check one: ☐ Existing Supplier ☐ Potential Supplier

9. Justification for application (explain reason for hardship or need for product):

(attach additional page(s) if required)

10. Describe end use of the product. (If for heating, state total floor space. If for industrial use, state type of equipment and consumption per hour. If for transportation, describe vehicle(s), miles to be driven, and purpose. If for resale, state customer(s)' end uses and basis for need.)

(attach additional page(s) if required)

11. I CERTIFY That all of the above information is true and accurate, and that, if any or all of the quantity requested is granted, it will be used for purposes here described, and will not be diverted to other uses. I further certify that I have an energy conservation program in effect.

_____   _____
(Applicant's Signature)   (Date)

Title 18 U.S.C. Section 1001, makes it a crime for any person knowingly and willfully to make to any department or agency of the United States any false, fictitious, or fraudulent statements or representations as to any matter within its jurisdiction.

FEO-20 (1-74)

GPO 871-626

Source: Federal Energy Commission.

Figure 5B-1. FEA Form 20: Application to State for Petroleum Product Supply Assistance.

Appendix 5C: Excerpts from the FEA Act of 1974 Relative to Federal-State Liaison in Energy Policy

Section 19. The Administrator may, for a period not to exceed thirty days in any one calendar year, provide for the exercise or performance of a management oversight review with respect to the conduct of any Federal or State (with consent of the Governor) energy program conducted pursuant to this Act. Such review may be conducted by contract or by any Federal department or agency. A written report shall be submitted to the Administrator concerning the findings of the review.

Section 20. (a) The Administrator shall—
(1) before promulgating any rules, regulations, or policies, and before establishing any programs under the authority of this Act, provide, where practicable, a reasonable period in which State governments may provide written comments if such rules, regulations, policies, or programs substantially affect the authority or responsibility of such State governments;
(2) provide, in accordance with the provisions of this Act, upon request, to State governments all relevant information he possesses concerning the status and impact of energy shortages, the extent and location of available supplies and shortages of crude oil, petroleum products, natural gas, and coal, within the distribution area serving that particular State government; and
(3) provide for a central clearinghouse for Federal agencies and State governments seeking energy information and assistance from the Federal Government.

(b) Pursuant to his responsibility under this section, the Administrator shall—

(1) provide technical assistance—including advice and consultation relating to State programs, and, where necessary, the use of task forces of public officials and private persons assigned to work with State governments—to assist State governments in dealing with energy problems and shortages and their impact and in the development of plans, programs, and policies to meet the problems and shortages so identified;
(2) convene conferences of State and Federal officials, and such other persons as the Administrator designates, to promote the purposes of this Act, and the Administrator is authorized to pay reasonable expenses incurred in the participation of individuals in such conferences;

(3) draft and make available to State governments model legislation with respect to State energy programs and policies; and

(4) promote the promulgation of uniform criteria procedures, and forms for grant or contract applications for energy proposals submitted by State governments. . . .

Appendix 5D: Model State Statutes on Energy Emergency Management

Establishing Priority Users: State of Washington, Electric Power Act of 1973

Section 3

There is hereby created and established an electric emergency curtailment and/or allocation committee composed of five members to be appointed by the governor to serve at his pleasure. . . .

Section 4

The committee shall have the following powers and duties:

(1) To gather and review pertinent information from whatever source available relating to electric power supply conditions;

(2) To make recommendations to the governor of appropriate emergency curtailment and/or allocation plans and procedures of electric power usage. In developing its recommendations the committee should consider the economic, social and environmental impact of a curtailment and/or allocation program;

(3) To advise the governor of the time or times, if any, based on pertinent information, when the electric power supply conditions require execution of emergency curtailment and/or allocation procedures, and also the time or times when such procedures can prudently be terminated.

(4) To monitor and review compliance with and effectiveness of orders of the governor issued under this chapter: PROVIDED. That compliance by regulated electric companies shall be reviewed by the Washington utilities and transportation commission and the results thereof shall be reported to the committee;

(5) To require submission by any electric utility, for review and approval by the committee, of a plan for curtailment and/or allocation of electric usage in the event of an emergency . . .

Establishing Emergency Powers for the Governor: State of Maine, Granting Energy Emergency Powers to the Governor, Act of 1974

Section 57, Part 2

A. Proclamation. Whenever an actual or impending acute shortage in usable energy resources threatens the health, safety or welfare of the citizens of the State, the Governor shall, by proclamation, declare that an energy emergency exists in any or all sections of the State. . . .

B. Powers. Upon the issuance of an energy emergency proclamation and after consulting with the Director of the Office of Energy Resources, the Governor is authorized to exercise all the powers granted in this chapter, except as may be specifically limited by this subsection and such powers shall include without limitation the authority to:

(1) Establish and implement programs, controls, standards, priorities and quotas for the allocation, conservation and consumption of energy resources;

(2) Regulate the hours and days during which nonresidential buildings may be open and the temperatures at which they may be maintained;

(3) Regulate the use of gasoline and diesel-powered land vehicles, watercraft and aircraft;

(4) After consulting, when appropriate, with the New England governors, and upon the recommendations of the Maine Public Utilities Commission, regulate the generation, distribution and consumption of electricity;

(5) Establish temporary state and local boards and agencies;

(6) Establish and implement programs and agreements for the purposes of coordinating the emergency energy responses of the State with those of the Federal Government and of other states and localities;

(7) Temporarily suspend truck weight and size regulations, but not in conflict with federal regulations;

(8) Regulate the storage, distribution and consumption of home heating oil.

C. Exclusions. In dealing with a declared energy emergency, the following powers granted by this chapter may not be invoked:

(1) The eminent domain powers granted in section 58;

(2) [N]o enforcement action may be taken pursuant to this paragraph

without publication of the order authorizing such action in a manner reasonably calculated to give persons affected thereby adequate notice of the order, rule or regulation to be enforced and the sanctions to be applied.

D. Environmental regulations. (1) [N]othing contained in this subsection shall be construed to authorize the Governor to suspend or to modify orders, regulations, standards or classifications issued or enforced by the Department of Environmental Protection or the Land Use Regulation Commission.

(2) At any time an energy emergency proclamation is in effect, the Governor may call the Board of Environmental Protection into extraordinary session to consider temporary waivers or suspensions of rules and standards related to air and water quality necessary to relieve then existing energy shortages. Thereupon, the board is empowered notwithstanding any other provision of law to approve such suspensions or waivers as it determines are necessary to relieve or avoid an energy shortage and will not result in environmental degradation of a permanent or enduring nature. . . . No such waiver or suspension shall remain in effect longer than 60 days or after the date on which the board renders a further order issued pursuant to the regular procedures specified in Title 38, whichever shall first occur.

**Establishing Emergency Conservation Programs:
State of Wisconsin, Emergency Energy
Conservation Act of 1973**

Section 1

The legislature hereby determines that:

(1) Disruptions in the availability of energy supplies, particularly crude oil and petroleum products, and the secondary effects of such disruptions pose a serious risk to the economic well being, health and welfare of the citizens of this state and the nation.
(2) A primary responsibility for developing and enforcing fuel shortage contingency plans to meet this risk lies with this state.
(3) This risk can be averted or minimized most efficiently and effectively through prompt action by the executive branch of government.

Section 2. Legislative Purpose

The purpose of this act is to:

(1) Grant to state executive agencies specific, temporary authority to deal with energy shortages;

(2) Provide authority to state government to implement the national program to conserve scarce energy resources;

(3) Minimize the adverse effects of energy shortages on the economic well-being, health and welfare of the people of this state; and

(4) Encourage all state agencies to take necessary actions to conserve energy through existing administrative authority.

Section 7. Energy Conservation Advisory Council

The governor or his designee shall establish an energy conservation advisory council to study and propose specific legislation on long-term energy conservation. The governor or his designee shall appoint to the council members of his staff and members of the general public with knowledge of energy conservation in the following areas: engineering, architecture, transportation, land use planning, agriculture, business and industry, and tourism and recreation. Two members shall also be appointed from each house of the legislature, including one member from the most predominant political party in each house and one member from the second most predominant political party in each house, to be appointed as are standing committees in the respective houses. The council shall report its specific proposals for legislation to the legislature and governor. . . .

Hawaii's Energy Data Disclosure Act of 1974

Section 1

The legislature finds that during the 1973-1974 energy crisis, the lack of solid information available concerning the distribution of liquid fuel within the State was appalling. This lack of information led to uncertainties and difficulties in the State's efforts to assess and cope with the energy crisis. The legislature further finds that although the crisis may have abated, the problem of fuel shortages will continue into the future. The State needs to develop and have available pertinent information on liquid fuel distributions in order to be prepared for future contingencies. Such information is vital to the safety, health, and welfare of the people.

It is the purpose of this bill to require information concerning liquid fuel distributions to be made available to the State.

Section 416

Each distributor shall on or before the last day of each calendar month, file with the director, on forms prescribed, prepared, and furnished by him, a notarized statement showing separately for each county . . . within which and whereon liquid fuel is sold or used during the last preceding month of the calendar year, the following:

(1) The total number of gallons of liquid fuel refined, manufactured, or compounded by the distributor within the State and sold or used by him, and if for ultimate use in another county or on either island, the name of that county or island;

(2) The total number of gallons of liquid fuel imported by him or sold or used by him, and if for ultimate use in another county or on either island, the name of that county or island;

(3) The total number of gallons of fuel sold as liquid fuel, avitation fuel, diesel fuel, and such other types of fuel as required by the director; and

(4) The total number of gallons of liquid fuel and the types thereof sold to: federal, state, and county agencies, ships stores, or base exchanges, commercial agricultural accounts, commercial nonagricultural accounts, retail dealers, and such other customers as required by the director.

All statements submitted to the department of regulatory agencies under this section shall be a public record.

Hawaii's Emergency Reallocation Powers Act of 1974

Section 125-2. Powers in an Emergency

—If the governor declares that an emergency as defined in section 125-1 exists, he or his authorized representatives, to make available commodities necessary to the public health, safety, or welfare, or to insure the availability of commodities required to maintain commerce to or within the State under normal conditions, may:

(1) Whenever the availability of shipping space depends upon determination by the governor or his authorized representatives, of the emergency needs of the population, allocate space to and among types of commodities and consignees, such distribution of space among consignees to be upon an equitable basis so far as reasonably practicable.

(2) Charter or affreight a ship or ships, make any other arrangements, including contracts of guaranty, for the procurement of ships and any other means of transportation, and transport cargoes to the State. Cargoes from the State may be transported on any return voyage.

(3) Purchase and resell, or otherwise distribute commodities.

(4) Control the distribution of commodities by rules and regulations . . .

Appendix 5E: State Multipurpose Energy Agencies

Excerpts from California's Energy Conservation Act of 1974

Chapter 1, Section 25006. It is the policy of the state and the intent of the Legislature to establish and consolidate the state's responsibility for energy resources, for encouraging, developing, and coordinating research and development into energy supply and demand problems, and for regulating electrical generating and related transmission facilities.

Section 25007. It is further the policy of the state and the intent of the Legislature to employ a range of measures to reduce wasteful, uneconomical, and unnecessary uses of energy, thereby reducing the rate of growth of energy consumption, prudently conserve energy resources, and assure statewide environmental, public safety, and land use goals.

Chapter 3, Section 25200. There is in the Resources Agency the State Energy Resources Conservation and Development Commission, consisting of five members appointed by the governor. . . .

Section 25202. The Secretary of the Resources Agency and the President of the Public Utilities Commission shall be ex officio, non-voting members of the commission, whose presence shall not be counted for a quorum or for vote requirements.

Section 25203. Each member of the commission shall represent the state at large and not any particular area thereof, and shall serve on a full-time basis.

Section 25216. In addition to other duties . . . the commission shall do all of the following:

(a) Undertake a continuing assessment of trends in the consumption of electrical energy and other forms of energy and analyze the social, economic, and environmental consequences of these trends; carry out directly, or cause to be carried out, energy conservation measures . . . and recommend to the governor and the legislature new and expanded energy conservation measures as required. . . .

(b) Collect . . . forecasts of future supplies and consumption of all forms of energy, including electricity, and of future energy of fuel production and transporting facilities to be constructed; independently analyze such forecasts in relation to statewide estimates of population, economic, and other growth factors and in terms of the availability of energy resources, costs to consumers, and other factors; and formally specify statewide and service area electrical energy demands to be utilized as a basis for planning the siting and design of electric power generating and related facilities.

(c) Carry out, or cause to be carried out . . . research and development into alternative sources of energy, improvements in energy generation, transmission, and siting, fuel substitution, and other topics related to energy supply, demand, public safety, ecology, and conservation. . . .

Section 25216.3. (a) The Commission shall compile relevant local, regional, state, and federal land use, public safety, environmental, and other standards to be met in designing, siting, and operating facilities in the state; . . . adopt standards, except for air and water quality, to be met in designing or operating facilities to safeguard public health and safety, which may be different from or more stringent than those adopted by local, regional, or other state agencies, or by any federal agency if permitted by federal law; and monitor compliance and ensure that all facilities are operated in accordance with this division. . . .

Section 25216.5. The commission shall do all of the following:

(a) Prescribe the form and content of applications for facilities; conduct public hearings and take other actions to secure adequate evaluation of applications; and formally act to approve or disapprove applications, including specifying conditions under which approval and continuing operation of any facility shall be permitted.

(b) Prepare an integrated plan specifying actions to be taken in the event of an impending serious shortage of energy, or a clear threat to public health, safety, or welfare.

(c) Evaluate policies governing the establishment of rates for electric power and other sources of energy as related to energy conservation, environmental protection, and other goals and policies established in this division, and transmit recommendations for changes in power-pricing policies and rate schedules to the Governor, the Legislature, to the Public Utilities Commission, and to publicly owned electric utilities.

(d) Serve as a central repository within the state government for the collection and storage of data and information on all forms of energy supply, demand, conservation, public safety, and related subjects. . . .

Chapter 9. Section 25800. There is in the General Fund in the State Treasury the State Energy Resources Conservation and Development

Special Account. On and after the effective date of this division, each electric utility shall add a surcharge of one-tenth of a mill ($0.0001) per kilowatt-hour to the cost of electric power sold to consumers in the state. . . .

Section 25802. Each person who submits to the commission a notice of intent for any proposed generating facility shall accompany the notice with a fee of one cent (0.01) per kilowatt of net electric capacity of the proposed generation facility. Such fee shall only be paid on one of the alternate proposed facility sites which has the highest electrical designed capacity. In no event shall such fee be less than one thousand dollars ($1,000) nor more than twenty-five thousand dollars ($25,000).

For any other facility, the notice shall be accompanied by a fee of five thousand dollars ($5,000). Such fee shall only be paid on one of the alternate proposed facility sites.

Section 25803. . . . All funds in the account shall be expended for purposes of carrying out the provisions of this division, when appropriated by the Legislature in the Budget Act.

Essentials of Local Government Energy Policy

Fundamentally, there are only three things a government can do in an attempt to alleviate an energy crisis: increase supply, reduce demand, or reallocate available supply among existing demand. Each of these strategies may be pursued by dozens of different tactics ranging in severity from public awareness programs to stockpiling and condemnation proceedings. Governments are also obliged to deal with the symptoms of a crisis: black and grey markets, unemployment, strikes, economic dislocations, and threats to public safety.

This chapter will first deal with "energy policy," then with "symptomatic relief."

Energy Policy

What is done in the area of energy policy will depend upon the seriousness of the crisis as the local government sees it and thus on information available to them on energy supply and demand in their jurisdiction. Consequently, the first requirement of energy policy is adequate information.

Needed information includes data on supply and demand plus some related areas such as the energy storage, transportation, and distribution systems in the jurisdiction. Chances are that much of this information is already collected by local or regional businessmen and officials who market petroleum products, electricity, gas, and coal; if local dealers cannot help, get in touch with the trade association to which they belong or the federal or state energy offices. In many instances local officials will find ready access to the required information; in others, they will encounter resistance. In either case, the acquisition, handling, and use of this sort of information should be regulated by ordinance. Perhaps the simplest approach to acquiring the necessary information is to amend the local public health, sales tax, or business licensing ordinance to require the periodic reporting of the outlook for energy supply, demand, and related issues. Alternatively, a separate "energy regulation" ordinance may be passed. A sample ordinance with annotations is appended to this chapter. The city attorney may easily adapt it for use as an amendment to a relevant ordinance.

In some jurisdictions efforts at establishing mandatory reporting of energy flows may be unfeasible for political or other reasons. The natural substitute for mandatory reporting is voluntary reporting system. Voluntary efforts may work well and have the advantage of flexibility over mandatory approaches. Before adopting a voluntary reporting scheme, however, energy suppliers in the jurisdiction should be polled to determine the extent to which they would cooperate. Another approach is to encourage the state to pass a reporting statute and to gather the appropriate information for local governments. The very best system, of course, would be one in which local officials were not notified or otherwise involved unless and until a potential problem arose.

Information about the flow of energy in a jurisdiction is only valuable if it is presented in a meaningful form and properly used. Someone must be charged with the responsibility of sorting through it and gleaning the policy implications from it on a regular, periodic basis. In small jurisdictions local officials will want to reduce to a minimum the number of times they go through this process: once in the fall to insure adequate winter supplies of home heating fuels and a few other necessities, and once in the spring to insure supplies for the agriculture, recreation, and other industries vital to the local economy. Larger communities may want to have energy information available more often. In addition, it may be necessary to review the situation for specific purposes, such as assuring adequate preparation for strikes or other anticipated disruptions in the industry.

The best way to guarantee regular and thoughtful treatment of energy information is to create an advisory unit statutorily required to file periodic reports and recommendations with the city's governing commissions or council. In some cases, such a unit might be a single part-time individual employed in a related job, such as in the county or city clerk's office, the local office of the electrical or gas utility, etc. In other instances an unpaid citizen's advisory board might be created. In any case, the unit should, at the proper times, file an "energy budget report" consisting of:

1. an energy needs forecast for the period beginning with the filing of the report and ending on the next filing date,
2. a forecast of energy availability for the same period,
3. a set of recommendations for action if a shortage appears possible, and
4. additional information as appropriate, such as energy prices, storage facilities available, contingency planning arrangements and so forth.

One possible arrangement for the advisory unit is embodied in the Energy Advisory Board Ordinance appended to this section. Several other models might be used for an ordinance, including those passed by the New York City or Los Angeles city councils, or perhaps some of the state statutes establishing similar organizations should be examined. (California's is discussed in chapter 5.) A discussion on preparing the Energy Budget Report appears in chapter 8.

Symptomatic Relief

The symptoms of a crisis cannot be precisely forecast without detailed information about the character of the energy economy in a jurisdiction. Nonetheless, the crisis of the winter of 1973-74 revealed that the most serious symptoms are likely to be the social problem sparked by the economic dislocations of the crisis. Thus, certain industries shut down or reduced operations temporarily, energy prices skyrocketed, and the allocation program generated a black market in which prices rose even higher. Rising prices can be a serious burden to people on relatively fixed incomes (elderly, welfare clients, public employees, etc.) and can threaten performance of contracts. Delivery problems result in cold homes and the threats to health from exposure, particularly for the young and the elderly. Other health problems follow when shortages affect power-driven sanitary and water utilities, refrigerated storage facilities, and the delivery or manufacture of medicines, food, and clothing. Public safety can be threatened by looting and street crime in periods of electrical blackout or reduced commercial activity generally.

But the most damaging impact of a shortage is the economic dislocation caused by price explosions. Shortages often drive prices up; prices soared in the 1973-74 season even under government wage and price controls. Energy prices are expected to rise more rapidly than the consumer price index for some years to come. Maine, the coldest continental state, experienced an explosion in No. 2 heating oil and kerosene prices—from 19 cents in 1973 to 49 cents in early 1974. Since the average Maine home used 2000 gallons of oil, heating bills soared from under $400 to almost $1000 in only twelve months. In Georgia, the price of propane rose 400 percent before stabilizing at a 300 percent increase. In Kentucky the price of coal, used for heating by many low-income groups, jumped 300 to 500 percent between 1972 and 1974.

Small increases in the relative price of energy can be absorbed by most individuals simply by reallocating their budget; however, there are innate dangers. Beyond a certain point people will buy heating fuel at the expense of medical, dental, nutritional, and other necessities, thus creating a public health problem. At inflation rates for energy prices of several hundred percent, you can expect politically serious social problems to develop first with low-income groups, but soon with the politically more significant middle-income groups. Under such circumstances a public information program explaining these dangers and how to watch for them could be very important in preventing irrational responses; for example, buy a sweater and give up a little heat rather than nutritious food or medical care.

There is not much that can insulate the middle-income classes from energy bill inflation short of the city going into the energy business itself. City-owned fuel yards, retail gasoline and related businesses have been operated in the past (some were eventually found unconstitutional). The main value of such tactics is not their declared intention (keeping prices down), for it seems clear that most government services are at least as expensive as privately operated equivalents. Rather, their main value is their demonstration effect, the appearance of government action to meet popular expectation. Demonstration effects are important sources of governmental power and popularity; it matters little that they failed or were eventually enjoined by the courts. Moreover, in a serious crisis such morale boosters can make important, perhaps critical contributions to public confidence in government, and that can mean all the difference in getting through the crisis with a minimum of permanent damage. Keep in mind that when facing an economic crisis, a holding action is the strategy most likely to succeed. Incomes, wages, and even Social Security payments are eventually adjusted to new prices, and before that, most individuals can do something with their own budgets to stave off disaster.

However, independent from, or in association with, some demonstration action, you may want to alleviate some of the most serious economic burdens of the crisis. These are most likely to fall upon the elderly, the poor, and those out of work for any reason. An important source of help, and one that carries demonstrational impact as well, is private charity; churches, service groups, and private individuals can often be enlisted to help defray fuel costs for the neediest, many of whom can adjust to the higher price if given more time.

Private charity, however, is not a reliable source of enduring aid. Any serious relief effort must incorporate elements of public assistance. There are two areas in which the federal and state governments provide you with some help: control of discrimination by suppliers and helping low-income families meet or adjust to higher energy costs.

Controlling Discriminatory Practices

The FEA strives to guarantee that every householder using petroleum-based fuels for home heating will receive an adequate supply and that the price of that fuel will be fair. Thus, you may direct some individuals seeking help or relief from discrimination directly to the FEA. The petroleum fuels are allocated to classes of end-users (e.g., residential) with equal priority. This is because the allocation scheme is based on the assumption that enough fuel is available to satisfy all customers at the *specified allocation levels*. To meet these specified levels, residences may be required to reduce thermostat settings or achieve a fuel-use savings equivalent to a specified reduction. 1973-74 allocation rules, for example, called for settings no higher than 68 degrees.

For those who heat with natural gas there has been less of an availability problem. Even though natural gas is in short supply nationwide and the Federal Power Commission has taken steps to allocate natural gas supplies at the wholesale level, residential users are by law and tradition given the highest priority of all firm contract holders. Moreover, the law regulating retail utilities obligates them to provide continuous and adequate service; they are liable for damages resulting from failure on their part to provide such service. In case of an interruption of service for reason other than nonpayment, a simple call should straighten the matter out. Service discontinuation for nonpayment is permissible in some states.

Another area of the allocations affecting the low- and fixed-income groups is gasoline, though only about half own cars. Gas retailers in low-income areas should be made aware that there have been a number of cases in which similarly situated dealers have received less fuel than their entitlement. In these cases, complaints should be filed through the regional FEA office. Other retailers may be eligible for increased allocations if population in their area has grown, or a number of gasoline stations in their vicinity have closed, resulting in a situation where those retailers remaining are responsible for more potential customers. Again contact the FEA.

Gasoline shortages and high prices present a special problem to migratory farm workers, who depend on gasoline to move up the migrant stream. Being transients, they have no regular dealers and do not receive consideration for state setasides from the states through which they move. The Department of Labor, the Department of Agriculture, HEW, and FEA are working together to try to solve the special problems of the migrant. But no programs are currently operational. However, under FEA allocation regulations the growers for whom the migrant workers work receive 100 percent of current need. Growers may be urged to consider the needs of their migratory workers as included in their own needs, even though they should be advised that FEA regulations do not allow for this.

Financial Assistance for Energy Bills

The largest energy budget item for low-income groups is space heating. A typical study of residential energy consumption showed that energy costs can run as high as 25 percent of income for the poorest households, and of that nearly 90 percent is for heating. It is generally believed that increasing energy prices across the board will have a considerable dampening effect on household consumption due largely to the pronounced impact of price increases on middle-income groups. However, such an action will have a seriously deleterious impact on lower-income groups unless coupled with some price relief for these groups. Price relief could come in the form of subsidies, income-progressive rate structures, or other alternatives. At this writing, legislation to provide subsidies has been introduced in Congress but not acted upon.

A major current source of help for individuals is the public welfare system. Contact your local office. If no funds are available in your state, you might suggest a state program be initiated. An interesting and apparently successful model was Maine's Project Fuel. Project Fuel demonstrated that the key to a successful program was not direct subsidy for fuel bills but rather assistance in improving residential winterization: installation of insulation, caulking, plastic membrane storm windows, etc. (See Chapter 9.) One-time winterization assistance by the project cost some $280,000 (not including volunteer labor mobilized by project workers) and saved an estimated one million gallons of fuel in one heating season. If a straight fuel bill subsidy program had been adopted, a program with equivalent impact would have cost in the neighborhood of $750,000 annually. Thus, the cost-benefit ratio for a winterization program is at least twice as attractive as that for direct subsidy program. However, in states with less severe winters, the ratio may not be as attractive, and even Maine found that direct fuel grants could not be avoided in some instances.

The principle of Project Fuel holds, however, even beyond Maine's special environment. Thus, the most cost-effective programs for assistance to truck-dependent southern migrants may be a new more efficient truck rather than an "energy stamp" program.

A number of other federal programs are also relevant to relieving the financial strain of energy prices on individuals.

AFDC (Section 403 of the Social Security Act). Emergency cash and special assistance can be provided to AFDC families directly by welfare offices. The AFDC program is administered by each state's designated agency, usually the welfare department. Benefit amounts are set at state (not federal) discretionary levels and can be modified to: (a) Provide recipients with increased fuel allowances (Vermont has raised fuel allotments by 50 percent); and (b) increase the proportion of the subsistence needs standard.

The Social Security Act also allows states to provide up to $500 for home repairs which can be used for winterizing. State welfare departments administer this provision.

The Emergency Assistance Program.   Most states now participate in the EAP, and other states can elect to do so. This program authorizes cash payments for emergencies to: (a) families with a female head-of-household not eligible for AFDC; (b) needy families with a male head-of-household; and (c) non-AFDC migrants. Under EAP, the state must raise 5 percent of the amount.

Farmers Home Administration (504) Loans.   Under Section 504 of the Housing Act of 1949, small, low-interest, long-term loans may be made by FmHA to eligible rural residents. Recipients do not have to be farmers. Loans can be used for insulation materials and general winterizing.

Department of Housing and Urban Development.   Support may be available for municipally designed and run programs of winterization under the Community Development Act of 1974. Contact your local or regional HUD office.

Appendix 6A: Energy Regulation for Information Purposes: A Model Ordinance

The following ordinance is designed to facilitate the collection of information relevant to energy consumption and availability. It was compiled for use as a model only and should be reviewed by a competent attorney before consideration for passage; authority for the actions in this ordinance may not exist under some state constitutions. The ordinance empowers a municipal corporation to issue licenses regulating the sale and exchange of energy within the corporate limits and requiring they be recorded.

The purpose of the license is to provide municipal officials with necessary information concerning the use, storage, distribution, transfer, and sale of energy. This information may be used in formulating policies. Two types of licenses are required in this ordinance: a Class A License and a Class B License. Class A licenses regulate those who profit from the sale, transfer, or distribution of energy, otherwise stated as dealers and producers. A Class B license regulates those who use energy in production, which production may result in profit. License fee levels are established by this ordinance but are not included. In general, any reasonable fees may be charged. The administration may wish to charge no fee; or to develop enough revenue to defray certain administrative costs; or it may wish to charge fees that are high enough to deter some energy uses or users. Additionally, some classes of licensees might be exempted from paying fees: churches, hospitals, etc.

In the event this type of ordinance is not politically feasible in the jurisdiction, a voluntary energy information reporting system might be feasible. If desired, this ordinance or portions of it may be incorporated in the business licensing, sales tax, or other related ordinance.

AN ORDINANCE

TO REGULATE ENERGY AND FUELS WITHIN THE CONFINES OF (CITY) IN TIMES OF ENERGY CRISIS, IN ORDER TO REDUCE THE DELETERIOUS EFFECTS OF SUCH AND TO REPEAL ALL ORDINANCES OR PARTS OF ORDINANCES IN CONFLICT WITH,

BE IT ORDAINED BY THE (CITY COUNCIL OR COMMISSION) OF (CITY) (STATE) AS FOLLOWS:

Section 1: Short Title

This ordinance shall be known as the Energy Regulation Ordinance of (City) (1974) and may be so cited and pleaded.

Section 2: Definitions

For the purposes of this chapter the following phrases, terms and words shall have the meanings given herein: Words used in the present tense include the future; words in the singular number include the plural and the plural the singular.

(a) ENERGY. "Energy" shall mean any material such as uranium, coal, coke, gas, petroleum liquid, peat or wood used to produce heat or power or that heat or power in any form, including but not being thereby limited to hot water, steam, and electricity.

(b) ENERGY ADVISORY BOARD. "Energy Advisory Board" shall mean any local advisory board however designated, created or empowered by the (City Council or Commission) to advise them on energy policy.

(c) PERSON. "Person" shall mean any firm, individual, estate, trust, sole proprietorship, partnership, association, company, joint venture, corporation, governmental unit or instrumentality thereof, or any charitable, educational or other institution.

Section 3: Purpose

This ordinance is enacted to aid the government of (City) in combating the pernicious effects of an energy crisis by causing information regarding the sale, transfer, storage, distribution, and use of energy within the jurisdiction of (City) to be provided to (City) in association with other business licensing information.

Section 4: Licensing

No person shall engage in a business as a wholesale or retail merchant dealing with the sale, transfer, storage, distribution, or use of energy except that he use said energy for private, individual, or nonprofit purposes, or except that he hold a valid license issued under the provisions of this ordinance.

Regulations Governing the Issuance of Licenses

1. No applicant shall be deprived of a license under the provisions of this ordinance except for the nonpayment of required license fees. Nothing contained herein shall limit the power of (City) to deny, suspend, or revoke a license under the provisions of any other valid ordinance of (City).

2. The (City Council or Commission) of (City) shall designate by resolution an official responsible for the enforcement of this ordinance and who shall prepare the necessary application forms for licenses. Said official shall take care that said forms require the inclusion of all information deemed necessary by (City) to carry out the purpose of this ordinance.

3. Fees for application for license under this ordinance shall be as follows: (fee schedule not included; see headnote)

Class A License

1. No person shall engage in the production, acquisition, or purchase of energy for purposes of resale as a dealer in energy for profit except that said person hold a valid Class "A" License.

2. Issuance of a Class "A" License shall be made on submission of an application for license to (City) along with the required application fee. The application shall be approved and the license issued within a period of not more than one week. The Class "A" License shall be valid for a period of six months from date of issuance.

3. Renewal of Class "A" License shall be approved upon payment of the required fee and submission of reports by the applicant on forms provided by (City) listing the amount and value of energy sold, transferred, stored, or distributed under any immediately expired or expiring license

and the estimated amount and value thereof to be sold, transferred, stored, or distributed under the license applied for.

Class B License

1. No person shall seek to acquire or purchase energy for any commercial or industrial use except resale for profit as a dealer in energy or except that said person hold a valid Class "B" License.

2. Issuance of a Class "B" License shall be made on submission of an application for license to (City) along with the required application fee. The application shall be approved and the license issued within a period of one week after application. A Class "B" License shall be valid for a period of one year from the date of issuance.

3. Renewal of a Class "B" License shall be approved upon payment of the required fee and submission of reports by the applicant on forms provided by (City) listing the amount and value of energy acquired or purchased and the person from whom acquired or purchased under any immediately expired or expiring license and the estimated amount and value thereof to be purchased or acquired under the license applied for.

4. No Class "B" Licensee who does not also hold a Class "A" License shall sell, transfer, or otherwise dispose of energy in his possession or under his control except that he have a valid Energy Disposal Permit to do so. Energy Disposal Permits shall be issued upon submission of proper application forms to be obtained from (City) indicating the amount and value of the energy sought to be transferred and the persons party to the transfer.

Other Energy Users

Any person who shall use energy for any purpose other than those specified for a Class "A" License or a Class "B" License shall not require a license.

Section 5: Confidentiality

The information filed by individual persons, as defined herein, except such information as is requested to be held confidential by the person providing said information, shall be open to the public. Divulgence of such information as is requested to be held confidential except upon order of a court of competent jurisdiction or except to an officer of the state entitled to receive the same in his official capacity shall be a misdemeanor. Nothing herein shall be construed to prohibit the publication, or divulgence by other means, of reports derived from confidential information provided that report does not identify individual applications or breach any lawful and reasonable request for confidentiality.

Section 6: Repeal of Conflicting Ordinances

All ordinances or parts of ordinances which shall conflict with this Energy Regulation Ordinance are declared to be repealed.

Section 7: Supervision

All power with respect to this ordinance shall be vested in the (City Council or Commission). No delegation of authority, except as to ministerial acts shall be made.

Section 8: Appeals

Any person aggrieved by an action undertaken by authority of this ordinance may file an appeal with (City). An appeal shall be in writing and signed by the applicant, be designated clearly as an appeal, contain a concise statement of grounds for the appeal and requested relief, be accompanied by briefs, if any; and be marked on the front page "Appeal."

Section 9: Penalties

Any person who violates any provision of this ordinance shall be guilty of a misdemeanor.

Section 10: Separability

Should any section, clause, or provision of this ordinance be declared by the courts to be invalid, the same shall not effect the validity of the ordinance as a whole or any part thereof, other than the part so declared to be invalid.

Section 11: Emergency Clause

In the opinion of the (City Council or Commission) of (City), a public emergency exists in connection with the matters in this ordinance contained, and it is necessary to the peace, safety, and general welfare of the inhabitants of (City) that this ordinance become effective upon publication.

Section 12: Effective Date

This ordinance shall take effect upon its adoption and publication.

Passed by the (City Council or Commission) (City) (State), this _____day of_____, 197__.

Appendix 6B: The Energy Advisory Board: A Model Ordinance

The following ordinance establishes a three-member board (with provision for staff and budget if desired) charged with analyzing the energy situation in a jurisdiction. The board described here is formed to compile and present periodic reports on energy supply and demand and to submit recommendations for action along with an analysis of their efficacy. Authority to create such a board is intrinsic to local government's legal personality in most states. However, this ordinance was compiled as a model only and should be reviewed by a competent attorney before consideration for passage.

AN ORDINANCE

CREATING AN ENERGY ADVISORY BOARD, SPECIFYING THE DUTIES THEREOF, AND PROVIDING FOR THE ORGANIZATION AND PROCEDURES OF SAID BOARD.

BE IT ORDAINED BY THE (CITY COUNCIL OR COMMISSION) OF (CITY) (STATE) AS FOLLOWS:

Section 1: Short Title

This ordinance shall be known as the Energy Advisory Board Ordinance of (City), (1974) and may be so cited and pleaded.

Section 2: Definitions

For the purposes of this chapter the following phrases, terms and words shall have the meanings given herein:

(a) ENERGY. "Energy" shall mean any material such as uranium, coal, coke, gas, petroleum liquid, peat or wood used to produce heat or power or that heat or power in any form, including but not being thereby limited to hot water, steam, and electricity.

(b) ENERGY SUPPLY. "Energy supply" shall mean the amount of energy available for immediate delivery within (City), during any specific, given period of time.

(c) ENERGY DEMAND. "Energy demand" shall mean the amount of energy needed for consumption within (City), during any specific, given period of time.

(d) ENERGY CRISIS. "Energy Crisis" shall mean the onset of any situation or the reasonable expectation thereof, in which energy demand exceeds energy supply.

(e) PERSON. "Person" shall mean any firm, individual, estate, trust, sole proprietorship, partnership, association, company, joint venture, corporation, governmental unit or instrumentality thereof, or any charitable, educational or other institution.

Section 3: Purpose

This ordinance is designed and enacted for the purpose of promoting the health, safety, morals, order, convenience, prosperity and welfare of the present and future inhabitants of (City) by providing for prepared leadership and needed information in times of an energy crisis, by establishing an Energy Advisory Board to advise the (City Council or Commission) on energy management matters herein defined, as shall be directed by the (City Council or Commission).

Section 4: Creation of Board

There is hereby created and established within (City) an Energy Advisory Board, the composition, powers, and duties of which are hereinafter specified.

Section 5: Duties

Reports

On every September 1 and every March 1, and other dates as from time to time established by (the City Council or Commission) the Energy Advisory Board shall submit to the (City Council or Commission) three reports as hereinafter described.

Report Number One: Energy Needs of (City) for the Period (date) to (date). The Energy Needs Report shall summarize the energy demand statistics of (City) and its inhabitants during the six-month period prior to the filing date of the report and forecast the same demand statistics for the six-month period following the filing date. Demand summaries and forecasts will be made for each type of energy. Specific categories of energy types to be used in this report shall be determined by the Energy Advisory Board and approved by (the City Council or Commission). Particular attention shall be paid in the report to determining which needs are discretionary and, therefore, could be eliminated without deleterious effect in a severe shortage and which needs are necessary to the maintenance of the public safety and health. Additionally, this report may contain such other information as the Board or (the City Council or Commission) deems appropriate.

Report Number Two: Availability of Energy in (City) for the Period (date) to (date). The Availability of Energy Report shall summarize the energy supply statistics of (City) and its inhabitants during the six-month period prior to the filing date of the report and forecast the same supply statistics for the six-month period following the filing date. Supply summaries and forecasts will include estimates of the quantity, availability, price, and quality of supplies of energy in or immediately deliverable to (City), including those in storage facilities. Specific categories of energy types to be used in this report shall be determined by the Energy Advisory Board and approved by the (City Council or Commission). Particular attention shall be paid in this report to identifying underutilized suppliers and supplies, and suppliers and supplies that would be available or become available under emergency conditions. Additionally, this report may contain such other information as the Energy Advisory Board or the (City Council or Commission) deems appropriate.

Report Number Three: Recommendations of the Energy Advisory Board for Action During the Period (date) to (date). In its report on Recommendations the Energy Advisory Board shall summarize and evaluate the effectiveness of any energy policy actions taken by (City) during the six-month period prior to the filing of this report. Additionally, the Board shall make recommendations for action on the part of (City) and its agents for the six-month period following the filing of the report. This report shall include the recommendations of the Board in each of the following areas in addition to such other recommendations for action as the Board deems necessary and prudent. The Board shall make recommendations regarding,

a. additions to and withdrawals from the stocks of energy in the possession of, under contract to, or otherwise controlled by (City) or its agents;
b. provisions and facilities for the storage of energy, in the possession of, under contract to, or otherwise directly controlled by (City) or its agents;
c. the advisability of entering into, modifying, or terminating contracts, agreements, or other instruments with persons including but not limited to school districts and counties for the purpose of pooling energy to insure against shortages or other strategies to insure the public safety, health, order, prosperity, and welfare by mitigating the effects of deleterious shortages of energy;
d. the amount of available energy which should be retained under the control of the municipal corporation and the amount which should be declared surplus and sold if otherwise permissible to priority users in the event of the imminent threat or advent of a deleterious shortage of energy within the jurisdiction of (city); and
e. the identification of priority users to whom surplus fuel should be sold if otherwise permissible in the event of such a crisis. (Any such identification should take into consideration the nature, duration and timing of the expected shortage and the essential functions governing the health,

safety, welfare, order and prosperity of the entire jurisdiction of (City) for the future as well as the present.)

Voting

The Energy Advisory Board shall not transmit any report to the (City Council or Commission) unless it be approved for transmittal by at least two Board members. A dissenting member shall list the points of dissent and state his position in a minority report to be appended to the instrument of transmittal.

Public Meetings

The Energy Advisory Board shall not transmit any report to the (City Council or Commission) unless it be presented in its substantive part of parts for comment by all affected parties at a public meeting or by some other means of publication.

Section 6: Budget

The Energy Advisory Board shall submit a request for an operating budget in the manner prescribed and applicable to other city departments. The request shall be considered in the annual budget act of the city. The Board's budget proposal will include requests for funds to defray all ordinary and necessary anticipated expense.

Section 7: Composition

Term Lengths

The Energy Advisory Board shall consist of a chairman and two board members appointed by the (City Council or Commission). The chairman shall be appointed for a term beginning (date) and ending (the same day three years hence) when the (City Council or Commission) shall review and act on his appointment for a second term. This procedure shall be followed in all successive terms. One board member shall be appointed for a term beginning (date) and ending (the same date two years hence) when his reappointment shall be considered in the same manner used in reviewing the reappointment of the chairman. A second term and any future terms shall be for a period of three years. A second board member shall be appointed by the same procedure as the first board member with the single exception that his first term shall be from (date) to (the same day one year hence).

Qualifications

One member of the Board shall have knowledge of energy supply or conversion systems and environmental protection; one member shall be an attorney or have knowledge of the law; and one member shall be from the public at large.

Recall

Any member of the Energy Advisory Board may be recalled from his position for any cause, by the majority vote of the (City Council or Commission). His term shall be filled by temporary appointment by the (City Council or Commission). At the end of this term, reappointment shall be made according to the procedures and term lengths set down in this section. This same procedure shall be applied in the case of death or resignation of any board member.

Section 8: Staff

The (City Council or Commission) shall provide for the staff needs and organization of the Energy Advisory Board, which shall be financed according to the procedures set down in the budgetary section. All civil service rules and regulations shall be adhered to by the Energy Advisory Board with regard to this staff.

Section 9: Repeal of Conflicting Ordinances

All previous ordinances which conflict with this Energy Advisory Board Ordinance are declared to be repealed.

Section 10: Separability

Should any section, clause, or provision of this ordinance be declared by the courts to be invalid, the same shall not affect the validity of the ordinance as a whole or any part thereof, other than the part so declared to be invalid.

Section 11: Emergency Clause

In the opinion of the (City Council or Commission) of (City), a public emergency exists in connection with the matters in this ordinance contained, and it is necessary to the peace, safety, and general welfare of the inhabitants of (City) that this ordinance become effective upon publication.

Section 12: Effective Date

This ordinance shall take effect upon its adoption and publication.

Passed by the (City Council or Commission) (City) (State), this _____day of_____, 197__.

7

Policy Alternatives

Policies aimed at the symptomatic relief of such side effects of an energy crisis as economic dislocation and threats to the public health and safety were discussed in the previous chapter. Here we deal with policy alternatives aimed directly at resolving an energy crisis. The three policy objectives open are: increase supply, reduce demand, and reallocate available energy. These three general objectives encompass such specific objectives as: (1) direct supply distribution; (2) determination of priority uses; (3) limitation of consumption; (4) requisition for essential needs; (5) prohibition of certain energy consuming activities; (6) requiring or permiting the use of alternate fuels; (7) requiring the performance of certain contracts over others; (8) imposition of surtaxes; and so forth.

Supply Policy

If a survey of the energy situation in the jurisdiction (see chapters 6 and 8 on the Energy Budget Report) shows the possibility of a shortfall in supply, early intervention should be considered to improve the supply picture. There will be considerably greater difficulty improving supply as the forecast shortage looms nearer and others begin competing on the spot market for uncommitted stocks.

Available approaches to improving supply depend upon the energy commodity in dearth. The principal approaches to supply improvement are building stockpiles during periods of loose supply and acquiring the capability to burn alternate fuels. Most small jurisdictions do not have facilities for the storage of natural gas or electricity and cannot afford to build them (though technologies for such units are available). Many months supply of natural gas can be stored in underground formations or large tanks. Typically, such installations cost many millions of dollars to construct and install. Electricity is "stored" by using it to pump water uphill during off-peak periods. During peak periods or when supply is short, the water is allowed to run back downhill through a generator. Such facilities are typically ten or more times as expensive as those that store natural gas. Smaller amounts of electric power can be stored against blackouts for considerably less money by storage batteries, gas, or diesel electric generators and more recently capacitor banks and flywheels. All such systems, however, require careful engineering before purchase and installation.

Local storage of coal and petroleum products is well within the means of any local government. If you choose to develop such stockpiles, you will want to encourage some key facilities (hospitals and clinics, churches, perhaps some schools, etc.) to install and keep up equipment that will allow them to make use of the stocks on hand in an emergency. This encouragement should be especially directed to users of natural gas, a fuel in short supply nationwide and likely to remain so for a number of years.

Acquisition of stocks presents certain financial risks, particularly with regard to price fluctuations. A serious drop in price could cost holders of stocks a great deal. The risks of holding stocks, however, must be evaluated by each jurisdiction against the background of their needs.

Where stockpiling is not feasible, survey the contracts under which energy is delivered to local constituents to insure that critical users cannot be cut off arbitrarily especially when (and if) the mandatory allocation program now guaranteeing fair distribution of available supplies expires. Local governments may face some difficulties in dealing and bargaining with large corporate entities—especially public monopolies—for adequate firm contracts, in getting valid information on supply availability, and the like. With regard to dealing with private nonmonopolistic corporations, an effort should be made to deal with a number of different corporations, and encouragement should be given to as many as possible to operate in the local area as a means of raising supply reliability. With regard to public utilities, the bargaining position of local officials may seem weak, but remember that public monopoly requires franchises, rights of way, licenses, and other permits from the local government. When these items are renegotiated (every few years in many states) they may be revised in favor of local control. Also, public utilities are legally bound to supply consumers with adequate, continuous, and reliable service. Failure to do so may render the utility liable whether or not it was negligent.

A word on the legal character of stockpiles: they may be owned by local governments or private persons. If owned by government, acquisition for, and sales from, such stockpiles may be subject to challenge on constitutional grounds if not done properly. In general, local jurisdictions may purchase, receive, hold, sell, lease, convey, and dispose of property only for purposes that in the judgment of the governing authority will provide for the safety, preserve the health, and promote the prosperity of the inhabitants. Most municipal corporations may engage in stockpiling, sanctioned by ordinance, provided that distributions from stock are in keeping with the law. Distribution for consumption in public facilities (police stations, jails, courthouses, and etc.) presents no problem; in an emergency, distribution for consumption, by private organizations such as hospitals also falls within the law in most states. Other distributions (such as those to low-income families) might also be acceptable if done through a public housing or similar agency or if they meet two criteria: (1) they provide for the safety, preserve the health, promote the prosperity of the inhabitants; and (2) no other agency, private or public, can or will make such distributions. In short, caution must be exercised in the management of public stockpiles that they do not compete with private enterprise; direct competition between private enterprise and a public agency invites legal action by aggrieved businessmen. Stockpiling fuel against periods of shortage, however, cannot be construed as competition with private (or other public) suppliers.

Put another way, it has been held that municipal corporations may not engage in private enterprise, strictly speaking, except when that enterprise is for public purpose: reducing unemployment during a depression, using raw materials of the state, etc. Thus, the compilers of *American Jurisprudence* write:

It was, until fairly recently at least, looked upon as a well-established principle of law that a municipal corporation could not constitutionally be authorized by the legislature to engage in the business of selling and distributing to its inhabitants, at reasonable rates and without discrimination, the conveniences or even the necessities of life, if the business was of such a nature that it could be and ordinarily was carried on by private individuals without the aid of any franchise from the state. It was for this reason that it has been held that it is not within the power of the legislature to authorize municipal corporations to establish fuel yards and to purchase coal and wood to resell to their inhabitants—even at a time when fuel is scarce and the prices are high, so that the cost to consumers might be expected to be reduced by such an undertaking on the part of the municipality—or to buy and resell at retail gasoline, oil, and lubricants. . . . There were, from the beginning, some exceptions recognized. . . . Even the courts which deny the power of the legislature to establish municipal fuel yards concede that *if a condition arose in which the supply of fuel would be so small, and the difficulty of obtaining it so great, that persons desiring to purchase it would be unable to supply themselves through private enterprise, since it is conceivable that agencies of government might be able to obtain fuel when citizens generally could not, the government might constitute itself an agent for the relief of the community;* consequently, the money expended for the purpose would be expended for public use.[1]

In such an instance, it might be held that the stock has been rededicated; what was once only for corporate purpose has been at least in part put to public purpose. Reasonable and fair rules must govern the use of property for public purpose.

An additional problem with stockpiles arises in the case of petroleum stocks: rededication as well as hoarding of fuel may be prohibited by the Mandatory Petroleum Allocation Regulations. An FEA officer reviewing this handbook wrote that stockpiling

> *may* be in conflict with the provisions of Section 211.13 (f) of the Regulations. . . . There are other sections of the Regulations as well which I believe would preclude any stockpiling of petroleum fuels. Prior to recommending this . . . I would strongly recommend that it be reviewed as to legality under the Federal Regulations.[2]

Section 211.13 (f) appears to prohibit rededication:

> [Applications to suppliers] shall contain a statement that increased allocations shall be used only for the purpose stated in the application, shall not be diverted for other uses; and that if its needs decline, the purchaser shall file an amended application for a downward adjustment to its base period use.[3]

Other parts of the regulations appear to prohibit hoarding:

> No wholesale purchaser shall accept an adjusted base period volume initiated by a supplier under this paragraph which, when combined with the adjusted base period volumes supplied to the wholesale purchaser by its other base period suppliers, would exceed the wholesale purchaser's actual unusual growth for a base period. A wholesale purchaser offered such an adjusted base period volume shall immediately notify FEO in accordance with forms and instructions issued by FEO. The FEO may require suppliers of the wholesale purchaser to adjust the wholesale purchaser's base period volume as adjusted by its suppliers under this paragraph and to adjust the wholesale purchaser's future allocations to compensate for any excess product received by the wholesale purchaser.[4]

It appears to us that the mandatory regulations may prohibit excessively large one-time purchases of fuel to fill stockpiles. They do not seem to prohibit the construction or operation of stockpile facilities. Thus, public utilities are permitted to maintain stockpiles and, in fact, can apply for additional supplies long before stocks are depleted. An official of the city of Denver explained Denver's stockpiling program:

> During the exceedingly cold winter of 1972-73 a number of cus-
> tomers, including the City and County of Denver . . . were required
> to shift from gas to alternate fuels, usually fuel oil. . . . All found
> that the capacities of the operating fuel holding facilities were in-
> adequate and because of this a number of them found difficulty in
> procuring fuel oil fast enough to meet their increased daily operating
> requirements.
>
> To prevent a similar situation arising again many of the interruptable
> customers in this area, including Denver, took steps to increase the
> capacity of their operating fuel holding facilities and to fill them all to
> their new capacities. Stockpiling *per se* was not considered.[5]

Again, the issue seems to be political rather than legal. In essence, excessively large purchases in times of scarcity (when allocation levels are
below 100 percent) invite trouble; politically sensitive management is
the answer.

In regard to rededication, the diversion of stocks during a demonstrable
emergency could not be effectively prevented by the FEA, nor would it
be easy for FEA or any other agency to impose sanctions after the fact
if such diversion were in the public interest. In order to impose such
sanctions they must prove that municipal officials were not acting in good
faith, and local official actions are presumed valid unless proven otherwise.

Other conflicts with FEA regulations are, of course, possible. It would
appear, however, that none of these objections is substantive provided
public stocks are managed with reasonable care.

Privately owned stockpiles present fewer management problems but
have other drawbacks. First, it is difficult to encourage the construction
and stocking of private facilities. Property and other local tax incentives
to do so may not be sufficient encouragement and may face difficult constitutional challenges as well. Second, it is difficult to influence the rate
of acquisitions to and withdrawals from private facilities. In addition,
private stockpiles face the same problems with the mandatory program
regulations as do public ones. Public officials can expect that private
facilities will be used for private purposes (residential and commercial
heating, agricultural production and so forth) that seldom coincide with
the demands upon public stocks. In sum, adequate private facilities usually do not eliminate the need for public facilities. A model ordinance
establishing and regulating a public energy stockpiling facility is appended
to this chapter.

The second major area of supply policy is that of substitution of plentiful for scarce supplies. There are two major opportunities for substitution:
substituting lower-quality for higher-quality supplies (where quality in-

cludes but is not limited to sulfur content), and substituting other types of fuel.

Substitution of the latter type, coal for oil being the primary instance, may face difficult environmental and economic problems. Most of the substitution opportunities available are in boiler applications, where expensive modifications may be required. In addition, the increased use of coal may cause serious environmental degradation, although the FEA has power to order such conversions.

An attractive and underutilized area of substitution is the encouragement of the use of solar energy, something the government is just beginning. Solar energy technology for application to space heating, crop drying, and some commercial and industrial processes is available now. The main obstacles to the wider use of solar technology, particularly in space heating, are: (1) conservatism and ignorance on the part of investors (especially loan officers); (2) lack of judicial recognition of one's right to sunlight; (3) environmental impact worries (every home facing South?) and (4) lack of experienced contractors. Some of these obstacles might be removed or at least lowered by municipal government programs.

The most accessible and reasonable opportunity for substitution involves the establishment of a program of standby low-quality-fuel permits allowing such fuels to be burned during an emergency with a waiver of emission standards providing weather conditions permit. The Clean Air Act has been temporarily amended to allow the FPA administrator to "temporarily suspend any stationary source fuel or emission limitation as it applies to any person. . . ." An applicant must approach the state authorities for a variance, which they must in turn submit for EPA approval. Many states have simplified their variance application procedures to accommodate fuel emergencies.

Demand Policy

Energy conservation programs are aimed at reducing demand for energy so that a reduced supply may become adequate. There are at least three approaches to implementing a conservation program: public appeals to use less energy, regulation by ordinance of energy consumption practices, and manipulation of energy prices by taxation.

Public information programs are well developed, and a great deal of help is available for the asking. Lists of energy conservation tips for almost every situation, occupation, and activity are available from various federal and state agencies. (A large number appear in chapter 9). Assistance with preparing radio and television presentations and advertising materials is available from your state extension service, the state energy office, or the Federal Energy Administration. Public information programs depend upon the promotion of energy-saving tips—tips that generally have two weaknesses. First, the relative or even absolute effectiveness of most energy-saving tips is not known; hence, much public effort may be wasted promoting ineffectual activities. For example, more conservative use of hot water may in some cases save more energy than turning down the thermostat. Second, the cost effectiveness of most tips is either not known or seldom published; insulating the walls in a home may take twenty years or more to pay for itself, or it may pay for itself in the first month. Careful thought should be given to any tips provided by or through public authorities.

Regulation by ordinance of energy-use patterns to reduce consumption is not well worked out and may not be fully constitutional in every state. Nonetheless, certain techniques thought to be effective have been implemented elsewhere, including: reduction or elimination of decorative and/or street lighting; reduced hours of operation of service stations and commercial establishments generally; providing priority supply of gasoline to emergency vehicles, public transit, and transport of essential commodities; limiting the use of official vehicles; banning the use of nonessential and recreational gasoline-consuming equipment; reducing speed limits; imposing fuel surcharges; restricting commuter traffic by means of closing some roads, parking bans, etc.; preferences for car pools in parking, toll fees, through or express lanes, etc.

The power to implement such programs may come from one or a host of grants to local jurisdictions. Any locality may, of course, pass resolutions calling for citizen cooperation with almost any scheme, but voluntary schemes may not be fully effective and cannot be enforced. Mandatory schemes derive their authority either from a special direct grant from the state (as with a declaration of emergency) or from standing grants of state power. In the latter case, authority must be specifically related to the proposed program. For example, even-odd alternate-day fuel sales may be allowable as a means of regulating traffic (preventing long waiting lines at service stations that constitute traffic hazards); full rationing might be construed as a means of maintaining public order and health; decorative lighting may be declared a public nuisance. In considering whether to make use of any of these regulatory policies, their questionable legality may not be important. If a court determination of the unconstitutionality of such an ordinance would create no legal liability or political consequences for the local government—that is, if the only effect of the court's order is to terminate the program—then enactment will, at worst, do no harm. Moreover, the worst part of the crisis may have passed by the time a restraining order can be issued. Two more points: first, if a program works well and has only minimal side effects, court challenges may simply not arise; second, restraining orders are not necessarily bad—they may be the most acceptable way from a purely political standpoint of terminating a program or eliminating an apparent but impractical possibility that enjoys some citizen support.

A primary example of conservation regulated by ordinance were the programs adopted by Los Angeles in 1973-74. During Phase I of the city's Emergency Energy Curtailment Program, users of electricity were required to cut back by an average of 15 percent (10 percent for residential and industrial, 20 percent for commercial). Enforcement provisions of questionable legality would have allowed the city to order all power to be shut off to violators for up to one month. However, enforcement was to be delayed by a few months, and in the meantime consumption dropped from 14 percent to 18 percent. Phase II of the program was never initiated; it required greater cutbacks.

Manipulation of energy consumption by taxation may have either of two objectives: the elimination of waste in some or all energy uses or the total elimination of some uses. It is generally felt that the pattern of energy use will not change much until the price increase exceeds 10 percent or more. Since the percentage levy of sales and use taxes are fixed by most state laws, at levels less than 10 percent, local jurisdictions must make use of license taxes; license taxes are based on the police power to regulate or prohibit a particular business and not upon the power to raise revenue. Generally, a license tax is applied to the seller and is passed on to the user by him, thus controlling, albeit indirectly, the price of energy to the user. Beneficial use of such taxes by local governments today is perhaps limited to discouraging nonresidential uses of natural gas. Nonetheless, local jurisdictions could make use of their powers to regulate businesses as a lever to manipulate energy prices.

There are, however, two problems with the use of price policy on the local level that may reduce its effectiveness in certain situations. First, the Balkanization of energy prices may lead to a high price for energy in one locale and low price in an adjoining one. In the long run, such differentials are likely to affect decisions on location of new investments and thus the economic health and character of the jurisdiction. In short, the economic and social impact of adopting any tax policy needs to be carefully and fully examined before enactment. Second, price-induced conservation policies have different impacts on different users. Consumption habits of the middle-income groups are the most responsive to price changes. High-income groups and big users are somewhat less responsive. Least responsive are the lower income groups, which may also suffer most from price increases. Thus, a tax policy raising the price of energy is likely to be interpreted as antipopulist and thus to pose serious local political problems. Also, tax-inspired tax increases may conflict with federally imposed pricing regulations, delivery contracts, and other activities.

Reallocation Policy

Reallocation is one of the most powerful and useful energy-crisis management tools. Reallocation refers to the confiscation or removal of a source of supply from one user and its rededication to another. Reallocation policy also includes the distribution of secondary stocks to end-users; secondary stocks are stockpiles of fuel owned or controlled by persons not engaged in the energy marketing business, i.e., coal piles in the backyard of the local school, large propane tanks belonging to a local vegetable canning firm, etc. The justification for reallocation lies in an adaptation of the doctrine of beneficial use. If sufficient supply is available for only one of two uses, it is the public responsibility to insure that the most beneficial of the uses is served first.

It is a problem of the greatest political difficulty to determine which are and which are not beneficial uses. No one can make this determination but responsible local officials. There is, however, some general lore (and that's all it is) on priority problems. To some extent, the priority of use depends upon the type of energy being reallocated, the expected duration and severity of the shortage occasioning the reallocation, the politics and economic character of the jurisdiction, and perhaps other factors as well. A tentative list of priority uses for petroleum and natural gas products was prepared in 1973 as a policy aid for the federal government in developing their crisis policy, which finally emerged as the mandatory allocation program; it may be some help in formulating other lists:

The following list of activities considered as priority uses of petroleum products is recommended as guideline for use in state programs to allocate petroleum products.
(1) Farming, ranching, dairy, and commercial fishing.
(2) Services directly related to the cultivation, production, processing, preservation, or distribution of food.
(3) Oil, gas and coal industry operations and related suppliers and services.
(4) Health and sanitation services.
(5) Police, firefighting and emergency aid services.
(6) Public passenger transportation, including school buses and other buses, intercity and mass transit rail systems, and airline passenger services, but excluding taxicabs and tour and excursion services.
(7) Rail, highway, sea and air freight transportation services.

(8) Public utilities, except for substitute natural gas feedstocks and fuels required for conversion from coal and residual fuel oil other than those necessary to meet primary air standards.

(9) Telecommunications.[6]

Two cautions about using this list. First, it is obviously incomplete and specific to a limited situation: for example, in some situations, home heating (which is not even listed), might be the highest priority. Second, the list given reflects a national perspective of priorities not a local one. A local perspective may emphasize categories of users more appropriate to local life (tourism, hothouse gardening, etc.).

The approach to reallocation policy may be mandatory or voluntary. In a crisis or near crisis perhaps the most effective approach in a small jurisdiction is simply to call together the relevant persons, present them with the situation, and ask for their voluntary cooperation. By such an approach, large industrial plants, school districts, and others have voluntarily shut down and redistributed their energy supply to "more beneficial" uses. Such informal approaches should always be given early consideration; they have the advantage of eliminating the need for the complex legal and administrative trappings of mandatory arrangements.

More formal approaches to reallocation policy may also involve the prior execution of contracts with suppliers or others (school districts, trucking firms, etc.) for reallocation in the event of an emergency. The principle here is to develop an energy pooling arrangement among a number of major users. Thus, if one user expected to fall, say, 10 percent short, others would cut their consumption somewhat so that no members of the pool would fall more than, say, one percent short. Such an agreement might be modeled upon the agreement among the twelve big energy-consuming nations (the International Energy Program). The agreement provides that when supplies among the twelve taken as a whole drop below 93 percent of unconstrained demand, each of the twelve will immediately promulgate conservation programs designed to achieve 7 percent demand reduction. If supply fell to 88 percent, curtailment programs would have to achieve 10 percent reduction. If only one or two of the twelve were experiencing a shortfall, the remainder would, under the agreement, export supplies to eliminate or more equitably distribute the shortage.

An additional approach to effectuating reallocation is to use the city's power to force sales to priority users. It is an established principle of the application of municipal police power that individual property rights, e.g., the right to hold for private use a supply of fuel, are subject to certain restrictions. In particular, it is reasonable that a city in a dire situation may: by executive order, order any individual subject in its jurisdiction to sell, at a fair price, a supply of fuel in his possession to a priority user; or by due process and with just compensation, take or condemn for its own or other public use any supply of fuel within its jurisdiction.

There are two fundamental limitations of these powers. First, the regulation or infringement of private rights must not be arbitrary, unnecessary, or unreasonable. In essence, the effect of infringement upon the one must be to conserve rather than restrict the rights of all. Second, care must be taken not to infringe upon the federal or state governments or by infringing upon individuals to compromise a federal or state action.

Appendix 7A: Energy Stockpiling Ordinance

The following ordinance sets up a facility, to be owned and operated by a municipal corporation, in which stocks of fuels may accumulate. In an emergency these stocks can provide relief. Authority for this ordinance rests with the power of jurisdictions to acquire and dispose of real and personal property for corporate purposes and by lawful means. Such a stockpiling facility must be carefully managed for reasons explained in the text of this chapter. This ordinance was compiled as a model only and should be reviewed by a competent attorney before consideration for passage.

AN ORDINANCE

AUTHORIZING THE ACQUISITION OF ENERGY SUPPLIES IN ANTICIPATION OF EMERGENCY NEEDS, PROVIDING PROCEDURES FOR THE DETERMINATION OF PRIORITY NEEDS, PROVIDING FOR THE APPOINTMENT OF AN ENERGY MANAGER AND SPECIFYING THE DUTIES THEREOF,

BE IT ORDAINED BY THE (CITY COUNCIL OR COMMISSION) (CITY) OF STATE OF (STATE) AS FOLLOWS:

Section 1: Short Title

This ordinance shall be known as the Energy Stockpiling Ordinance of (City) (State), (1974) and may be so cited and pleaded.

Section 2: Definitions

For the purposes of this chapter the following phrases, terms and words shall have the meanings given herein:

(a) ENERGY. "Energy" shall mean any material such as uranium, coal, coke, gas, petroleum liquid, peat or wood used to produce heat or power or that heat or power in any form, including but not being thereby limited to hot water, steam, and electricity.

(b) ENERGY SUPPLY. "Energy supply" shall mean the amount of energy available for immediate delivery within (City), during any specific period of time.

(c) ENERGY DEMAND. "Energy demand" shall mean the amount of energy needed for consumption within the (City) during any specific period of time.

(d) ENERGY CRISIS. "Energy Crisis" shall mean the onset of any situation or the reasonable expectation thereof, in which energy demand exceeds energy supply.

(e) ENERGY ADVISORY BOARD. Shall mean any local advisory board or examiner designated, created or empowered by the (City Council or Commission) of (City) to collect and analyze energy data for the purposes of advising the (City Council or Commission) on energy policy, or, in lieu thereof, the (City Council or Commission) of (City).

(f) PERSON. "Person" shall mean any firm, individual, estate, trust, sole proprietorship, partnership association, company joint venture, corporation, governmental unit or instrumentality thereof, or any charitable, educational or other institution.

(g) ENERGY RESERVE. "Energy Reserve" shall mean any and all energy supplies either owned by, or otherwise under the exclusive control of (City).

Section 3: Purpose

This ordinance is enacted to provide for the health, safety, morals, order, convenience, prosperity and general welfare of the present and future inhabitants of (City), by authorizing (City) to buy, sell, transfer, store and distribute energy to provide for the necessary and ordinary needs of (City) and to provide, in times of energy crisis, an energy reserve to be applied to any purpose deemed necessary, by the (City Council or Commission) to the promotion of the safety and prosperity, the preservation of health, and the improvement of morals, peace, order, comfort and convenience of the inhabitants of (City), provided that such application is lawful and does no harm to any person except that person be fully, fairly, and expeditiously compensated under provisions hereinafter stated and in accordance with law.

It is not the purpose of this ordinance to authorize (City) to enter into private commerce to buy or sell energy to any person except for corporate purpose or in the event common energy suppliers cannot meet the needs of the inhabitants of (City) during an energy crisis.

Section 4: Provision for the Acquisition and Use
of Energy Supplies

A. (City) shall acquire energy by purchase, consignment, or any other lawful means for municipal purposes including, but not limited to, the lighting and heating of city offices and other public buildings, operation of city vehicles, street lights, water and sewer systems, emergency equipment and any other city owned or operated equipment, utilities or property. The city shall acquire and store such additional amounts of fuel as the (City Council or Commission) with the advice of the Energy Advisory Board determines to be necessary and prudent to meet priority needs during times of energy crisis. These priority needs shall include but not be limited to the operation of health care, police, and emergency aid facilities, the maintenance of telecommunications, water, and sewer systems, the provision of adequately heated and lit space for any persons displaced or inconvenienced by the energy crisis.

B. The facilities for the storage and production of energy by the city shall be surveyed by the Energy Advisory Board. The Board will report its findings and make recommendations for action by the (City Council or Commission), if any be required, to improve the city's facilities for storing energy to meet the needs stated in 4 (A) above, as well as any additional requirements the Energy Advisory Board deems necessary and reasonable.

C. The (City Council or Commission) shall appoint to serve at its pleasure an Energy Manager to act as its agent in the performance of the following duties:

1. discover supplies of energy which may be purchased for municipal use;
2. represent the (City Council or Commission) in the negotiations for and purchase of these supplies;
3. arrange for the timely delivery of these supplies to the appropriate storage facilities;
4. manage those storage facilities, providing for their maintenance, safety and utility, the proper rotation of the stocks therein stored and other necessary and proper related duties;
5. arrange for the timely delivery of energy from city stores to such users and for such purposes as the (City Council or Commission) with the advice of the Energy Advisory Board lawfully directs; and
6. report to the Energy Advisory Board and to the (City Council or Commission) on these activities with a frequency and in a manner directed by them.

Section 5: Power with the Council

All power with respect to this ordinance shall be vested in the (City Council or Commission), who shall have power to overrule all decisions made pursuant to this ordinance by any agent or agency created herein.

Section 6: Appeals

Any person aggrieved by any actions undertaken by authority of this ordinance may file an appeal with the (City Council or Commission). An appeal shall be in writing and signed by the applicant, be designated clearly as an appeal, contain a concise statement of grounds for the appeal, be accompanied by briefs, if any; and be marked on the front page "Appeal." Decision by the (City Council or Commission) shall be final.

Section 7: Repeal of Conflicting Ordinances

All previous ordinances which conflict with this Energy Advisory Board Ordinance are declared to be repealed.

Section 8: Separability

Should any section, clause, or provision of this ordinance be declared by the courts to be invalid, the same shall not affect the validity of the ordinance as a whole or any part thereof, other than the part so declared to be invalid.

Section 9: Emergency Clause

In the opinion of the (City Council or Commission), a public emergency exists in connection with the matters in this ordinance contained, and it is necessary to the peace, safety, and general welfare of the inhabitants of (City) that this ordinance become effective upon publication.

Section 10: Effective Date

This ordinance shall take effect upon its adoption and publication.

Passed by (City Council or Commission) (City) (State), this____day of_____, 197__.

8

The Energy Budget Report

The first requirement of an effective energy policy is information, a summary of the patterns in which energy is supplied and consumed in the jurisdiction. Because this information is similar in form to the economic information on a financial balance sheet, we refer to it as the information required for *energy budget* management. The collection of information for an energy budget may be required by ordinance, e.g., an amendment to the business licensing, sales tax or other act; such an ordinance is discussed in chapter 6. In this chapter we describe the Energy Budget Report and how to compile it.

The Energy Budget Report (EBR) should be a periodic report to local government authorities summarizing: (1) the forecast demand for critical energy commodities for the period beginning with the filing of the report and extending into the future some predetermined length of time, (2) the forecast supply for the same period, and (3) a set of recommendations for action if supply and demand are not expected to clear. This section of the handbook describes the EBR and how to compile it.

Collecting Data

Most energy policy agencies collect data by having users and suppliers fill out forms. These forms vary with the type of user or supplier. For example, one such form in use by a state agency is aimed at determining energy consumption in residential buildings. Among the questions are: name, location, age, number of stories, and square footage, etc. of the building; its total twelve-month consumption of electricity, natural gas, fuel oil, steam, and other energy forms for each of four years preceding the filing date; the number and description of major appliances, including air conditioners, hot water heaters, furnaces, etc. Another form aimed at suppliers of liquid petroleum gas (LPG) asks them to report for the coming quarter: the total number of LPG they require, the amount of shortfall they expect, the name of the suppliers, and the amount supplied by each, their total storage capacity, their present supply on hand, the distribution of their customers by locale and type (residential, commercial, industrial, etc.). Some forms inquire about prices, forms of payment, and firmness of contractual obligation. Two examples of supply survey forms and one user survey form are included as appendixes to this chapter.

Not all information you require must be gathered by you; the Federal Energy Administration, the Department of the Interior, and other agencies as well as private companies publish periodicals of data. Among the most useful periodicals is *Monthly Energy Review,* published by, and available from, the National Energy Information Center, an office of the FEA. Introducing the *Review,* an FEA official writes:

> The Federal Energy Administration is charged with the responsibility for collecting, analyzing, and disseminating energy-related information. Through FEA's National Energy Information Center, a variety of technical reports have been published. This new report, *Monthly Energy Review,* incorporates the energy information previously published in the *PIMS Monthly Petroleum Report,* the supplements to the *PIMS,* and *Monthly Energy Indicators.* Other data elements will be included as they are developed. The introduction of *Monthly Energy Review* is part of our continuing effort to meet your information needs.[1]

Other valuable data periodicals include: the Bureau of Mine's *Mineral Industry Surveys* and three privately published periodicals that have statistical sections: *Energy Controls* (Prentice-Hall), *Energy Management* (Commerce Clearing House), and *Energy Users Report* (Bureau of National Affairs). In addition, many of the energy industry groups have publications, notably the *Oil and Gas Journal, The Oil Daily,* the Institute of Electrical and Electronic Engineers' *Spectrum,* the annual reports of your local electric companies, natural gas companies, oil companies, and the National LP-Gas Association and others. (See the bibliography in chapter 2.)

Forecasting in General

The short-term forecasting (six months or less) required for an EBR need not be a sophisticated computerized science nor a black art. It is merely a simple process of extending the past into the future. Moreover, much of the work may be done for the forecaster if he designs his survey forms correctly. In any case, excluding war and national emergencies, massive shifts in supply and demand patterns do not occur in such short time spans as six months; for example, the nation typically has more than a three-month supply of energy at all times. If patterns of demand change only by a few percent from quarter to quarter, forecasts are likely to be near the mark. The real purpose of the forecast is to satisfy local officials that they won't be short of fuel by 50 percent or more; being off a few percent either way cannot be easily measured much less forecast and in many instances may not matter much.

In order to compile an EBR the forecaster will need to develop two separate kinds for forecasts: one for demand and one for supply. Each requires its own forecasting technique.

Demand Forecasts

The key forecasting technique on the demand side involves establishing historical patterns for critical fuels and *extrapolating* them (extending them forward) into the future. For local governments, critical fuels will almost always include electricity, diesel and home heating oil (these are somewhat interchangeable), gasoline, natural gas, coal, and some bottled gases. Other fuels and energy sources may be or may become important in a particular jurisdiction—especially if a major employer requires them.

In most areas of the country, consumption of these critical fuels under-

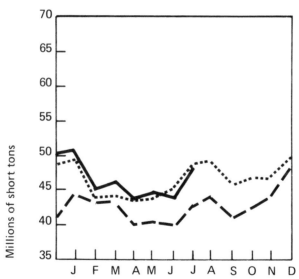

Note: The broken line represents 1972 data, the dotted line 1973, and the solid line 1974.

Source: Federal Energy Administration, National Energy Information Center, *Monthly Energy Review*. Washington, D.C., Federal Energy Administration, October 1974, p. 25.

Figure 8-1. Domestic Consumption of Coal

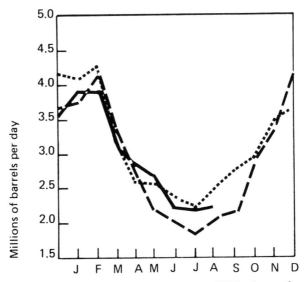

Note: The broken line represents 1972 data, the dotted line 1973, and the solid line 1974.

Source: Federal Energy Administration, National Energy Information Center, *Monthly Energy Review*. Washington, D.C., Federal Energy Administration, October 1974, p. 19.

Figure 8-2. Domestic Demand for Petroleum Distillates

goes a seasonal cycle (see figures 8-1, 8-2, and 8-3): sales of coal reach a peak once during the summer air conditioning season (coal is the primary fuel for electrical utilities) and once during the winter heating season; diesel and home-heating oils peak during the winter; electricity demand peaks in step with coal. To forecast demand, ask all wholesale purchasers in your jurisdiction to submit records by month for each fuel. Graph a year's worth of these records (figures 8-1, 8-2, and 8-3). This graph can constitute your forecast. That is, to forecast coal demand for June, merely read off the graph the June figures. You may want to include your best guess as well as to what you think might be the range of demand above or below that point, perhaps, say, as a function of the weather. There is no good formula for making best guesses; they should be based on judgment and familiarity with the situation. The only advice is *use common sense;* for example, if the jurisdiction has undergone significant change during the data-collection period in terms of number of tourist visitor days, number of motor vehicles, or just the number of resident population, an attempt should be made to estimate the impact of that

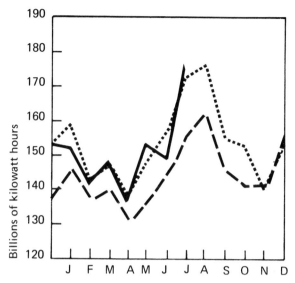

Note: The broken line represents 1972 data, the dotted line 1973, and the solid line 1974.

Source: Federal Energy Administration, National Energy Information Center, *Monthly Energy Review.* Washington, D.C., Federal Energy Administration, October 1974, p. 29.

Figure 8-3. Demand for Electricity

change on the forecast. You might try doing the forecast in terms of per capita demand, sales per motor vehicle, and etc.

Consumption of many fuels is strongly influenced by the weather. For example, the greatest determinant of heating-fuel consumption is temperature. To improve the accuracy of your forecast, you may want to include some correction for the expected weather. The simplest approach is again extrapolation from historical data; thus, if you expect a colder than normal winter, insert a question in your survey of, say, retail fuel oil dealers such as "What do you expect demand to be if this winter is: (1) much colder than last year? (2) much warmer than last year? (3) the same as last year?" A more sophisticated, though perhaps less reliable, approach is to make use of the "degree-day" measurement. For example, in order to forecast residential heating requirements, you need to know the amount of fuel (cubic feet, pounds, gallons) used per *heating degree-day* in your jurisdiction.

Heating engineers developed the heating degree-day statistic as a useful integrator of temperature and fuel consumption early in the century. The heating degree-day statistic is a simple method, using only outdoor air temperature, and neglecting the other factors such as solar radiation and wind. Numerous studies have established the fact that when the daily mean air temperature is 65° or higher, most buildings require no heat to maintain an inside temperature of at least 70°. The daily degree-day statistic is calculated by subtracting the mean temperature for the day from a base temperature of 65° as follows:

$$65° - \frac{\text{Max Temp} + \text{Min Temp}}{2} = \begin{array}{l} \text{Daily Heating} \\ \text{Degree-Days} \end{array}$$

Thus, each degree of mean temperature below 65° is one degree-day unit. If the mean temperature is 45°, 20 heating degree-days would be accumulated. If the daily mean temperature were 25°, 40 degree-day units were accumulated. Twice as much fuel would be required on a day with 40 heating degree-days than a day with 20 heating degree-days. If the mean temperature is greater than 65°, the heating degree-day value is set equal to zero (0) for the day. The degree-days for any given period are obtained by totaling the degree-days for each day of the period.

Salt Lake City (thirty-year average of airport data) has 6052 heating degree-days per year. Typically, Salt Lake City consumes 1.13 million cubic feet of natural gas per degree-day for residential heating. Although the rate of consumption of home-heating fuels is not exactly proportional to rate of accumulation of degree-days, it is very nearly so. Similar data can be amassed to forecast demand for other jurisdictions. Degree-day measurements are taken continually by the National Oceanic and Atmospheric Administration and reported weekly in their *Weekly Weather and Crop Bulletin* (available from Agricultural Climatology Service Office, South Building Mail Unit, U.S.D.A., Washington, D.C., 20250). Sample pages from the bulletin appear in Figures 8-4 and 8-5.

Winter weather is extremely variable in most of the United States; the rate of accumulation of heating degree-days may vary from the mean by 100 percent or more. Thus, it is important to have some idea of whether to expect a severe or a mild winter in a given jurisdiction. Long-term forecasts are not very reliable, but they are available and should be used—though with great caution. The National Weather Service prepares thirty-day and ninety-day forecasts which are also published in their *Weekly Weather and Crop Bulletin* (Figures 8-6 and 8-7).

In sum, techniques for forecasting demand will depend upon the use to which the fuel is put. The general principles of demand forecasting, however, require that the forecast be based on historical data plus any contemporary factors that might have a significant effect. Research de-

Table 8-1

Excerpt From Heating Degree-Days Reporting Chart
Heating Degree Days (Base 65°) For Week Ending Dec. 1, 1974

States and Stations	Weekly		Seasonal Accumulation †		
	TOTAL	Departure*	TOTAL	Departure*	Departure From 1973-74
. . . . .	.	.	.	.	.
. . . . .	.	.	.	.	.
KANS. Concordia	231	27	1077	⊢ 9	82
Dodge City	228	37	974	⊢ 8	61
Goodland	255	37	1405	83	38
Topeka	223	30	1036	30	165
Wichita	204	25	880	4	96
KY. Lexington	207	32	1072	148	367
Louisville	196	22	1009	107	382
LA. Baton Rouge	125	59	289	17	176
Lake Charles	111	53	246	24	149
New Orleans	112	55	244	16	134
Shreveport	140	52	386	25	173
MAINE, Caribou	322	41	2317	77	86
. . . . .	.	.	.	.	.
. . . . .	.	.	.	.	.

* Based on 1941 = 70 Normals.   † Accumulation July 1, 1974

Source: National Oceanic and Atmospheric Administration of the US Department of Commerce and Statistical Reporting Service of the US Department of Agriculture, *Weekly Weather and Crop Bulletin* (Agricultural Climatology Service Office, South Building Mail Unit US Department of Agriculture, Washington, D.C. 20250), December 3, 1974, p. 13.

partments from the various energy industries can often provide help in formulating forecasts, as can FEA.

Supply Forecasts

Supply forecasting is simpler than demand forecasting because energy consumed in January is, quite often, produced and posted to accounts in August or earlier. Supply forecasts for the nation as a whole are available for almost every fuel. Some of these forecasts are released periodically by the FEA; others are made available by private groups and other government departments. FEA forecasts are, in general, the most reliable and are often broken down by regions. However, shortfalls at the national or regional level do not always imply local shortfalls. During the severe gasoline shortages of the winter of 1973-74, many western states had no gasoline waiting lines and experienced no problems. Thus, while a na-

132

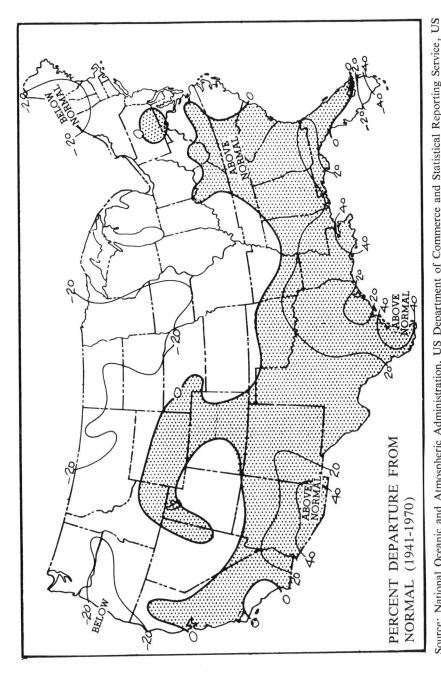

PERCENT DEPARTURE FROM
NORMAL (1941-1970)

Source: National Oceanic and Atmospheric Administration, US Department of Commerce and Statistical Reporting Service, US Department of Agriculture. *Weekly Weather and Crop Bulletin*, December 17, 1974. p. 10.

Figure 8-4. Weekly Heating Degree-Day Map.

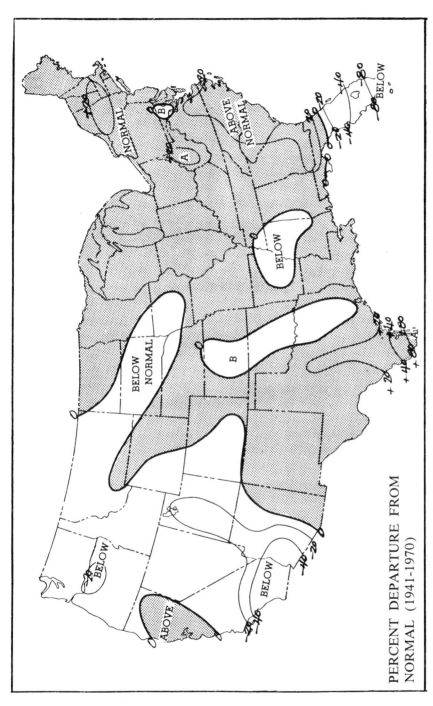

PERCENT DEPARTURE FROM
NORMAL (1941-1970)

Source: National Oceanic and Atmospheric Administration, US Department of Commerce and Statistical Reporting Service, US Department of Agriculture. *Weekly Weather and Crop Bulletin*, December 3, 1974. p. 12.

Figure 8-5. Map of Seasonal Accumulation of Heating Degree-Days.

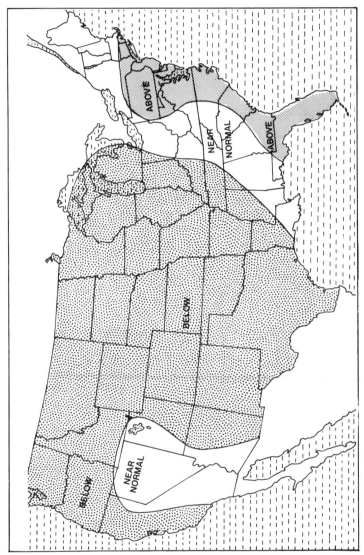

Note: The chart shows the expected average temperature.

Source: National Oceanic and Atmospheric Administration, US Department of Commerce and Statistical Reporting Service, US Department of Agriculture. *Weekly Weather and Crop Bulletin*, December 3, 1974, p. 10.

Figure 8-6. Average Monthly Weather Outlook.

135

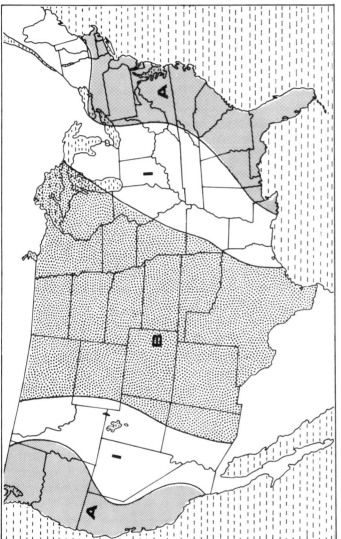

Note: The shaded areas, A (above normal) and B (below normal) each carry a 60 percent probability of deviating from the 30 year average for the month. The areas marked I (indeterminate) are forecast to have a 50 percent probability of deviating from normal (either above or below normal).

Source: National Oceanic and Atmospheric Administration, US Department of Commerce and Statistical Reporting Service, US Department of Agriculture, *Weekly Weather and Crop Bulletin*, December 3, 1974, p. 15.

Figure 8-7. Outlook for Winter Average Temperatures.

tional shortage creates an imminent danger for local jurisdictions, local problems do not always follow. Nonetheless, forecasts of national shortage should trigger local action. Again the most useful periodical is the FEA's *Monthly Energy Review*. The monthly energy "Overview" section in this periodical will alert the reader to many problems months before they appear on the local or even regional scene, and the remainder of the publication will give additional details.

A reasonable approach to writing the supply forecast portion of the EBR is to begin by summarizing the national outlook. Next, summarize any important impacts that the national situation might have upon the situation in the particular jurisdiction. Add a third section summarizing any information derived from efforts to collect supply information locally through survey questionnaires and licensing ordinances.

Appendix 8A: Sample
Energy Survey Forms

Natural Gas Supply Survey Form

1. What is the commitment of your company to "firm" contracts in:
   January_____MCF   February_____MCF
2. What is the commitment of your company to "interruptibles" for:
   January_____MCF   February_____MCF
3. At what temperatures do you interrupt your "interruptible" customers?
   What volume of gas are they using at that temperature?

Class of Customer	Cut-Off Temperature	Volume of Gas Used at That Temperature (MCF)
_____	_____	_____
_____	_____	_____
_____	_____	_____

4. Can you maintain your "interruptibles" on gas at a lower temperature than the cut-off temperature? What is the cost to them?
   No_____   Yes_____   Cost ($MCF)_____
5. What is your storage capacity?
   Natural Gas_____MCF   Liquid_____   Propane_____
6. What is your present storage reserve?
   Natural Gas_____MCF   Liquid_____   Propane_____
7. What is your maximum daily transmission line contract?_____MCF
8. What is your maximum daily propane-air peak-shaving capability?_____ MCF
9. What is your daily peak demand requirement?_____MCF
10. What is the amount of your contract for propane delivery through February?_____gallons
11. At the average daily temperatures given below, how many gallons of propane do you use to deliver your requirements?

Average daily temperature	Gallons of propane required for peak shaving
−15°F.	_____gallons
−25°F.	_____gallons
−30°F.	_____gallons

12. During December 3 to 23, 1972 did you have to buy propane on the "spot" market?   Yes_____   No_____
    If so, how much did you buy?_____gallons

Source: State of Minnesota, Department of Public Safety, Civil Defense Division

Oil Supply Survey Form

1. What is the total number of gallons of #1 and #2 fuel oil that you require through February 28th?   #1_____   #2_____
2. What is the total number of gallons of #1 and #2 fuel oil that you will be short through supplier reduction?   #1_____   #2_____
3. What is the total number of gallons that you will be able to replace through other supply sources?_____
4. What are the net gallons you expect to be short?_____
5. Who is your major supplier?_____
6. Who are the suppliers you use for replacement supplies?_____
_____
7. What is your storage capacity in gallons?_____
8. What is your present reserve by type of oil?
    #1_____   #2_____   #3–#6_____
9. What is the makeup on your deliveries among the three classes, residential, commercial, and industrial?

	Percent of business	Vol. of #1 fuel oil	Vol. of #2 fuel oil
Residential	_____	_____	_____
Commercial	_____	_____	_____
Industrial	_____	_____	_____

10. Please list your five largest volume customers and their #1 and #2 fuel oil requirements for January and February with their capabilities of using any other type of fuel oil (i.e., #5 or #6).

Name of Company	Address	Jan. #1	Jan. #2	Feb. #1	Feb. #2	Other oil burning capability 3,4,5,6
1.						
2.						
3.						
4.						
5.						

11. If we call for a program to conserve fuel by requesting that people cut down on usage, would you be able to use this as an opportunity to store fuel for a time of greater demand? That is, if we ask customers to skimp on usage now, would that help you to build up storage for the cold months in late January and early February?_____
_____

12. Fuel Supply Status
    Name of Company_____
    Type of Fuel_____
    Address_____
    Phone_____Name of Person_____

Source: State of Minnesota, Department of Public Safety, Civil Defense Division

Household Energy Use Survey Form

1. Do you have any of the following items in your home?
   Heating_____gas_____electric_____other_____
       What temperature do you set it at?_____
       How often do you change it?_____
2. Air Conditioning_____central_____window_____other_____
       What temperature do you set it at?_____
       How often do you change it?_____
3. Stove_____gas_____electric_____other_____
4. Water heater_____gas_____electric_____capacity_____
5. Television(s)_____screen size(s)_____
       How many hours per day is/are it/they on?_____
6. Do you have any of the following items in your home?   dishwasher_____
   washing machine_____dryer/type_____
   _____

7. Do you own your home or are you renting?_____
       Are your utilities paid by your landlord?_____
8. If gas and electric prices were raised by 10 percent would you use less,
   the same, more or don't know?_____
       How would you use less?_____
       If you used the same, more or not enough less to offset the extra cost,
       where would the extra money be taken from?_____
   _____

9. If gas and electric prices were raised by 50 percent would you use less,
   same, more or don't know?_____
       How would you use less?_____
       If you used the same, more or not enough less to offset the extra cost,
       where would the extra money be taken from?_____
   _____

10. If gas and electric prices were raised by 100 percent would you use less,
    same, more or don't know?_____
        How would you use less?_____
    _____

        If you used the same, more or not enough less to offset the extra cost,
        where would the extra money be taken from?_____
    _____

11. The government has suggested several ways to reduce consumption of
    fuels, such as gas and electricity, so that we will not run out. Which of
    these ways do you think would be good or bad, rating them from one to
    five, one being very good and five very bad with three in the middle being
    neither good nor bad?
    A. Raise the cost of fuels to everyone?_____

    B. Set a maximum amount that any household could use?_____

    C. As you use more the cost per unit increases?_____

    D. Advertise to reduce consumption?_____

12. Here is a card with some average income groups for Americans. In which group does your family fit?

Source: John M. Verburg, "The Impact Public Utility Rate Alterations Could have for Energy Conservation and Household Consumption Patterns." Unpublished Master's Thesis, 1974.

Appendix 8B: Sample of "Overview" Section from *Monthly Energy Review*

The *Monthly Energy Review* is a monthly publication of the National Energy Information Center, an office of the Federal Energy Administration, Washington, D.C., 20461. The following is reprinted from pages 4 and 5 of the October 1974 issue:

The domestic production of energy for the first 8 months of 1974 was comparable to the output during the same period of 1973. Minor changes did occur in the mix of domestically produced fossil fuels. As of the end of August 1974, the portion of total U.S. energy production contributed by coal was 23.9 percent, a 1 percent increase above coal production for the first 8 months of 1973. For the same period in 1974, natural gas production represented 40.4 percent of the total, a decline from 41.2 percent in 1973. Petroleum production declined from 29.8 percent of the total in 1973 to 29.2 percent in the 1974 period.

The domestic production of crude oil declined in 1974 by 3 percent from the level achieved in the first 8 months of 1973. Imports have tended to compensate for the decrease in domestic production, especially from April through August of this year. Crude oil stocks in 1974 have been maintained at levels comparable to those held in the same period of 1972, and above those recorded for 1973.

With natural gas production declining by 3 percent from last year and imports declining by 7 percent, significant shortages are expected for this coming winter. The shortage of natural gas is further complicated by the recent Canadian Government announcement that natural gas export prices will be increased on January 1, 1975, from the current price of $0.60 to $1.00 per thousand cubic feet. U.S. importers have the option of either accepting the price increase, or continuing to pay the current price with termination of Canadian imports after 2 years. Nearly all U.S. imports of natural gas are from Canada. All U.S. imports are equivalent to 5 percent of the total natural gas domestically produced. Therefore, the higher import price will have an impact on prices and supplies of fuel this winter.

The production of electricity at public utilities appeared to level off during the first 8 months of 1974 when compared to the same period in 1973. This is in contrast to the 7 percent growth rate attained each year since 1971.

August 1974 stocks of both distillate and residual fuel oils were well above the supplies held a year ago. Coal stocks, as of the end of July,

141

were slightly lower than those held in 1973. As of the end of July, oil stocks at public utilities were more than 55 percent higher than the supplies in 1973, and coal stocks were a little higher than the 1973 level.

At the end of August, oil and coal stocks were approximately the same as in 1973. No significant gasoline shortages were noted during the peak demand season, and stock levels were at record highs. Gasoline consumption from June through August of 1974 was 2.6 percent less than for the same period in 1973. Part of the reason for this decline can probably be attributed to the higher gasoline prices this year when compared with those in 1973. Prices this summer for regular gasoline averaged 43 cents per gallon, less tax, or about 60 percent higher than the average price for last summer. Retail gasoline prices in August 1974 declined for the first time in over a year, although the purchase price to dealers continued to edge upward. Average dealer margins declined on all gasoline products, with those of independent dealers showing decreases of as much as 0.7 cents per gallon for regular gasoline.

In resource development, oil and gas exploration showed a dramatic increase in activity for the first 8 months of 1974. Rotary drilling rigs were utilized at near capacity for the period. An average of 1,575 rotary rigs were in operation, an increase of 23 percent above the activity for the same period in 1973. The number of wells drilled so far in 1974 totals 19,868, a significant increase over the 1973 total of 16,295 and the 1972 total of 17,419. The 1974 figures on wells drilled and rotary rigs operating confirm the upswing in oil and gas exploratory activities. However, with only 123 new rigs estimated to be available for domestic use through 1973, a shortage of drilling rigs may develop and place a constraint against further expansion of drilling activities in the near future.

9

Conservation Programs

By far the best course open to local governments fighting an energy crisis is to cut energy consumption. The general problem of regulating demand for energy is introduced in chapter 7. Fundamentally, one or both of two approaches is possible. First, consumption cuts such as reducing thermostat settings, turning off decorative lighting, etc. may be recommended or ordered. Such cuts actually infringe upon the utility and comfort people derive from energy, but those infringements are either tolerable or occur in noncritical areas. Second, conservation may be achieved by measures that reduce the amount of energy used to produce an unchanged amount of comfort or utility; according to FEA sources Americans waste nearly 30 percent of energy they use. Better home insulation and radial tires are examples of such efficiency improvement measures.

Since the energy crisis of 1973-74 numerous organizations have been compiling energy conservation suggestions. An extensive list of these suggestions appears in this chapter. From it, plans can be prepared for energy conservation in any community. However, a word of caution is in order. Not all these suggestions are well tested or well suited to every community. Many require investment in such things as insulation, storm windows, and the like. And some of them may be marginal at best. Program developers should weigh the cost of each suggestion against the savings that might reasonably be expected from its implementation. It would be well to have users set up monitoring committees to check their own actual energy savings for a period of time. If consumption is not being reduced, perhaps a city consultant could be assigned to help check out the systems in question and discover the problem.

An energy conservation plan may aim at nothing more than a published list of practical conservation practices for various sectors of the community (farms, homes, etc.). On the other hand, it may include mandatory requirements via city ordinances concerning speed limits, temperature settings, and fuel delivery allocations or rationing. The factor that determines whether the voluntary or the involuntary alternative or any of infinitude of combinations in between is chosen will be the seriousness of the energy crisis itself. The formation of energy conservation policy, therefore, is something that will have to be "played by ear." This does not mean that city officials cannot conceive of, and work on, contingency plans and major objectives well in advance. They can. This is especially true of plans that involve the use of commodities that may become short in a fuel crisis: insulation materials, small electric space heaters, warm clothes, and the like.

In this chapter we discuss briefly voluntary programs and comprehensive mandatory conservation programs generally, followed by programs aimed specifically at (1) the residential, (2) the commercial and industrial, (3) the transportation, and (4) the agricultural sectors.

Voluntary Conservation Programs

Although voluntary programs are often thought to be ineffectual, that is not so in a crisis. In fact, voluntary programs may be more effective in a crisis than mandatory programs, which tend to be complicated and expensive.

Voluntary programs require strong leadership, and thus, most have two leadership techniques in common. First, the programs tend to be led or supervised by a blue-ribbon citizen's commission. Because of their familiarity with the problems of energy consumption at work and at home, the input of citizens is encouraged; they provide valuable suggestions, and citizen participation enhances the effectiveness of the program. A news release from the city of Denver that illustrates a program including such a commission "Project Energy" appears in an appendix to this chapter. Second, almost all voluntary programs make use of mandatory cutbacks among government agencies and personnel as a means of providing an example. Just such a program is outlined in the appendix to this chapter entitled "An Internal Conservation Program for Local Governments."

Incentives have played a role in some programs. Examples are contests for best conservation ideas, public recognition for persons with good conservation habits, tax incentives or subsidies for installing insulation, storm windows, and the like. Many programs have emphasized that good conservation practices can actually save money on fuel and electric bills. In fact, many may want to implement these programs during periods of adequate energy supplies simply to conserve funds.

Ultimately, the key to success in voluntary energy conservation is getting conservation suggestions to the people who will use them. A printed handout distributed with the local newspaper is one idea. Perhaps a TV or radio spot or a full program could be used in some areas. Specialized approaches might be made to certain industries. Whatever the method, it is best to state each suggestion in terms of specific instructions. "Turn down the heat" is not enough. "A 6 degree reduction in the thermostat setting will result in an up to 20 percent reduction in your annual fuel bill" is more motivating.

Comprehensive Mandatory Conservation Programs

Mandatory program efforts fall into two categories: temporary emergency efforts, and permanent long-term programs. Long-term programs tend to be limited to efficiency improvement measures, while emergency programs

Table 9-1

Evaluation of Possible Elements for Governmentally Imposed Conservation Programs

Short-Term Conservation Measures	Annual Savings Quadrillion Btu by 1975
Transportation	
1. Accelerate improvement of motorized mass transit including measures to improve traffic flow.	0.4
2. Improve automobile energy efficiency through use of low loss tires, improved engine tuning.	0.9
3. Inject energy issue into appropriate national programs (environmental, health, urban reform, etc.).	—
4. Promulgate energy efficiency standards for transportation.	—
Residential/Commercial	
1. Tax incentives for adding insulation and storm windows in existing homes.	0.1
2. Educational program to encourage good energy conservation practices in the home.	0.05
Industry	
1. Raise energy prices by tax and/or regulation.	1.6
2. Increase recycling and reuse of materials and products.	0.2
Electric Utilities	
1. Alleviate construction delays.	0.5
2. Smooth out daily demand cycle by shifting some loads to off-peak hours.	0.5
Environment	
1. Review regulations and programs with objective of meeting environmental standards while using least energy and avoiding scarce fuels.	—

Medium-Term Conservation Measures	Annual Savings Quadrillion Btu by 1980
Transportation	
1. Expand intercity surface transportation service.	0.9
2. Expand high speed and motorized mass transit service. Implement feeder service.	0.3

Table 9-1 (cont.)

3. Improve freight handling systems through freight consolidation and containerization.	0.9
4. Emphasize transportation issue on urban development (pedestrian oriented clusters).	0.2
5. Improve automobile energy efficiency through improved automobiles traffic flow and maintenance.	0.3
Residential/Commercial	
1. Upgrade insulation standards for new single and multi-family dwellings.	0.9
2. Increase price of fuel by tax levied at the point of production.	Large
3. Utilize above revenues for energy conservation in residential/commercial sector.	Large
4. Establish minimum efficiency standards for furnaces, air conditioners and appliances	0.6
5. Require energy efficiency labeling of all appliances.	0.6
Industry	
1. Raise energy prices by tax and/or regulation.	3.8
2. Increase recycling and reuse of materials and products.	0.4
Electric Utilities	
1. Alleviate construction delays.	0.5
2. Smooth out daily demand cycle by shifting some loads to off-peak hours.	0.5
3. Increase research and development efforts.	Large
Environment	
1. Review regulations and programs with objective of meeting environmental standards while using least energy and avoiding scarce fuels.	—

Long Term Conservation Measures	Annual Savings Quadrillion Btu by 1990
Transportation	
1. New freight handling systems	2.0
2. New mass-transit systems.	2.0
3. Improved urban design.	2.0
4. New engines (hybrid, nonpetroleum).	1.0
Residential/Commercial	
1. Develop nonfuel energy sources (solar and wind energy.	Large
Industry	
1. Raise energy prices by tax and/or regulation.	5.5
2. Increase recycling and reuse of materials and products.	1.1
Electric Utilities	
1. Increase research and development efforts	Large

Source: Adapted from *The Potential for Energy Conservation: A Staff Study*, Executive Office of the President, Office of Emergency Preparedness (Government Printing Office stock number 4102-00009, October, 1972), pp. viii–xiii.

tend to focus on measures that may result in temporary cuts in the utility and comfort derived from energy. A recent study by federal officials identified a range of program tactics of both types; we have reproduced their summary in table 9-1. Many of their suggestions make sense at the local as well as the federal level.

Among the most extensive emergency programs promulgated at the local level was that of Los Angeles. Los Angeles's Emergency Energy Curtailment Program included mandatory consumption cuts in all sectors of the economy as well as reductions in outdoor lighting, comfort heating and cooling of businesses, indoor business lighting, swimming pool use, and other recreational and cultural uses. The city considered but rejected the idea of adding to the program a reduction in business hours and the use of rolling blackouts. (The original ordinance establishing the Los Angeles program is included in an appendix to this chapter.) The legal authority for emergency programs as drastic as that of Los Angeles may not be available except if an emergency is officially declared either by the state or, where so empowered, by the city. Each proposed measure should be reviewed by a competent attorney.

Long-term efficiency improvement programs have recently focused on improving the energy efficiency of buildings. Several states and cities have enacted stricter insulation requirements for new construction in an effort to conserve energy. Studies show that at today's prices the additional investment in insulation these requirements imply will be recouped in about ten years. One such ordinance was passed in Wooster, Ohio. (See appendix to this chapter.) Other efficiency improvement areas where there is great potential but little action involve municipal investments in "total energy systems" (see encyclopedia index), mass transportation, better regulation of traffic patterns, industrial processes and others.

Conservation Programs in Specific Sectors

Whatever overall approach to conservation policy is taken, voluntary, mandatory, etc., local officials will need a specific set of program objectives and mechanisms by which they can be achieved. What constitutes a reasonable set of objectives depends upon the purposes of the program. For example, Los Angeles based its program objectives on the need to save a specific amount of residual fuel in order to maintain continuous electrical service. Los Angeles pegged their objectives to a 10 percent reduction for residential and industrial users and a 20 percent reduction by commercial users. That is, Los Angeles made the political and economic judgment that commercial establishments could absorb a greater portion of the shortage with less impact than residential, industrial, or other users.

Once such a determination is made, tactics must be selected to achieve the objectives. While a complete list of conservation opportunities is not possible in this volume, we have included in this section a list of the most commonly mentioned opportunities by way of illustration. The list includes ideas from the residential, commercial and industrial, agricultural, and transportation sectors.

Suggestions for Energy Conservation: Residential

In the United States 21.5 percent of the energy consumed is used in the home, shown in table 9-2.

Space Heating. Table 9-2 clearly shows that improvements in the efficiency of space heating may provide the greatest opportunity for energy savings in the home. In an extensive study conducted for the US Department of Housing and Urban Development, it was found that a series of modifications to existing designs could reduce residential energy consumption from 23 to 36 percent. Included were (1) modifications in the dwelling structure, such as additional insulation, the use of storm windows and doors, etc., (2) modifications in the heating and cooling equipment, and

Table 9-2

Typical Residential Energy Load Distribution

Use	Percent of Total Load
Space Heating	60.2
Hot Water Heating	12.3
Outdoor Gas Lamp	8.2
Central Air Conditioning	5.6
Lights	3.1
Range	1.8
Refrigerator-Freezer	2.8
Clothes Dryer	1.5
Color TV	0.8
Furnace Fan	0.6
Dishwasher	0.6
Clothes Washer	0.2
Iron	0.2
Coffee Maker	0.2
Miscellaneous	1.9

Source: Residential Energy Consumption-Phase I Report, US Department of Housing and Urban Development, Office of the Assistant Secretary for Research and Technology, March 1972, US Government Printing Office stock number 2300-00262.

Table 9-3

Annual Energy Savings Possible for Improved Dwellings (Percent savings in primary energy over characteristic structure)

	Single Family	Town-house [a]	Low Rise [a]	High Rise [a]
Combined Structural Modifications	17.5	23.0	18.0	16.0
Heating and Cooling Systems Modifications	10.7	10.7	0 [b]	0 [b]
Internal Factors Modifications	8.0	11.4	10.3	7.7
Totals	36.2	45.1	23.3	23.7

[a] Values shown in these columns are for the whole building.
[b] Heating and cooling systems in these characteristic structures were the best of those analyzed.
Source: Hittman Associates, *Residential Energy Conservation* (Columbus, Md., July 1974), p. 4.

(3) modifications in such internal factors as appliances, lights, etc. The savings effected by these modifications are shown in table 9-3.

The HUD study group continued on to analyze the cost effectiveness of their modifications:

To perform this [cost effectiveness] analysis we used the approximate incremental initial cost of each modification (that cost in excess over the conventional costs for construction, systems, and appliances) and the value of the energy saved. This latter factor was considered in two ways: first with a constant value of energy; and second with the cost of energy increasing 10 percent per year during the pay-back period. A 10 percent interest rate compounded annually was assumed for the initial capital. Using a constant cost of energy, the $1010 initial investment would pay for itself in energy savings in about seven years with a net return on investment of $684 realized after 10 years. If one assumes that the cost of energy will increase 10 percent per year over the next 10 years, the pay-back period is 5.3 years and the net return on investment over a ten-year span is $2024. Thus, on a single-family house energy conservation is an excellent investment with an average return ranging between seven and 20 percent per year over a ten-year span.[1]

On existing structures the most effective means of improving heating efficiency is probably to increase the amount of insulation. A three-inch blanket of insulation in an uninsulated attic may decrease heat consumption 33 percent. A six-inch blanket in the attic and a three-inch blanket in uninsulated walls plus storm windows and doors could yield a 55 percent saving. Other commonly mentioned heat-saving tips are:

1. Lower thermostats to 65-68 degrees during the day and 60 degrees at night. If these settings are 6 degrees lower than they were last year, heating costs should run almost 15 percent less.

2. Service furnace once a year, preferably each fall. Adjustment could mean a saving of 10 percent in family fuel consumption.

3. Consider the advantages of a clock thermostat which will automatically turn the heat down at a regular hour before you retire and turn it up just before you awake. This can save upwards of 20 percent of your fuel costs.

4. If you use electric heating, consider a heat pump system. The heat pump uses outside air in both heating and cooling and in some climates can cut electric heating costs by as much as 60 percent. Not every climate is well suited to heat pumps.

5. Dust or vacuum radiator surfaces frequently; keep vents open and free.

6. Open draperies and shades in sunny windows; close them at night to prevent drafts and give a warmer feeling.

7. For comfort in cooler indoor temperature, use the best insulation of all—warm clothing.

8. Caulk and weatherstrip doors and windows. This inexpensive measure, which the householder can do, could reduce the family's fuel costs by 10 percent or more.

9. Install storm windows and doors. Combination screen and storm windows are the most convenient because they do not require removal when the temperature is moderate and open windows are desirable. Conventional storm windows are expensive, but a sheet of clear plastic film tightly taped to the frames can be equally effective, and the entire cost for the average home typically runs less than $10. (Renters might prefer this low-cost method.) Either type of protection could reduce individual fuel costs by about 15 percent and make the home more comfortable year round.

10. Use bath and kitchen ventilating fans only as needed.

11. Turn off furnace pilot lights in summer. (Do not just blow them out; shut off the valve.) It is estimated that nearly 9 percent of all energy used in the home goes to run pilot lights.

12. Concerning the heating plant: clean the heat exchange surfaces, insure proper and regular maintenance, and clean filters.

13. Close air leaks into the attic.

14. Repair hot water faucets.

15. Close fireplace dampers when not in use so warm air can't escape up the chimney. If your fireplace doesn't have a damper, consider having one installed. Also, consider installation of a glass fireplace screen to minimize heat losses when the fireplace is in use as well as when it's not.

16. Do not place thermostats on cold or outside walls.

17. Set thermostat to 50 thru 55 degrees if going away for a few days or more.

18. Minimize use of portable space heaters.

19. Keep humidity at a proper level with humidifiers or with a water supply near the furnace vents. It is a well established physical and psychological fact that it takes more heat to make you comfortable if the air is dry.

20. Set up a zoning system, if your house is large enough to warrant one, so that a separate thermostat can be used to control the temperature in each zone. Shut off heat to rarely used rooms and close their doors.

21. Avoid excessive readjustment of thermostats.

Air Conditioning. As in the winter, the best way to avoid energy waste in the summer is through insulation. This makes insulation a doubly good investment. The air conditioning system can also be made more efficient. Consumers should buy the right size air conditioner for the job. If the unit is too large it wastes energy, because it cools a room too frequently and can't dehumidify the room properly. Look for the "Energy Guide" label now being affixed to many air conditioners; it tells you the energy efficiency ratio (EER) rating of the air conditioner. The EER is the ratio of the number of Btu's of cooling power of the unit to the number of watts it takes to run it. The higher the EER, the more efficient the unit, and the less it costs to run it. The additional purchase cost can be paid for in a short time by the savings on your electric bill; estimates of the amount of annual savings for many models are available from the US Department of Commerce's National Bureau of Standards; ask any dealer to see the National Bureau of Standard's publication 1053 or write to National Bureau of Standards, Washington, D.C., 20234. Roughly, EERs on air conditioners today are running from 5 for the poorest units to over 12 for the best units. Other commonly heard suggestions for a more efficient cooling system include:

1. Set air conditioning thermostats no lower than 78-80 degrees. These temperatures are judged to be reasonably comfortable and energy efficient. If they are an average of 6 degrees higher than last year's summer settings, home cooling costs should drop about 47 percent. (The federal govern-

ment is enforcing a strict 78-80 degree temperature setting in all its buildings.)

2. Run air conditioners only on really hot days. On hot days set the fan speed at high. In very humid weather set the fan at low speed to provide less cooling but more moisture removal. On cooler days or during cooler hours open windows instead of using the air conditioner fan.

3. Turn off air conditioning equipment in unused rooms and close them off.

4. Clean air conditioning filters at least once a month, and replace them when they're worn out.

5. Turn off as many electric lights as you càn, and concentrate the light where it is most needed—in reading and work areas and for safety. Lights add heat.

6. Deflect daytime sun with vertical louvers or awnings on windows, or draw draperies and shades on sunny windows. Keep windows and outside doors closed during the hottest hours of the day.

7. Dress for the higher temperatures. Sports clothes, including shirts with open collars for men and light fabrics for women, are most comfortable and are acceptable almost everywhere during the summer.

8. Shut the air conditioner off late at night and start it early in the day before heat builds up inside the house.

9. Be certain that all outside doors and windows are closed when air conditioners are on and seal all areas leading from air-conditioned spaces to the attic. Allow air to flow freely into and out of the air conditioner. Don't let indoor draperies or outdoor shrubbery get in the way. Use electric fans to circulate air even if you have air conditioning. By so doing, you can operate air conditioners at higher temperatures and still be comfortable.

10. When cooking, use covered pots and low settings when possible.

11. Use television sets, radios, and appliances wisely. They generate heat.

12. If possible, confine use of ranges or dryers to morning or evening hours, when it's cooler.

13. Plant trees to provide shade for the house.

14. Use a bathroom exhaust fan or open the bathroom window, with the door closed, before bathing or showering to remove the heat and moisture so that the air conditioners will not have to use valuable energy to do the same job.

Electricity and Water. Loads on electricity and water reach their peak in the late afternoon and early evening. The smaller peak occurs between 8:00 and 10:00 in the morning. When these peaks occur, electric companies have to turn on inefficient and energy-wasting temporary generators. To help curtail this problem, citizens should be encouraged to schedule household chores during off-peak-load hours. Other suggestions relate to the more efficient use of lighting, water, refrigerator, clothes washer and dryer, range, dishwasher, and other appliances.

Lighting. Although individual lamps consume very little energy, all the home lighting put together adds up to over 16 percent of all electricity used in residences. Some conservation suggestions include:

1. Always turn lights off when not in use.
2. Don't use larger bulbs than necessary.
3. Switches for attic, cellar, and outdoor lights—as well as heating cables and outdoor pool pumps—should be equipped with indicating lights so that you know when they're on.
4. Use three-way bulbs instead of regular bulbs in table lamps. Turn on high for reading; low for conversation.
5. Use light-color paint or paper on walls and light-colored rugs, draperies, and upholstery to reflect more light and make it possible to use lower-wattage bulbs and reduce the amount of artificial lighting required.
6. Put fluorescent lighting in kitchen (or other) ceiling fixtures. A double 40-watt fixture will do the same lighting job more economically with less energy than one 150-watt incandescent, two 75-watt incandescent, or three 60-watt incandescent bulbs.
7. Standard-life bulbs conserve more energy than so-called long-life bulbs and usually give the most life for the lighting dollar. Use long-life incandescent lamps only in hard-to-reach places. They are less efficient than ordinary bulbs.
8. Consider the new low-watt night lights to replace the regular 7-watt night lights.
9. Remove one bulb out of three (replace it with a burned-out bulb for safety). Replace others with bulbs of the next lower wattage, but concentrate light in reading and working areas and where it is needed for safety. The average electric cost should drop about 4 percent.
10. Keep lamps and lighting fixtures clean. Dirt absorbs light.
11. Reduce or eliminate ornamental lights.
12. Use outdoor lights only when essential.

Water. Heating water accounts for 12 percent of the energy used in homes and 3 percent of all energy used in the United States. A water heater should be no larger than necessary. Oversizing wastes energy. A forty-gallon hot water tank is sufficient for the average family of four. Other tips include:

1. Don't overheat water for your needs. A good hot-water temperature for a normal house with a dishwasher is 140°F; without a dishwasher,

110°F. For every 10 degrees the water temperature is raised above 140 degrees, hot water costs increase 3 percent.

2. To conserve hot water, take showers instead of baths unless you're a shower lingerer. An average shower takes 5 gallons of water; a bath averages 10 gallons. If you let the hot water run while shaving or rinsing dishes, you can waste from 10 to 30 gallons of hot water per day. Rinse the dishes under cold water and use cold and warm cycles as often as possible for dishwashers and washing machines. Switching to cold cycles can lower gas or electricity costs by up to 4 percent.

3. Install a flow restrictor in the pipe to the showerhead. This easy-to-install device can save a considerable amount of hot water in a year. It costs under $10, fits into the pipe to the showerhead, and restricts the flow to an adequate four gallons of water per minute.

4. Run dishwashers and washing machines only when they are fully loaded. A half load uses just as much electricity and hot water.

5. Turn the water heater off when you are away for extended periods of time.

5. Replace worn washers on leaky faucets. One leaky faucet can waste up to 5000 gallons of water per year.

7. Make sure your hot water heater is working efficiently.

8. Insulate hot water tank and piping.

9. Drain and flush hot water heater once a year (prevents buildup of sediments).

Refrigerator. The average cost for running American kitchen appliances is $47 per year. Of this, between $30 and $40 goes to running the refrigerator. Following are some ideas for using it wisely:

1. Some refrigerators have heating elements in their walls to prevent condensation on the outside. These heaters need only be turned on when the air is extremely humid. When buying such a refrigerator, be sure it has a switch to turn off these heaters. Better yet, buy one without heaters.

2. Defrost as soon as necessary to keep the internal cooling coils operating efficiently.

3. Use proper defrosting methods for manual-defrost refrigerator-freezers. These appliances consume less energy than those which defrost automatically, but they must be defrosted frequently and as quickly as possible to maintain that edge. Frost should not be allowed to build up to more than one-quarter of an inch.

4. When you are away for extended periods of time, turn the refrigerator dial two or three settings warmer, or empty the refrigerator, disconnect it from the power outlet, clean thoroughly, and leave the door ajar.

5. Check seals around the refrigerator to make sure they are airtight; if not, adjust the latch or replace the seal.

6. Keep the external coils, fins, and motor free from dust.

7. When using the refrigerator, don't overfill it. Good air circulation is necessary for efficient operation. Don't block the air vents. Keep the freezer full, on the other hand, to prevent icing.

8. If you're going to buy a new refrigerator, consider one with a power-saver switch that reduces the operating cost by letting you select an operating level that corresponds to the outside weather.

9. Cool foods and food containers to room temperature before placing them in the refrigerator or freezer and cover all liquids stored in the refrigerator (to prevent frost build-up).

10. If you're going to purchase a freezer, get a chest type (if you have the floor space for it) rather than an upright. A chest freezer loses less cold air when you open it than an upright.

11. Keep refrigerators away from heat (equipment and sunlight).

Clothes Washing and Drying. It costs less to wash clothes than to dry them. Drying clothes outside the old-fashioned way, then, is the biggest energy saver in this category. Other savers are:

1. Wait until you have a full load before you run the washer.

2. Sort laundry if you've got several loads. Since lighter materials take less drying time, the dryer doesn't have to be on as long for these loads. Use the correct time and temperature for each particular load.

3. To help remove heavy dirt, use presoak or prewash cycles.

4. Spin-dry wash before putting it in the dryer.

5. Don't overload the washer or dryer. They'll have to work harder and longer and use more energy in the process. Also, overloading the dryer causes wrinkles that have to be ironed out later.

6. Keep the lint filter on the dryer clean to permit air to move freely. Clean the filter after each use.

7. Fill washers and dryers, unless they have small-load attachments or variable water levels.

8. Dry your clothes in consecutive loads. Once the dryer is warm, it cuts down on initial energy consumption.

Range. Next to the refrigerator, the range is the largest energy consumer in the kitchen, using $10 in electricity a year. The energy wastage of the range can be cut in a number of ways:

1. Use covered pots and low settings whenever possible.

2. Bake two cakes or pies at one time. Freeze one for future use.

3. Use the right size pan for the cooking unit. Pans that are too small allow unused heat to escape into the room.

4. When using the self-cleaning feature on an oven, use it right after cooking, while the oven is still hot.

5. Have faulty elements or switches serviced as soon as possible.

6. Make sure the pilot light on a gas range is adjusted properly.

7. Put pots and pans on the range before the heat is turned on.

8. Choose meals that use the oven instead of the surface units since less heat is lost in a confined area.

9. If you've got the cash, buy and learn how to use a microwave oven. Microwave cooking uses much less energy.

10. Reduce oven peeking to a minimum. Everytime the oven door is opened, the oven temperature drops 25 to 50°F.

11. When heating or boiling a large amount of water, start with hot tap water rather than cold.

12. If you have a pressure cooker, use it when possible.

13. Clean heat reflector below the heating element.

Dishwasher. Conservation practices with the dishwasher are particularly effective because it uses both electricity and hot water. Some suggestions include:

1. Scrape and rinse dishes under cold water and use the cold and warm water cycles as much as possible.

2. Be sure the dishwasher is full, but not overloaded, before you turn it on. An average dishwasher uses fourteen gallons of hot water per load.

3. Keep the dishwasher drains and filters clear of debris.

4. During the summer, use the dishwasher at night to avoid extra heat in the house during the day.

Other Appliances. When it comes time to replace an entertainment product, you can ensure future energy savings by buying an all solid-state appliance rather than one using tubes or a combination of tubes and solid-state circuits. It costs $13.32 per year to operate, 5.7 hours per day, a 19-inch color television receiver with a hybrid circuit (combination tube and transistor circuit), but only $7.74 per year for a 19-inch all solid-state color set with an instant-on feature.

When using any of the many other electrical appliances not already discussed, there are ways to save energy. Mostly, it's just common sense. For example, small appliances such as toasters, electric skillets, and popcorn poppers generally use less energy than a range or oven would for specialized jobs. And all appliances use less energy if they're maintained so that they operate at peak efficiency. A vacuum cleaner, for instance, will use more energy when operating with a nearly full bag than when the bag is empty.

Outdoor Activities. Unless you have a swimming pool, outdoor energy savings don't amount to much. Some things that may help are:

1. Maintain electrical tools in top operating shape, clean and properly lubricated.

2. Keep cutting edges sharp. A sharp bit or saw cuts more quickly and therefore uses less power. Oil on bits and metal cutting compounds on saws also reduce power required.

3. Buy the power tool with the lowest horsepower adequate for the work you want it to do.

4. Remember to turn off shop lights, soldering irons, gluepots, and all bench heating devices as quickly as possible.

5. When using gasoline-powered yard equipment, do not allow it to idle for long periods. Turn it off and restart when ready to resume work.

6. Plant deciduous trees and vines on the south and west sides of homes to provide protective shade against summer sun and to let in natural light in the winter.

7. Use manure or a natural compost from your own yard cuttings for fertilizer. Petroleum and natural gas are used as raw materials and for fuel in the manufacture of artificial fertilizers.

Designing a New Home. If designing a new home or apartment building, some of the following suggestions save money and fuel:

1. When designing a new house, design for the climate and take advantage of sun and shade.

2. Limit window areas to 10 percent of the floor area. In cool climates, install fewer windows in the north wall, where no solar heating gain can be achieved in winter. In warm climates, put the largest number of windows in the north wall to reduce the heating gain from the sun.

3. Install windows you can open, so that you can use natural ventilation in moderate weather.

4. Use double-pane glass throughout the house. Windows with heat-reflecting or heat-absorbing glass in south and west windows provide additional energy savings.

5. Insulate walls and roof to the highest specifications recommended for your area, but provide a minimum of 6 inches in the attic and 3 inches in the walls. Insulate floors, too, especially those over cold basements and garages.

6. Install water heater as close as possible to areas of major use. When buying a new water heater, select one with thick insulation on the shell. Avoid purchasing a tank with greater capacity than needed; have the dealer advise you on the size suitable for the number of people in your family.

7. Install louvered panels or wind-powered roof ventilators rather than motor-driven fans to ventilate the attic.

8. Select light-colored roofing in warm climates.

9. When buying a house, ask for a description of the insulation and data on the efficiency of space heating, air conditioning, and water heating plants, or have an independent engineer advise you about the efficiency of the equipment provided. Consider the need for additional insulation or replacement of equipment.

10. Build "skirts" around exposed base of house, especially mobile homes.

11. You might consider using some of the more exotic heating schemes; the technology for solar and geothermal plants is fully adequate.

Shopping Suggestions. The following suggestions are for the energy-conservation-minded consumer purchasing things for home use:

1. Whenever possible, buy products made of recycled materials or those which offer opportunities for recycling, such as steel, aluminum, paper and glass. More energy is used in production of products from virgin materials than from recycled or reclaimed materials.

2. When you buy fabrics or garments, try to choose those that require little or no ironing to conserve energy-cost of up-keep.

3. Try to buy products that will last. Less durable products require earlier replacement, and this wastes energy. Over a period of time, your dollar cost for a product also increases with more frequent replacement.

4. Buy operating equipment, such as automobiles, appliances, pumps, fans, compressors, and boilers, on the basis of initial cost plus operating expenses (the "lifetime cost" concept) rather than on the basis of purchase price alone. Often a piece of equipment that is more expensive initially, but is energy-efficient, will cost less over a period of years than a similar lower-priced but less energy-efficient unit.

5. Ask for information about the energy-efficiency of the products you buy. Under a voluntary labeling program, automobiles and air conditioners bear labels approved by the federal government, showing their energy consumption. Other products will soon bear such labels. Ask for comparative information if a label does not appear on the product.

Energy Conservation in Commerce and Industry

A wide variety of literature and other supporting items for commercial and industrial establishments interested in energy management and conservation programs is available. Implementation of such programs may require the services of a competent consultant in engineering, accounting, economics, or other field. A resource of significant value is the *Energy Conservation Program Guide for Industry and Commerce* (National Bureau of Standards Handbook 115, September 1974) which includes an updating service. In the introduction, the authors write:

Many companies are finding that an organized energy conservation program can hold down both energy use and energy costs without disrupting plant production. It has been repeatedly demonstrated that conservation measures can reduce energy use by 15 to 30 percent, or more, with justifying cost savings. More importantly, if by energy conservation your company can maintain production despite a reduction in energy supply, or increase production in the face of frozen fuel allocations, the effect on your sales and profits is obvious.[2]

Many small commercial and industrial establishments consume energy in many of the same categories as do residences. Those firms might profit from the previous section. Larger firms with more complex problems should be encouraged to get a copy of the NBS Handbook. Perhaps the local Chamber of Commerce should acquire NBS and other materials and set up a program to deliver conservation information to local businessmen. A partial bibliography of conservation-related materials for commerce and industry is appended to this chapter.

A second and equally important aspect of energy management is the control of utility costs. Several good cost-accounting systems exist. Excellent examples are *A Guide to Monitoring and Controlling Utility Costs,* by Seymour G. Price (Washington, D.C.: BNA Books, 1973) and *How to Profit by Conserving Energy,* by the U.S. Department of Commerce (U.S. G. P. O.).

Steps to an Energy Conservation Program

The following outline for establishing an energy conservation program in a commercial or industrial establishment is reprinted from the NBS Handbook.[3]

I. TOP MANAGEMENT COMMITMENT
A. Inform line supervisors of:
 1. The economic reasons for the need to conserve energy
 2. Their responsibility for implementing energy saving actions in the areas of their accountability
B. Establish a committee having the responsibility for formulating and conducting an energy conservation program and consisting of:
 1. Representatives from each department in the plant
 2. A coordinator appointed by and reporting to management
  Note: In smaller organizations, the manager and his staff may conduct energy conservation activities as part of their management duties.

C. Provide the committee with guidelines as to what is expected of them:
1. Plan and participate in energy-saving surveys
2. Develop uniform record keeping, reporting, and energy accounting
3. Research and develop ideas on ways to save energy
4. Communicate these ideas and suggestions
5. Suggest tough, but achievable, goals for energy saving
6. Develop ideas and plans for enlisting employee support and participation
7. Plan and conduct a continuing program of activities to stimulate interest in energy conservation efforts
D. Set goals in energy saving:
1. A preliminary goal at the start of the program
2. Later, a revised goal based on savings potential estimated from results of surveys
E. Employ external assistance in surveying the plant and making recommendations, if necessary
F. Communicate periodically to employees regarding management's emphasis on energy conservation action and report on progress

II. SURVEY ENERGY USES AND LOSSES

A. Conduct first survey aimed at identifying energy wastes that can be corrected by maintenance or operations actions, for example:
1. Leaks of steam and other utilities
2. Furnace burners out of adjustment
3. Repair or addition of insulation required
4. Equipment running when not needed
B. Survey to determine where additional instruments for measurement of energy flow are needed and whether there is economic justification for the cost of their installation
C. Develop an energy balance on each process to define in detail:
1. Energy input as raw materials and utilities
2. Energy consumed in waste disposal
3. Energy credit for by-products
4. Net energy charged to the main product
5. Energy dissipated or wasted
   Note: Energy equivalents will need to be developed for all raw materials, fuels, and utilities, such as electric power, steam, etc., in order that all energy can be expressed on the common basis of Btu units.

D. Analyze all process energy balances in depth:
1. Can waste heat be recovered to generate steam or to heat water or a raw material?
2. Can a process step be eliminated or modified in some way to reduce energy use?
3. Can an alternate raw material with lower energy content be used?
4. Is there a way to improve yield?
5. Is there justification for:
   a. Replacing old equipment with new equipment requiring less energy?
   b. Replacing an obsolete, inefficient process plant with a whole new and different process using less energy?
E. Conduct weekend and night surveys periodically
F. Plan surveys on specific systems and equipment, such as:
1. Steam system
2. Compressed air system
3. Electric motors
4. Natural gas lines
5. Heating and air conditioning system

III. IMPLEMENT ENERGY CONSERVATION ACTIONS

A. Correct energy wastes identified in the first survey by taking in the necessary maintenance or operation actions
B. List all energy conservation projects evolving from energy balance analyses, surveys, etc. Evaluate and select projects for implementation:
1. Calculate annual energy savings for each project
2. Project future energy costs and calculate annual dollar savings
3. Estimate project capital or expense cost
4. Evaluate investment merit of projects using measures, such as return on investment, etc.
5. Assign priorities to projects based on investment merit
6. Select conservation projects for implementation and request capital authorization
7. Implement authorized projects
C. Review design of all capital projects, such as new plants, expansions, buildings, etc., to assure that efficient utilization of energy is incorporated in the design.
   Note: Include consideration of energy availability in new equipment and plant decisions.

IV. DEVELOP CONTINUING ENERGY CONSERVATION EFFORTS

A. Measure results:
1. Chart energy use per unit of production by department
2. Chart energy use per unit of production for the whole plant

   Note: The procedure for calculating energy consumption per unit of product is presented in "How to Profit by Conserving Energy."
3. Monitor and analyze charts of Btu per unit of product, taking into consideration effect of complicating variables, such as outdoor ambient air temperature, level of production rate, product mix, etc.

   a. Compare Btu/product unit with past performance and theoretical Btu/product unit

   b. Observe the impact of energy-saving actions and project implementation on decreasing the Btu/unit of product

   c. Investigate, identify, and correct the cause for increases that may occur in Btu unit of product, if feasible

B. Continue energy conservation committee activities
1. Hold periodic meetings
2. Each committee member is the communication link between the committee and the department supervisors represented
3. Periodically update energy-saving project lists
4. Plan and participate in energy-saving surveys
5. Communicate energy conservation techniques
6. Plan and conduct a continuing program of activities and communication to keep up interest in energy conservation
7. Develop cooperation with community organizations in promoting energy conservation

C. Involve employees
1. Service on energy conservation committee
2. Energy conservation training course
3. Handbook on energy conservation
4. Suggestion awards plan
5. Recognition for energy-saving achievements
6. Technical talks on lighting, insulation, steam traps, and other subjects
7. "savEnergy" posters, decals, stickers
8. Publicity in plant news, bulletins
9. Publicity in public news media
10. Letters on conservation to homes
11. Talks to local organizations

D. Evaluate program
    1. Review progress in energy saving
    2. Evaluate original goals
    3. Consider program modifications
    4. Revise goals, as necessary

Energy Conservation Suggestions

The following list of opportunities for energy conservation actions has been compiled from a wide range of publications. As in other sectors, space heating offers great potential for conservation.

1. Turn down heat during day to 65°-68°F; at night and on weekends to 60°F or less; in unused areas to 50°F (10°C).

2. Use minimum heat in warehouses and storage areas.

3. Turn on heat later than usual each day.

4. Lower cafeteria temperature immediately after lunch.

5. Reduce temperature in highly ventilated areas.

6. Ensure that all outside doors are self-closing.

7. Segregate special operations that require more heating or cooling than surrounding areas.

8. Keep doors closed to unheated or uncooled areas such as corridors.

9. Keep heaters clear of obstructions.

10. Seal thermostats to prevent unauthorized adjustments.

11. Use humidifiers to improve employee comfort at lower temperatures.

12. Maintain heating, air conditioning, and other heat transfer equipment in top condition.

13. Consider multiple fuel capability.

14. Upgrade inefficient boilers and power equipment.

15. Use small automatic steam generators at remote locations requiring steam.

16. Automate combustion system controls.

17. Recycle waste fuel.

18. Shut off chillers during winter months.

19. Discontinue use of some building entrances.

20. Close loading dock doors when not in use and use dock curtains when unloading trucks.

21. Use air curtains at doors that must remain open.

22. Pull drapes at sundown to cut heat loss.

23. Make maximum use of sunlight for heating and lighting.

24. Rearrange office furniture so that desks are close to heating systems and/or natural sunlight.

25. Inspect and repair insulation, weather stripping, and caulking.

26. Install additional insulation especially on ceilings.

27. Investigate more or better pipe and duct insulation in unheated areas.

28. Cover windows with plastic sheets or film or install storm windows or cover all or a portion of windows with insulating material and/or wall panels.

29. Install insulating glass in windows.

30. Consider infrared or other spot heaters in small work areas where general heating can be reduced.

31. Use heat recovery units on exhausts.

32. Install baffles to eliminate drafts.

33. Eliminate any unused roof openings and abandoned stacks.

34. Reduce makeup air during day; eliminate all makeup air at night.

35. Turn on ventilation later than usual each day.

36. Cycle ventilation equipment during day.

37. Paint roofs with reflective materials to reflect heat.

38. Pipe heat from machinery, ovens, etc. to cooler places in the winter.

39. Relax clothing requirements for employees.

The most universally used energy-saving measure has been electricity savings by the reduction of lighting, both interior and exterior. Brilliantly lighted signs, it has been found, do not aid a company's image during shortage periods. Reductions need not include plant security and safety lighting.

1. Turn off lights when not in use.

2. Use timers to control lighting cycle.

3. Put "lights out" stickers on room light switches.

4. Mark panels and switches so guards can monitor lighting.

5. Turn off parking lot lights after last shift; restrict parking to specific lots so lights can be kept off in unused lots.

6. Install photoswitches on lights that remain on at night.

7. Put timed shut-off switches on lights in transformer rooms and similar closed-off areas.

8. Deenergize some light fixtures; remove some light bulbs (and ballast where necessary).

9. Remove diffusers from lights.

10. Replace incandescent fixtures with fluorescent ones or with self-ballasting mercury or sodium bulbs.

11. Clean light fixtures on regular basis.

12. Reduce lighting in material storage areas and in corridors except where required for safety, production, and security needs.

13. Provide improved localized lighting but reduce overall lighting (abandon the uniform lighting concept).

14. Rearrange office furniture so that desks and chairs are close to natural sunlight.

15. Install additional light switches to control lighting in small areas.

16. Reschedule night-time cleaning operations to daylight hours.

17. Reduce water-heating temperatures in washrooms (110°) and commercial kitchens (140°).

18. Conduct a plant load survey to see that motors are properly loaded, that belts are adjusted, and that unnecessary shafting is eliminated.

19. Consider rescheduling work hours, production, or any special operations to off-peak periods.

20. Eliminate unnecessary power devices such as automatic doors, dryers in washrooms, and electric water coolers.

21. Limit use of elevators and slow down or turn off escalators.

22. Prohibit individual space heaters unless specifically authorized.

23. Turn off electric typewriters when not in use.

24. Eliminate weekend overtime; limit overtime to specific nights.

A good deal of energy can be saved by analyzing the industrial process for energy efficiency. Raytheon Corporation has pushed boiler efficiency to 90.75 percent (the average is 75 to 82 percent(by simply cleaning and changing burner elements frequently. The process-related energy conservation category is probably the one open to the most innovation; it is also the area where a consulting engineer may be of the most use. Encourage programs for new process practices.

1. Turn off process exhausts when not in use; schedule work so process exhausts are used less; improve efficiency of exhaust systems by re-designing hoods.

2. Substitute less toxic chemicals that require less ventilation.

3. Cut down on process use of hot water (rinses, etc.); check hot water systems for leaking valves and faucets.

4. Use plastic spheres on hot liquids in open top tanks.

5. Determine efficient "hold" temperatures on process tanks during overnight and weekend periods.

6. Reduce temperature of processing fluids.

7. Shut down gas burners in process equipment if not in use instead of idling them.

8. Eliminate some processing department if they are marginal operations (subcontract work).

9. Use ultrasonic leak detector to locate steam and/or compressed air leaks.

10. Reschedule work to require minimum usage of electrical equipment (test equipment, motors, fans, etc.).

11. Use submetering to monitor power usage within certain areas of the plant.

12. Deenergize excess transformer capacity whenever practical.

13. Provide proper maintenance and lubrication of motor-driven equipment for the most efficient operation.

14. Use alternative processing methods that require less energy, e.g., powder coating versus solvent based.

15. Substitute a plentiful for a scarce fuel. In general, coal is the most plentiful fuel, but its use requires expensive handling equipment and stack gas cleaning facilities.

Energy can be saved by encouraging employees to do the little things. Programs of compensation for "Energy Saver of the Month" can be effective. Large wall posters displaying conservation reminders are also common practice. Some things for employees to think about are:

1. Utilize minimum artificial lighting; keep unnecessary lights off; shut off lights when leaving office or work area.

2. Turn off window air conditioners before days end.

3. Close dampers that admit outside air.

4. Report leaky faucets and radiators.

5. Regulate blinds, draperies, etc. to make the most of sunlight.

6. Shut off typewriters, fans, coffee makers, etc. when not in use.

7. Use stairs rather than elevator when possible.

There are several other areas a company can explore in energy conservation. IBM has a program of recycling plastic keyboard buttons; Bell Laboratories initiated a computerized car pooling program for its employees, using maps of each employees' residential area. Another area for computers is reporting on machine efficiency. Some other ideas:

1. Post signs on company vehicles for 50 miles per hour maximum speed.

2. Encourage car pool use by awarding preferential parking spaces.

3. Arrange for bus service for employees.

4. Run shuttle service between adjacent facilities or outlying buildings.

5. Appoint "energy monitors" in all plant areas.

6. Train security guards and night watchmen to recognize and report wasteful energy usage.

7. Issue violation tickets for wasteful energy practices.

8. Give proper weight to energy consumption requirements in planning studies.

Energy Conservation in Transportation

The 100 million plus registered American family cars consume about one fifth of all energy used in the United States. The average car gets 13.7 miles per gallon (includes in-city driving) and consumes 700 gallons of gas annually. Experts estimate that some 30 percent of all fuel used in transportation is discretionary, in other words, it could be eliminated without serious effects. Perhaps as much as half of all private auto use is discretionary.

The most effective tactic to reduce consumption of motor gasoline is to reduce private automobile use. Encourage mass transportation, car pools, bicycles, and walking. Employers can be urged to set up car pool routes. This would be especially effective on a county level. The local government may help by placing parking restrictions on one-passenger cars, suspending or reducing tolls on full cars, and providing express lanes for buses and car pools in congested streets. Consider a program of establishing bicycle lanes.

Encourage individuals to study the market before they buy a new car. Either the dealer or the Environmental Protection Agency (Washington, D.C., 20460) can provide a free copy of the "Gas Mileage Guides for Car Buyers" available for most models back to 1973. Buyers should also review test results published by Consumers Union and motor industry magazines. Generally, the best fuel economy is associated with low vehicle weight, small engines, manual transmission, low axle ratio, and small frontal area (the width of the car times its height). Buyers should select within their size requirements on the basis of the combination of purchase price and estimated fuel costs for as long as they plan to keep the car—the lifetime cost of the car.

Here are some additional commonly mentioned conservation hints:

1. Have your car tuned as recommended by the manufacturer. Regular tuneups can save you as much as 10 percent on gasoline costs.

2. Keep the engine air filter clean. Insufficient air wastes gasoline.

3. Use the octane gasoline and oil grade recommended for your car. Multigrade oils are good for a wide range of conditions.

4. Check tire pressures regularly. Ten percent underinflation in your tires will reduce gas consumption about 5 percent; 40 percent underinflation will cost you nearly 60 percent of peak mileage.

5. Consider steel-belted radials when you buy new tires. They give several percent better mileage and last longer.

6. Remove unnecessary weight from the car. The lighter the car, the less gas it uses.

7. Don't buy an air conditioner unless you really need it; if you have one, use it sparingly. The cooling equipment reduces fuel economy an average of 10 percent, almost 20 percent in stop-and-go traffic.

8. Purchase only the optional equipment and accessories you really need. Items like automatic transmission and power steering require considerable energy, and all this energy is derived from the gasoline. Other equipment, such as power brakes and electric motor-driven windows, seats,

and radio antennas, requires less energy for operation; however, all accessories add to the vehicle weight and reduce fuel economy.

The automobile is the most inefficient method of passenger movement, and it is made even more inefficient by "fuelish" motorists. Of US commuters, 56 percent drive alone, 26 percent drive with passengers, and 14 percent use mass-transit systems. It is evident, therefore, that a major energy savings can be made by car pooling and eliminating unnecessary trips. Urge motorists to take one less short trip a week; do several errands in one trip; combine their trips with those of friends and neighbors. In other words, plan their trips beforehand.

The next best way to save money and energy with an automobile is to use good driving techniques. A careful driver can get at least 30 percent more mileage than the average driver and 50 percent more than the careless one. Some of the most important of these techniques are:

1. Drive at moderate speeds, especially on high-speed roads. Most automobiles get about 28 percent better fuel economy on the highway at 50 miles per hour than at 70 and about 21 percent better at 55 than at 70.

2. Accelerate smoothly to save engines, tires, and gasoline.

3. Avoid jack rabbit stops and starts: with automatic transmission, accelerate slowly; with manual transmission, get to high gear faster.

4. Minimize braking—anticipate speed changes.

5. Drive at a steady pace, avoid stop-and-go traffic, and slow down as soon as you see a red light ahead.

6. Don't let the motor idle for more than a minute. Turn off the engine. It takes less gasoline to restart the car than it takes to let it idle. Generally, there is no need to press the accelerator down to restart a warm engine.

7. Don't overfill your gasoline tank. By stopping at the first cutoff on the automatic valve you can eliminate any change of spillage.

8. Use brakes and not acceleration to keep car from rolling back when stopped on a hill.

Long trips usually yield better gas mileage statistics because of the reduction of stops and starts found in normal daily driving. Nevertheless, gasoline bills and total energy consumption will reflect the length of the trip. An energy-conscious vacationer could well keep several things in mind:

1. Vacation closer to home this year. Discover the nearby attractions which visitors to your area are eager to see.

2. A nearby hotel or campground can often provide as complete and happy a change from routine as one that is hundreds of miles away.

3. When you travel, try a train or a bus instead of the family car.

4. During your holiday rediscover the pleasures of walking, hiking, and bicycling.

Energy Conservation in Agriculture

Agriculture uses more energy than any other single industry. This great consumption of energy is responsible for the greatly increased agricultural production in the US (59 percent between 1950 and 1973). If we were to try to revert back to 1939 technology, experts estimate that it would take 31 billion man-hours rather than the 6.4 billion of today, 16.5 million laborers rather than today's 4.4 million, 1.5 million tractors instead of the present 4.5 million, and, finally, 27 million horses and mules. We would need 668 million acres of land instead of the 296 million now used —81 million just to feed the horses and mules.

Agriculture will probably continue to be society's largest energy-user. But the individual farmer can still employ energy-saving practices, which if multiplied collectively will substantially cut energy consumption at the national as well as local level. This section is separated into energy conservation practices in machinery handling, and energy conservation in farming methods.

Energy Conservation Practices in Farm Machinery and Equipment Handling. Proper maintenance of machinery could decrease fuel consumption of gasoline tractors by 14 percent and increase horsepower capability by 11 percent. Here are some suggestions:

1. Keep air filter clean.
2. Tune and service ignition system regularly.
3. Keep fuel filters, injectors, etc. in top condition.
4. Change oil regularly.
5. Check thermostat. Fuel consumption increases by at least 25 percent when engine is operated at 100°F, instead of 180°F. Use extra heat shields on the engine when doing light work in cold weather.
6. Engine testing—a good way to be sure engines will produce its best is to have it checked and tuned on a dynamometer.

One of the best ways to save fuel in tractor operation is to gear up and throttle back. This practice will reduce fuel consumption by more than 30 percent in some models. Farmers will have much higher fuel efficiency if they run the tractor harder and pull faster, according to agricultural experts. Light loads at low speeds are inefficient. Other energy conservation suggestions include:

1. Control slip—you can do a lot more work with a gallon of fuel if you don't spin your wheels (you get traction only by adding weight).
2. Reduce rolling resistance from tires sinking into soft soil. If rolling resistance is the problem, take weight off or distribute it over more soil

surface, go to wider or larger diameter tires, reduce inflation (but not too much), or add duals.

3. Consider duals, for increased flotation if wet or soft soils are a problem, for better sideways stability, for more weight, which means better traction, for less downtime (if you have to change a tire, you can move the tractor to a more convenient area), for more full-season tractor use. Check with a reputable farm tire dealer and your implement dealer before converting your tractor to duals.

4. Consider radial tires. They slip less than conventional bias-ply, doing more work per hour, and the tread lasts longer. They cost about 25 percent more than regular tires but can increase field efficiency up to 20 percent in terms of acres worked per gallon of fuel.

5. Match tractor to the job. Use small tractors for lighter jobs and diesel tractors when the gas supply is tighter than the diesel supply.

6. Shut engine off; idling wastes energy.

7. Move large equipment by truck if possible.

On-the-farm storage facilities for gasoline and diesel fuel suffer from evaporation. Construction of a sunshade for storage tanks is a simple measure which may cut evaporation from above-the-ground tanks by as much as 50 percent. Tanks should also be painted white to reflect heat (if law permits). Evaporation losses can be still further reduced by use of a *pressure-vacuum relief valve*. It can be used in place of a standard vented cap.

Conserving Energy in Farming Methods. Farming methods provide many opportunities for energy conservation. For example, minimum tillage means cultivating or turning the soil as little as possible in order to grow a crop. Some reduced tillage systems virtually eliminate the energy consuming plow, which requires some 19 hp-hrs/acre as compared to 5.5 to 6 hp-hrs/acre for a disk. No-tillage is the most recent advance in reducing tillage to an optimum. No-tillage is a way of planting crops in previously unprepared soil by opening a narrow slot, trench, or band only of sufficient width and depth to obtain proper seed coverage. No other soil preparation is done. Herbicides control unwanted weeds and grasses; that allows chemicals to substitute for tractor power. These methods require less than one gallon fuel per acre for on-row time and about one-third gallon for other engine time. Actually, there are several methods of reducing tillage on your farm. All contribute to saving energy. They include: plow-plant in one operation, wheeltrack planting in plowed or plowed and harrowed soil, lister planting or modified lister planting, strip-till planting, field cultivator planting, chisel-plow planting, aerial seeding, and stubble-mulch planting. Contact the Agricultural Extension Service for details. Other energy-conserving tillage practices:

1. Reduce plowing depth.

2. Add a plow packer or harrow behind the plow to reduce secondary tillage needed if tractor can pull added load.

3. Keep plowshares sharp. Dull shares increase draft up to 25 percent and cause soil compaction at the plow sole.

4. Plow when soil moisture is favorable.

5. Use proper plow adjustment so it runs level as viewed from the side as well as from the rear. Adjust rear furrow wheel to reduce landslide pressure.

6. Pull planter behind disk or digger to increase load on tractor and reduce trips over the field.

7. Harrow field in diagonal patterns when two passes are needed. Compared to working in lands, that helps save at least 25 percent in travel and eliminates excess tillage at ends.

8. Plow or drill around fields instead of in lands to reduce idle travel at ends.

9. Lay out odd number of lands 75 to 80 feet in width to reduce number of dead furrows to finish.

10. Consider layout of field so headlands may be plowed at same time as body of field by plowing around entire field to finish up.

11. Hitch roller packer behind grain drill for interseeding grain to eliminate an extra trip.

12. Postpone operation like ditch digging or land leveling if possible (until after peak periods).

13. Consider preserving crops with organic acid rather than drying them.

14. Consider drying crops with partial heat. Dry down to 21 percent, then finish drying with natural air.

15. Select seed for proper hybrid maturity; try to plant short-season varieties to allow a better chance to dry down in the field.

Appendix 9A: Denver's "Project Energy"

[Denver's "Project Energy" is] a twofold approach to obtain the maximum efficient use of all forms of energy within the city and the conservation of fuels.

The first segment of the project is within the city government, with each department cooperating through the project coordinator, to examine all facets of the city operation to achieve a total program of energy conservation within city government. This will entail a total look at fuel utilization, fuel oil consumption, and electricity consumption by all city departments.

The mayor is also naming an eighteen-member Citizens Energy Management Advisory Council. This group will work with the project coordinator to formulate plans to be implemented by the city in the private sector to provide for conservation of as much energy as possible by individuals and private agencies. There will also be a representative from the Colorado Broadcasters Association and the Colorado Press Association who will act as advisors to the energy council in matters of public dissemination of information.

This group will help coordinate the city's "Project Energy" plans with federal and state agencies and make periodic reports on the status of energy use and availability within the city. They will further be charged with the responsibility of advising the Mayor in regard to furnishing the people of Denver guidance in complying with energy conservation programs. This group, which represents a broad base of expertise and citizen input, will examine all possible ideas for maximum conservation of energy within the city and county of Denver.[4]

Appendix 9B: An Internal Conservation Program for Local Governments

The following outline of an internal conservation program for local government is aimed at conserving petroleum. It was adapted from one developed by the Office of Government Preparedness (General Services Administration) during the summer of 1973 and circulated for comment.[5] Shortages of other energy commodities might require somewhat different plans; local officials may wish to make use of the conservation suggestions listed elsewhere in this chapter for assembling programs.

A Suggested Message from the Mayor to Local Government Officers and Employees

The nation today faces increasing demands for fuel and electric power. Federal officials have announced that critical shortages of energy products exist. Our nation is now consuming more gas and oil than it produces, making us dependent upon foreign countries for our energy supply. A need exists to conserve energy.

This critical situation makes it desirable that we cooperate with state and federal government in the overall effort to conserve fuel and electric power.

The attached document is an outline plan for fuel oil conservation within the city and should be studied carefully.

Section I of the outline plan concerns the responsibilities of department heads. Section II lists measures to be taken by those actually in charge of operation of buildings and other facilities. Section III sets forth the measures to be taken by all employees.

The responsibility for implementing the plan will be coordinated through (city office). If any questions arise, please contact this office.

The performance of each government facility with respect to energy conservation is particularly important because of the example it sets for the rest of the community.

To be effective the plan requires the cooperation of major officials, facility managers, and all employees.

Implementation of the measures outlined will result in an appreciable reduction in energy usage with an accompanying savings in our utility bills without adversely affecting the performance of government functions.

Widespread adoption of similar measures by the industrial and commercial sector and by individual families could account for that crucial margin between demand and supply which spells the difference between adequacy and deficiency and could eliminate the need for more stringent emergency measures.

The measures listed are applicable to all types of government facilities: courthouses, municipal centers, school and college buildings, police stations, firehouses, hospitals, prisons. It is appreciated, however, that not every recommended measure will necessarily be applicable to each facility. Insofar as it is practical, however, I urge all of you to follow the measures included in this plan.

Suggested Actions for Department Heads

1. Advise all management officials, facility managers, and individual employees of this appeal by the Office of Emergency Preparedness to conserve our energy resources. Particular emphasis should be directed to, where appropriate, contingency plans developed to minimize its effects.

2. Assign a management official to monitor and supervise this government-wide energy conservation effort to reduce the consumption of fuel oil.

3. Publicize the use of strict conservation practices through announcements at staff meetings and notices and posters placed on bulletin boards and in facility newsletters.

4. Direct implementation of action items listed for accomplishment by occupants and facility managers.

5. Encourage the conduct of projects and seminars on fuel and electric power conservation through the state and local educational systems.

6. Develop a Fuel Consumption Reduction Plan to be implemented in the event that a shortage does develop. This plan should detail which equipment will be shut down. The order for shut-downs and later start-up should be set forth in detail to include, if required, restricted hours of operation of heating equipment with cut-on and cut-off times geared to outside temperatures. All employees should be given instructions beforehand on what action they should take during the emergency.

7. In some parts of the nation environmental considerations have accelerated the conversion of electric-power-generating plans from coal to oil fired. Such conversions have increased the consumption of fuel oil and accentuated the current fuel-oil shortages. Where such is the case, the conservation of electric power is equally as significant as the conservation of heat, and an all energy conservation effort should be implemented in those areas affected.

Suggested Measures for Facility Managers

1. Verify building occupant's heating needs. Based on these needs, establish scheduled hours of operation of the heating equipment to include cut-on and cut-off times to cover a range of outside temperatures.

2. Make sure that all heating equipment is in good operating repair.

3. Shut down heating equipment to the extent possible on weekends and holidays in buildings that are unoccupied during those periods.

4. Reduce heat to unoccupied space such as storerooms and unoccupied living quarters and barracks.

5. Reduce amounts of outside air used in ventilating systems.

6. Inspect and repair where necessary the wall and ceiling insulation, caulking, and storm windows of all buildings.

7. Verify that pipe insulation is provided and maintained in good repair on all steam or hot-water lines, particularly those passing through unoccupied or air-conditioned spaces.

8. Take little-used buildings out of service completely and shut off all utilities not needed for fire protection or security.

9. Set all heating thermostats at the lowest level consistent with health of personnel.

10. Keep fans, pumps, compressors, and other rotating equipment in good repair.

11. Implement, where required because of fuel-oil-fired electric-generating plants, an energy conservation plan, to include electric power.

Suggested Tear Sheet for Desk-to-Desk Distribution to All Government Employees

This message is intended to inform all employees of local government on how they can help their state and country by conserving our energy resources this winter, particularly fuel oil used for heating and electric-power generation.

The nation today faces increasing demands for fuel and power. A recent survey conducted by the Joint Board on Fuel Supply and Fuel Transport, under the direction of the President's Office of Emergency Preparedness, indicated that critical shortages of fuel oil are possible in many areas of the country this winter.

This critical situation makes it desirable that all employees of state and local governments cooperate in the overall effort to use our heating resources prudently and conservatively. This effort will set an example for the rest of the state.

Individual employees should take the following actions as the situation warrants.

1. Keep windows and outside doors closed, particularly loading docks and similar large entrance doors.

2. If individual heating units are provided, close the damper that admits outside air.

3. Turn off or cut back individual heating units shortly before end of business day when requested by your supervisor.

4. Draw or partially close blinds, shades, and draperies to conserve existing heat when appropriate.

5. Carry these same rules of energy conservation to your home and practice them there as well.

6. In some areas of the nation, conservation of electric power could contribute substantially to the nationwide effort to reduce fuel consumption, because fuel oil is used to generate electricity. If such is the case in your area, prudent and conservative use of electric lights and all equipment and appliances using electricity should be practiced.

Appendix 9C: Los Angeles Emergency Energy Curtailment Program

THE PEOPLE OF THE CITY OF LOS ANGELES DO ORDAIN AS FOLLOWS:

Chapter XIII—The Emergency Energy Curtailment Plan of the City of Los Angeles

SEC. 131.00. Scope. There is hereby established a City of Los Angeles Emergency Energy Curtailment Plan.

SEC. 131.01. Declaration of Urgency. The Council of the City of Los Angeles hereby finds and declares that there exists within this City an electrical energy emergency, and that as a result, there is an urgent necessity to take legislative action through the exercise of the police power to protect the public peace, health and safety of this City from a public disaster or calamity, to take effect immediately upon publication of this Ordinance.

SEC. 131.02. Declaration of Purpose. The purpose of this Chapter is to provide an energy curtailment plan to minimize the effect of a possible shortage of electrical energy to the inhabitants of the City and, by means of this Chapter, to adopt provisions that will significantly reduce the consumption of electricity over an extended period of time, thereby extending the available fuel required for the production of electricity, while reducing the hardship on the City and the general public to the greatest extent possible.

SEC. 131.03. Definitions. The following words and phrases, whenever used in this Chapter, shall be construed as defined in this Section unless from the context a different meaning is intended or unless a different meaning is specifically defined within the individual sections of this Chapter:

    a. "City" means The City of Los Angeles
    b. "Mayor" means the Mayor of The City of Los Angeles.
    c. "City Council" means the Council of The City of Los Angeles.
    d. "Board" means the Board of Water and Power Commissioners, unless some other board of the City is expressly described in a specific provision of this Chapter.
    e. "Department" means the Department of Water and Power unless some other department of the City is expressly described.
    f. "General Manager" means the General Manager and Chief Engineer of the Department of Water and Power of The City of Los Angeles.

179

g. "Section" means a section of this Chapter unless some other ordinance or statute is specifically mentioned.

h. "Customer" includes every person, firm and corporation, and any state or local governmental agency or public district using or receiving electrical energy from the Department.

i. "Chapter" means the ordinance providing for "The Emergency Energy Curtailment Plan of The City of Los Angeles."

j. "Officer" means every person designated in Section 5 of the Los Angeles City Charter as being an officer of The City of Los Angeles.

k. "Base period" means that period of time over which the base is computed.

l. "Base" means the amount of electrical energy used on customer's premises for the corresponding billing period between the months of September 1, 1972, and August 31, 1973. The Department, in its discretion, may adjust such base if the customer establishes, to the satisfaction of the Department, that the base, as herein provided, would cause him great hardship for reasons including but not necessarily limited to technological improvements to customer's premises since the base period, increased employment on customer's premises since the base period, and abnormal temperature changes, economic fluctuations, and occupancy factors occurring since the base period.

Any customer who was not a customer of the premises for which services billed by the Department during the base period, shall be assigned the same base for such premises as provided above, and the Department shall have the further discretion to adjust such base in the event such customer's use of the premises is substantially different from the previous use thereof during the base period.

SEC. 131.04. Authorization. The various officers, boards, departments, bureaus, and agencies of the City are hereby authorized to immediately implement the provisions of this Chapter upon the effective date hereof. (As Amended by Ord. 145,400, Eff. 12-27-73.)

SEC. 131.05. Application. The provisions of this Chapter shall apply to all customers and property situated within the limits of the City, and also shall apply to all property and facilities owned, maintained, operated or under the jurisdiction of the various officers, boards, departments, bureaus, or agencies of the City.

SEC. 131.06. Emergency Energy Curtailment Phases.

a. Phase I. Effective December 21, 1973, no customer shall make, cause or permit any use of electrical energy provided by the Department of Water and Power in a manner which is contrary to the provisions of subsections (i) through (ix) of this subsection a.

(i) *Street Light Reduction.*

(a) *Electrical energy supplied to city agencies*

The Director of the Bureau of Street Lighting of the Department of Public Works is hereby directed to develop, as soon as practicable, a plan which, upon implementation, will produce a twenty-five percent (25%) reduction in energy used for street lighting. Such plan shall be submitted to the City Council for approval at the earliest practicable date.

(b) *Electrical energy supplied to agencies of the County of Los Angeles and State of California.* The appropriate agencies of the County of Los Angeles and State of California are hereby requested to develop, as soon as practicable, a plan which, upon implementation, will produce a twenty-five percent (25%) reduction in energy used for street lighting. The Department of Water and Power of The City of Los Angeles is hereby directed to reduce by twenty-five percent (25%) the amount of electrical energy provided by the Department of the County of Los Angeles and State of California for street lighting.

(c) *Street lighting defined.* The term "street lighting" as used in this Chapter shall include every electric lamp erected or suspended on or over any freeway, highway, street, sidewalk or parkway, whether public or privately owned and which is open to public access at any time, and is used in the lighting thereof, or any wire or other apparatus immediately attached to such lamp. Utilitarian street lighting in residential areas shall not be deemed street lighting within the meaning of this Chapter.

(d) The Bureau of Street Lighting shall activate said plan promptly upon the approval thereof by the City Council, and shall immediately effect such twenty-five percent (25%) reduction in energy usage for all such street lighting.

(e) *Exception.* These subsection (i) prohibited uses of electrical energy from the Department of Water and Power for street lighting are not applicable to that lighting necessary for public safety, or for security purposes, or for essential governmental services such as Police, Fire, Health and communications. (*Added by Ordinance No. 145,351. Eff. 12-14-73: and further amended by Ordinance No. 145,400, Eff. 12-27-73.*)

(ii) *Prohibited Use of Outdoor Advertising and Decorative Lighting.*

(a) No customer shall at any time make, cause or permit any use of electrical energy for lighting of billboards, signs, advertising goods or services or to identify the providers of goods or services, displays of goods, objects or designs symbolic of commercial enterprises, trademarks or logo, or motors or devices to rotate or move advertising signs or operate pumps or other devices in fountains which are primarily decorative, building floodlighting, architectural or decorative lighting, or lights used for landscaping, or any similar form of lighting based upon the use of electrical energy supplied by the Department.

(b) Notwithstanding the provisions of subsection (ii)(a) hereof, each business establishment may operate its window and display lighting and illuminate one outdoor sign between the hours of sunset and 10:30 P.M. local time or one-half (½) hour after closing, whichever is the later in time, and each billboard may be illuminated between the hours of sunset and 10:30 P.M., local time. (*Added by Ordinance No. 145,352, Eff. 12-14-73; and further Amended by Ordinance No. 145,400, Eff. 12-27-73.*)

(iii) *Prohibited Use of Functional Outdoor Business Lighting.* No customer shall make, cause or permit any use of electrical energy from the Department for the floodlighting of outdoor business areas including, but not limited to, service stations, used car lots, new car lots, automobile parking lots, or similar businesses, between the hours of sunrise and sunset, and when not open for business. After sunset, when such businesses are open, the use of electrical energy for such purposes shall not exceed fifty percent (50%) of the energy used during the base period.

Exception. These subsection (iii) prohibited uses on the use of electrical energy from the Department are not applicable to that lighting necessary for public safety, or for security, or that required by law, or required for the lighting of essential governmental buildings utilized for police, fire, education, health and communications purposes. (*Added by Ordinance No. 145,353. Eff. 12-14-73; and further Amended by Ordinance No. 145,400. Eff. 12-27-73.*)

(iv) *Comfort Heating and Cooling.* No customer shall make, cause or permit the use of electrical energy from the Department for the purpose of comfort space heating or cooling in any commercial or industrial establishment when such premises are not open for business. During business hours, no electrical energy shall be used in such establishments to provide heat to raise the temperature therein above 68° F nor to provide cooling to reduce the temperature therein below 78° F, except where other temperatures are specifically required by law. (*Added by Ordinance No. 145,354. Eff. 12-14-73.*)

(v) *Prohibition of Electrical Use for Outdoor Public Exhibitions.*

(a) *Commercial recreational or cultural activities.* No customer shall make, cause or permit the use of electrical energy from the Department for commercial recreational or cultural activities in excess of seventy-five percent (75%) of the amount used by that customer in the base period for the same or similar activities.

(b) *Non-commercial recreational or cultural activities.* No customer shall make, cause or permit the use of electrical energy from the Department for non-commercial recreational or cultural activities between the hours of 9:00 P.M. and sunrise, local time.

(c) *Definitions.* As used in this subsection, "recreational or cultural activity" means an activity to which the public generally is admitted for the purpose of participating in or witnessing an exhibition, including but not limited to, sporting events, plays, concerts, amusement parks and similar enterprises. "Non-commercial recreational activities" means those recreational activities such as playgrounds, school or college athletics from which no profit is derived or expected to be derived for any or all of the persons engaged in each such activity. "Commercial recreational activities" means all other recreational activities.

Exceptions. The foregoing prohibitions on the use of electrical energy for outdoor public exhibitions shall not apply to drive-in theatres or to religious, educational and political assemblies, nor to any recreational cultural activity otherwise protected under the First Amendment to the Constitution of the United States. (*Added by Ordinance No. 145,355. Eff. 12-14-73; and further Amended by Ordinance No. 145,400. Eff. 12-27-73.*)

(vi) *Prohibited Indoor Business Lighting.*

(a) No customer shall make, cause or permit the use of electrical energy from the Department for lighting the interior of any business establishment during that period of time that said establishment is not carrying on the usual and customary activities of that business.

(b) Notwithstanding the foregoing provision, a business establishment may provide sufficient illumination at all times to insure a minimal level of protection and security.

(c) Nothing in this subsection shall be construed to prohibit ordinary and customary maintenance and janitorial services at times other than those during which the business establishment is carrying on the usual and customary activities of that business. (*Added by Ordinance No. 145,356, Eff. 12-14-73.*)

(vii) *Residential Restrictions.* No customer shall make, cause or permit the use of electrical energy from the Department for residential purposes in an amount in excess of ninety percent (90%) of the amount used during the base period, as defined in this Chapter. No such customer shall use electrical energy provided by the Department for the heating or lighting, or both, of swimming pools located on private residential premises. For the purposes of this subsection, a customer is deemed to be using electricity for residential purposes if he is receiving such electricity pursuant to the Department's D-1 Domestic Service schedule. (*Added by Ordinance No. 145,357, Eff. 12-14-73.*)

(viii) *Commercial Restrictions.* No customer shall make, cause or permit the use of electrical energy from the Department for any purpose whatever in the operation of a commercial enterprise in an amount in excess of eighty percent (80%) of the amount of electrical energy consumed by that customer in that commercial enterprise during the base period as defined in this Chapter. A customer is deemed to be using electricity for the operation of a commercial enterprise if he is receiving electricity pursuant to the Department's A-1 General Service schedule and is engaged in those activities described in Divisions F through K, inclusive, and Appendix "A" thereto, of the Standard Industrial Classification Manual, 1972 Edition, prepared by the Statistical Policy Division of the Executive Office of the President, Office of Management and Budget. (*Added by Ordinance No. 145,358, Eff. 12-14-73: and further Amended by Ordinance No. 145,000, 12-14-73.*)

(ix) *Industrial Restrictions.* No customer shall make, cause or permit the use of electrical energy from the Department in the operation of any industrial enterprise in an amount in excess of ninety percent (90%) of the amount of electrical energy consumed by that customer during the base period as defined in this Chapter. A customer is deemed to be using electricity for the operation of an industrial enterprise if he is receiving electricity pursuant to the Department's A-1 General Service schedule and is engaged in those activities described in Divisions A through E, inclusive, and Appendix "A" Thereto, of the Standard Industrial Classification Manual, 1972 Edition, prepared by the Statistical Policy Division of the Executive Office of the President, Office of Management and Budget. (*Added by Ordinance No. 145,359, Eff. 12-14-73; and further Amended by Ordinance No. 145,400, Eff. 12-27-73.*)

b. *Phase II.* At such time as the consumption of fuel by the Department's electrical generating facilities exceeds the amount of fuel in storage plus that fuel for which there is a substantial certainty of delivery by an amount which is deemed critical by the Department of Water and Power, such determination shall be promptly communicated to the Mayor and the Council. At any time, on or after January 15, 1974, and upon being informed by the Department of Water and Power of a critical fuel shortage, the Mayor, with concurrence of the Council by Resolution, may order that no customer shall make, cause or permit any use of electrical energy provided by the Department of Water and Power in a manner which is contrary to the provisions of subsections (i) through (iv) of this subsection b. Said order shall be made by public proclamation, and shall be published one time in a daily newspaper of general circulation, and shall become effective immediately upon such publication.

(i) *Prohibited uses.* No customer shall make, cause or permit the use of lighting powered by electrical energy from the Department for the following purposes:

(a) Any use prohibited in subsections (ii) through (vi) of subsection a of Section 131.06 of the Los Angeles Municipal Code.

(b) The illumination of billboards at any time whatsoever.

(c) Functional outdoor business lighting at any time, whatsoever.

(d) The illumination of or in connection with outdoor noncommercial recreational or cultural activities of any nature whatsoever at any time whatsoever.

(e) Outdoor commercial recreational or cultural activities of any nature whatsoever in an amount in excess of fifty percent (50%) of the amount used by that customer in the base period for the same or similar activity.

(f) Notwithstanding the provisions of the foregoing subsections (a) through (e), inclusive, nothing contained therein shall be deemed to require the reduction of lighting below a level necessary for public safety or for security. (*Added by Ordinance No. 145,360, Eff. 12-14-73.*)

(ii) *Residential Restrictions.* No customer shall make, cause or permit the use of electrical energy from the Department for residential purposes in an amount in excess of eight-eight percent (88%) of the amount used during the base period, as defined in this Chapter. For the purposes of this subsection, a customer is deemed to be using electricity for residential purposes if he is receiving such electricity pursuant to the Department's D-1 Domestic Service Schedule. No such customer shall use electrical energy provided by the Department for the heating or lighting or both of swimming pools located on private residential premises. (*Added by Ordinance No. 145,361, Eff. 12-14-73.*)

(iii) *Commercial Restrictions.* No customer shall make, cause or permit the use of electrical energy from the Department for any purpose whatever in the operation of a commercial enterprise in an amount in excess of sixty-seven percent (67%) of the amount of electrical energy consumed by that customer in that commercial enterprise during the base period as defined in this Chapter. A customer is deemed to be using electricity for the operation of a commercial enterprise if he is receiving electricity pursuant to the Department's A-1 General Service schedule and is engaged in those activities described in Divisions F through K, inclusive, and Appendix "A" thereto, of the Standard Industrial Classification Manual, 1972 Edition, prepared by the Statistical Policy Division of the Executive Office of the President. Office of Management and Budget. (*Added by Ordinance No. 145,362, Eff. 12-14-73; and further Amended by Ordinance No. 145,400, Eff. 12-27-73.*)

(iv) *Industrial Restrictions.* No customer shall make, cause or permit the use of electrical energy from the Department in the operation of any industrial enterprise in an amount in excess of eight-four percent (84%) of the amount of electrical energy consumed by that customer during the base period as defined in this Chapter. A customer is deemed to be using electricity for the operation of an industrial enterprise if he is receiving electricity pursuant to the Department's A-1 General Service schedule and is engaged in those activities described in Divisions A through E, inclusive, and Appendix "A" thereto, of the Standard Industrial Classification Manual, 1972 Edition, prepared by the Statistical Policy Division of the Executive Office of the President, Office of Management and Budget. (*Added by Ordinance No. 145,363, Eff. 12-14-73; and further Amended by Ordinance No. 145,400, Eff. 12-27-73.*)

c. *Improved Fuel Forecast.* At such time as the Department of Water and Power deems its fuel situation to be no longer critical, it shall promptly so notify the Mayor and the City Council and the Mayor, with the concurrence of the City Council by Resolution, may then order that the Phase II provisions of this Section shall no longer be in effect. Said order shall be made by public proclamation and be published in the manner set forth in subsection b hereof. Upon the suspension of Phase II provisions as herein provided, the provisions of Phase I shall immediately become reinstated and effective without further notice. (*As Amended by Ordinance No. 145,400, Eff. 12-27-73.*)

SEC. 131.07 *Failure to Comply.*

(a) *Penalties.* It shall be unlawful for any customer to fail to comply with any of the provisions contained in subsections a and b of Section 131.06 hereof. Notwithstanding any other provisions of the Los Angeles Municipal Code, the penalties set forth herein shall be exclusive, and not cumulative with any other penalty prescribed in any other section of this Code. The penalties for failure to comply with any of the provisions of this Chapter shall be as follows:

(1) On the first violation by an customer, a warning notice of the fact of such violation shall be issued by the Department and delivered to the customer as provided herein, and if the violation is of subsection (vii), (viii) or (ix) of subsection a of Section 131.06 or of subsections (ii), (iii) or (iv) of subsection b of Section 131.06 hereof, a surcharge shall be made to the customer in an amount equal to fifty percent (50%) of that customer's electrical bill for the billing period during which the violation occurred, and if the violation is of subsections (i), (ii), (iii), (iv), (v) or (vi) of Section 131.06 a hereof or of subsection (i) of Section 131.06 b hereof and the customer fails to comply promptly after receiving notice of said violation with the requirements of this Chapter, the Department shall terminate service to said customer until such time as compliance thereto is assured, as determined by the Department in its sound discretion. (*As Amended by Ordinance No. 145,400, Eff. 12-27-73.*)

(2) For a second violation by any customer during the effective dates of the particular phase during which the violation occurred or during the preceding twelve (12) calendar months, whichever is the shorter, the Department shall discontinue electrical service to that customer at the premises at which the violation occurred for a period of two (2) days, upon the giving of notice of the second violation to said customer in the manner herein set forth.

(3) For a third violation by any customer, during the effective dates of the particular phase during which the violation occurred or during the preceding twelve (12) calendar months, whichever is the shorter, the Department shall discontinue electrical service to that customer at the premises at which the violation occurred for a period of five (5) days,

upon the giving of notice of such violation to said customer in the manner herein set forth.

(4) For each subsequent violation by any customer during the effective dates of the particular phase during which the violation occurred or during the preceding twelve (12) calendar months, whichever is the shorter, the Department shall discontinue electrical service to that customer at the premises at which the violation occurred for a period of not less than five (5) days nor more than thirty (30) days, as determined by the General Manager.

b. *Notice.* The Department shall give notice of each violation to the customer committing such violation as follows:

1. If the penalty assessed is limited to the surcharge described herein above, by enclosing with the billing on which said surcharge appears a written notice of the violation.
2. If the penalty assessed is, or includes, the termination of service to the customer for any period of time whatever, notice of the violation shall be given in the following manner:
   (a) By giving written notice thereof to the customer personally: or
   (b) If he be absent from his place of residence and from his assumed place of business, by leaving a copy with some person of suitable age and discretion at either place, and sending a copy through the United States mail addressed to the customer at either his place of business or residence; or
   (c) If such place of residence and business cannot be ascertained, or a person of suitable age or discretion there cannot be found, then by affixing a copy to a conspicious place on the property where the failure to comply is occurring and also by delivering a copy to a person there residing, if such person can be found; and also sending a copy through the United States mail addressed to the customer at the place where the property is situated.

Said notice shall contain, in addition to the facts of the violation, a statement of the possible penalties for each violation and a statement informing the customer of his right to a hearing on the violation. (*As Amended by Ordinance No. 145,400, Eff. 12-27-73.*)

c. *Hearing.* Any customer against whom a penalty is levied pursuant to this Section shall have a right to a hearing on the merits of alleged violation upon the written request of that customer. The Council and Mayor shall adopt such regulations and rules as they, in their sound discretion, deem reasonable and necessary to the formation, procedure and operation of one or more appeal boards to conduct hearings pursuant to this subsection. (*As Amended by Ordinance No. 145,400, Eff. 12-27-73.*)

d. *Reservation of Rights.* The rights of the Department hereunder shall be cumulative to any other right of the Department to discontinue service.

SEC. 131.08. *Enforcement.* The Department of Water and Power shall enforce the provisions of subsections a and b of Section 131.06 of this Chapter.

SEC. 131.09. *General Provisions.*

a. *Exemption.* The provisions of subsection (viii) of Section 131.06 a and subsection (ii) of Section 131.06 b shall not apply to those domestic customers who are within the lowest one-third of all domestic customers as determined by the amount of kilowatt hours consumed during the base period.

b. *Relief from compliance.*

(1) *Prerequisites to relief.* Any customer who is dissatisfied with the application of any of the provisions of this Chapter, as the same relate to him, may seek relief as set forth below. No relief shall be granted to any customer in the absence of a showing by the customer that he has achieved the maximum practical reduction in electrical energy consumption in his residential, commercial or industrial energy usage, as the case may be, other than in the specific area in which relief is sought; in deciding what is the maximum practical reduction in electrical energy consumption, the appeal board shall take into consideration all relevant factors, specifically including, although not limited to, the particular question of whether any additional reduction in electrical energy consumption will result in a significant rise in unemployment. Any relief granted pursuant to this subsection shall be only to the extent minimally necessary to avoid a significant increase in the rate of unemployment and to achieve the ends reasonably sought in making the application. No relief shall be granted to any customer who, when requested by the Department, fails to provide the Department with information whereby the services provided to him can be classified for the purpose of establishing an appropriate base or classification pursuant to the provisions of this Chapter. (*As Amended by Ordinance No. 145,400. Eff. 12-27-73.*)

(2) *Relief Available.* A customer may seek relief as herein provided for any application of the provisions of this Chapter that adversely effect him at such times as Phase I of the curtailment plan are in effect. During Phase II or any subsequent phase which may hereinafter be imposed, a customer may seek relief as herein provided only as to the issue of whether that customer committed the particular act or acts, or omitted to perform the particular act or acts, as alleged by the Department.

(3) *Procedure for application for relief.* The Mayor, with the concurrence of the City Council, shall establish such number of appeal boards as he deems necessary. Each appeal board shall be composed of three members, one of which shall represent business, one of which shall repre-

sent labor, and one of which shall represent the general public. Applications for relief from the provisions of this Chapter shall be made to an appeal board in accordance with the rules and regulations established hereunder by the Mayor with the concurrence of the City Council. (*As Amended by Ordinance No. 145,400, Eff. 12-27-73.*)

(4) *Administrative remedies.* The filing by a customer of an application for a hearing before an appeal board, within five (5) days of the Departmental action complained, shall automatically stay the implementation of the proposed course of action by the Department pending the decision of the appeal board. No other or further stay shall be granted by the Department. Requests for relief hereunder may be filed immediately upon this Chapter becoming effective.

c. *Department Not to Discriminate.*

(1) *Department to give effect to legislative intent.* The Department shall provide electrical energy to its customers in accordance with the provisions of this Chapter, and in a manner reasonably calculated to effectuate the intent hereof.

(2) *Reduction in energy supplied.* If any customer fails to comply with any provision of this Chapter, the Department may, without notice, reduce the amount of electrical energy provided to that customer to the level which that customer would be using said energy if he were complying with the provisions of this Chapter. The provisions of this subsection shall be applied in lieu of, or in addition to, any other penalties provided in this Chapter, in the discretion of the Department, and shall be applied without regard to the status or nature of the customer.

d. *Public health and safety not be to affected.*

Nothing contained in this Chapter shall be construed to require the Department to curtail the supply of electrical energy to any customer when, in the discretion of the Department or any appeal board, such energy is required by that customer to maintain an adequate level of public health and safety. (*As Amended by Ordinance No. 145,400, Eff. 12-27-73.*)

SEC. 131.10 *Severability.* If any section, subsection, clause, or phrase in this Chapter or the application thereof to any person or circumstances is for any reason held invalid, the validity of the remainder of the Chapter or the application of such provision to other persons or circumstances shall not be affected thereby. The City Council hereby declares that it would have passed this Chapter and each section, subsection, sentence, clause, or phrase thereof, irrespective of the fact that one or more sections, subsections, sentences, clauses, or phrases or the application thereof to any person or circumstance be held invalid.

Sec. 3. The City Clerk shall certify to the passage of this ordinance and cause the same to be published in some daily newspaper printed and published in the City of Los Angeles.

BE IT ORDAINED BY THE COUNCIL OF THE CITY OF
WOOSTER, STATE OF OHIO:

SECTION I. (c) INSULATION REQUIREMENTS: The maximum
coefficient of heat losses through building sections shall not exceed the
following:

Ceilings
    (1) 0.05 for ceilings with heating panels. (Insulation R-19)
    (2) 0.08 for ceilings without heating panels (Insulation R-11)

Walls
    (1) 0.07 Exterior walls (Insulation R-11)
    (2) 0.10 Wall between habitable space and unheated garage (In-
        sulation R-7)

Floors
    (1) Over unheated basements, crawl spaces, breezeways and garages.
        0.07 insulation R-13.
    (2) A basement will be considered unheated unless it is provided
        with a positive heat supply equivalent to at least 15 percent of
        the total heat loss of the living unit, or contains the heating unit
        and uninsulated ducts or piping.
    (3) A crawl space is considered unheated unless it is (a) provided
        with a positive heat supply equivalent to at least 10 percent of
        the total calculated heat loss of the living unit or (b) contains
        uninsulated ducts or piping or (c) is used as a supply or return
        plenum.
    (4) A garage is considered unheated unless provided with a positive
        heat supply to maintain a minimum temperature of 50°F. (d)
        Crawl Space Plenums. When a crawl space is used as a supply
        or return plenum, the perimeter walls shall be insulated with
        material providing R values as follows: Supply Plenum R-7:
        Return plenum R-7.

Design temperature.
    The interior design temperature for habitable spaces shall be a mini-
mum of 70°F. with an outside temperature of minus 10°F.

Concrete slabs.
    Edge heat loss of concrete slabs around the perimeter of heated
spaces shall not exceed a maximum value per lineal foot of exposed
edge of 42 BTUh for unheated slabs and 50 BTUh for heated slabs.
    (4) Total width or depth of insulation shall be 24″.
        Insulation R. value for unheated slab 5.00
        Insulation R. value for heated slab 5.00

Appendix 9E: Bibliography of Conservation Literature for Commerce and Industry

The Conservation Foundation, *Citizens Action Guide to Energy Conservation*. Washington: U.S. Govt. Print. Off. Stock No. 4000,00300.

Department of Commerce, Office of Energy Programs. *Energy Management: Economic Sense for Retailers*. Washington: U.S. Govt. Print. Off., February 1974.

———. *33 Money Saving Ways to Conserve Energy in Your Business*. Washington: U.S. Govt. Print. Off., April 1974.

———. *Marketing Priorities and Energy*. Washington: U.S. Govt. Print. Off., May 1974.

———. *Industry's Vital Stake in Energy Management*. Washington: U.S. Govt. Print. Off., May 1974.

———. *Energy Conservation Handbook for Light Industries and Commercial Buildings*. Washington: U.S. Govt. Print. Off., May 1974.

———. *How to Start an Energy Management Program*. Washington: U.S. Govt. Print. Off., May 1974.

———. *Energy Conservation Programs*. Washington: U.S. Govt. Print. Off., April 1974.

———. *Energy Conservation Program Guide for Industry and Commerce*, NSB Handbook 115. Washington: U.S. Govt. Print. Off., September 1974.

Department of Housing and Urban Development, Office of Policy Development and Research. *The Modular Integrated Utility Systems*. Washington: U.S. Govt. Print. Off., 1974.

———. *Residential Energy Conservation*, HUD-HA1-8. Columbia, Md., Hittman Associates, Inc., July, 1974.

———. *Residential Energy Consumption Reports Series*. Columbia, Md., Hittman Associates, Inc., 1973-4.

Federal Energy Administration, Office of Communications and Public Affairs. *Tips for Energy Savers*. Washington: U.S. Govt. Print. Off., 1974.

———. *Federal Energy Reduction Program: Third Quarter Report*. Washington: U.S. Govt. Print. Off., June 1974.

General Services Administration, Public Buildings Service. *Conservation of Utilities*. Washington: U.S. Govt. Print. Off.

———. *Energy Conservation in Public Buildings—a Roundtable Discussion*. Washington: U.S. Govt. Print. Off., July 1972.

———. *Conservation of Energy in GSA Managed Buildings*, PBS 5800.33. Washington, U.S. Govt. Print. Off., August 14, 1973.

Office of Consumer Affairs. *7 Ways to Reduce Fuel Consumption in Household Heating through Energy Conservation*. Washington: U.S. Govt. Print. Off., December, 1972.

10 Managing an Energy Crisis

This chapter is a planning and operations guide for officials of local governments who may be confronted with a serious energy shortage. Other chapters of this handbook deal with how to avoid or ameliorate shortages; here we deal with contingency plans in the event a shortage becomes, or threatens to become, a disaster. In an energy emergency a two-pronged response is needed: on the one hand, the local officials will probably want to invoke an immediate conservation program to husband the remaining energy supply, and, on the other hand, they will want to take other steps similar to those required to protect the public safety, health, and welfare under other emergency conditions (flood, winter storm, etc.). Our discussion of emergency response is based upon some general recommendations for local disaster management put forth by the Defense Civil Preparedness Agency.[1] In accordance with these recommendations, we have divided this chapter into four sections covering: (1) planning for crisis management; (2) how to develop a basic plan for crisis management; (3) the supporting and supplementary information required for crisis management; and (4) actions the chief executive should take. An appendix presents additional information on managing specific kinds of shortages.

Planning for Crisis Management

For local officials, the distinguishing mark of a crisis is that it is a situation where you must be able to coordinate and direct simultaneously the operations of many—if not all—of the emergency and other services available in the community. It is the need for coordination that distinguishes crises from the emergencies that fire and police forces, or hospitals and doctors, deal with every day.

Many energy crises differ from other disasters in that local officials will often have many weeks or even months to prepare and plan. Even so, prompt action is desirable, especially with regard to the energy conservation aspect of the response. Remember, energy conservation is cumulative in many cases; what is not used now is available later. Thus, the earlier and the more stringent the conservation program, the better the chance of making it through an actual or threatened crisis.

To be properly prepared to handle an energy crisis, local officials

1. will need a "situation room" where they can direct and control the execution of contingency plans and, if it comes to that, emergency operations. All that's really needed here is someone manning a phone or a radio transceiver who can receive and pass on messages, answer questions and so forth;
2. should do some advanced planning for various types of energy crises; and
3. should be ready to give information on any developing crises to citizens. Citizens need and seek instructions so that they may avoid injury to themselves and their families and minimize damage to property.

Developing a Basic Plan of Operations

There are three steps local officials should take to develop a viable energy crisis management plan. First, they should write out a basic plan that covers the authority, organization, staffing, essential facilities, and general operations proposed for any energy crisis management program. Second, that basic document should be supported with materials such as maps, organizational charts, emergency call-up lists of key people, major sources and stockpiles of energy available locally, and any other information or data that would be useful. And third, they should develop specific checklists that cover the actions to be taken by the local chief executive, the local emergency and voluntary services, and others in the event a crisis develops. Existing emergency response plans, arrangements, and facilities should be examined for relevance and adaptability to energy crises and amended if necessary.

According to Civil Preparedness Officials, there are some things to keep in mind when developing an operations plan: most local leaders have no extraordinary powers to deal with emergencies; that is, they do not generally have the power to suspend civil rights or declare martial law, nor are they excused from liability by reason of an emergency situation. However, they do have broad powers and a duty to act to protect life and property by means of ordinances and proclamations. Also, they may operate their jurisdictions under what amounts to martial law, using only the ordinary powers of the police or sheriff department. This may be done simply by fielding sufficient policemen, firemen, and other officers to achieve the effect of martial law. If necessary, however, the state authorities (either the governor or the legislature) may declare true martial law in the jurisdiction, as well as supply local officials with additional manpower. However, the governor may send personnel, including detachments of the state militia, without declaring martial law.

It should be emphasized that the power to declare martial law is not absolute and is subject to judicial review. Nonetheless, several states have created various specific and limited forms of martial law to deal with energy emergencies. For example, Maine defined the extraordinary powers the governor could invoke during an energy crisis as including "without limitation" the authority to:

(1) establish and implement programs, controls, standards, priorities and quotas for the allocation, conservation, and consumption of energy resources;

(2) regulate the hours and days during which nonresidential buildings may be open and the temperatures at which they may be maintained;

(3) regulate the use of gasoline and diesel-powered land vehicles, watercraft and aircraft;

(4) regulate the generation, distribution, and consumption of electricity . . . ;

(5) regulate the storage, distribution and consumption of home heating oil.[2]

He could, in effect, delegate those same powers to local officials with regard to managing a crisis in their jurisdiction. Other states have similar arrangements.

Under existing powers and without delegation of extraordinary power from the state, local governing bodies can issue the orders and regulations needed to establish and regulate an emergency organization, assign personnel to key positions within those organizations, define their responsibilities, provide for the control and management of local resources during emergencies, and define interlocal mutual-aid agreements with other governmental units. A basic plan of operations, then, should provide for two kinds of emergencies: those in which local authorities exercise extraordinary powers and those in which they exercise only mundane authority.

The basic plan should contain a table of contents listing the types of energy problems covered (the list for your community may not be the same as for another). It should provide the steps and procedures for communitywide coordination of government and citizen actions before and during an energy crisis. A community must depend entirely upon its own resources during the initial period of any crisis or emergency. Assistance and additional resources should be obtained through channels only after local resources have been fully committed.

Assuming there is some lead time to plan for a crisis, local officials might consider the following points:

1. *An overall energy crisis management plan* could organize prospective actions into component parts, such as the voluntary and mandatory phases or according to a category or type of fuel. The concepts for implementation could be considered and presented in ascending order of stringency.

2. *Voluntary conservation measures* should be prepared which would encourage industry and the public to adopt practices to eliminate waste and realize economies in energy use. Parallel measures which local government offices may take should also be included. The emphasis in a campaign for voluntary cooperation should be upon the restraint necessary to avoid communitywide disaster in the near term; however, some mention should be made of cash savings that can be achieved by energy conservation practices. Fuel-saving adjustments in service by industries and utilities should be encouraged when such savings can contribute even indirectly to offsetting a shortage. For example, producers of electricity may be asked to reduce all nonessential use of electric power within the system and by their customers. Industrial plants may be requested to operate to the maximum all generators fired by fuels not in short supply. Utility systems, power tools, and bulk power suppliers should maximize energy transfers from adjacent systems or pools with capacity supplied by fuel not in limited supply.

Specific conservation and other emergency measures should be endorsed by municipal officials and emphasized to various categories of consumers. Press conferences and meetings with producer and consumer groups should be held with maximum media coverage, and public service announcements should be carried by radio and TV. The various departments of government should provide their "clients" with guidance and specialized materials to promote conservation in their respective sectors.

3. *Optimizing Alternate Fuel Use.* Many industries and utilities have the ability to switch from one fuel to another in shortage situations. In order to accommodate the burning of alternate fuels, procedures allowing temporary variances to air-quality standards should be included in plans. The Federal Environmental Protection Agency has reviewed its procedures for temporary variances that do not jeopardize the long-range objectives of the Clean Air Act and, under authority of the Energy Supply and Environmental Coordination Act of 1974, has set up simplified procedures that are executed by state officials. Priorities should be recommended for areas to receive fuel with low sulfur content. Plans should include the procedures by which public utilities may maximize energy transfers from adjacent pools. The capabilities of generating plants for alternative fuel operations should be determined to provide a quantified basis for decisions and implementation.

4. *Priorities and Allocations.* The technique of priority allocation may be used in both voluntary and mandatory schemes to distribute shortages. A list of priorities should be drawn up indicating the economic sectors, institutions, and activities to be given preference in the supply of available fuels. A mandatory program requires that certain contracts to secure fuel supplies will be honored before (but not exclusive of) all others. Similarly, it allows for others to be set aside during the period priorities are in effect. The plan's initial priorities list may have to be modified and refined as the crisis develops. If priority demand covers more essential activities than can be accommodated by available supplies, it will be necessary to establish allocations to identified users, including, as necessary, specific firms and institutions or types of private customers or areas of service. Allocation can only be accomplished by control over supply and distribution.

If the shortage worsens and threatens to become a disaster, local officials may have to initiate full emergency responsive capabilities, possibly including the acquisition of extraordinary powers. In any community, there are four departments that may have the capability to respond to emergencies twenty-four hours a day and are referred to as "emergency services": the police, fire, and public works departments and medical facilities. There are also volunteer rescue squads available, and an "emergency welfare service" can usually be quickly assembled to provide emergency food, lodging, clothing, and other essentials as required. The Red Cross, local church groups, affiliates of labor unions, and service organizations are its core. In the event of a disaster or imminent threat thereof, an Energy Crisis Management Team (ECMT) should be assembled. The executive head of local government, representatives of the "emergency services," and the news media are the main work force of an Energy Crisis Management Team.

Communications may be difficult in an energy crisis emergency, particularly if electrical shortages are involved. Thus, communications systems with independent power supplies (mobile units) are imperative. A practical approach is to make an inventory of all existing communications systems in the community and develop a simple plan to coordinate operations by using these existing facilities, being careful not to overload any of them. This inventory should include telephone switchboards, radio base stations, and mobile and portable radio units (one- and two-way), whether owned by government, business, or private citizens. Police, fire, and public works "emergency service" communications can be augmented by using commercial or amateur radio systems for supplementary or back-up purposes. Local broadcast stations (radio and TV), particularly those with emergency power equipment, can provide extensive one-way emergency information to the public. Local newspapers can be used to convey more complex information.

Providing good public information is often overlooked in emergency planning. It can be the most essential element in saving lives, alleviating suffering and hardship, protecting property, and aiding recovery. Even though the news media are not a part of government, they are vitally needed to provide fast, accurate, *official information and instructions* to the public. In addition to helping the people directly, this can also greatly ease the job of government.

A basic plan for energy crisis management should be supplemented by two types of "action checklists," plus information that can be used to prepare instructions to citizens for specific problems.

Executive Leadership Actions. This list of suggestions is intended to serve as guidance for the chief executive or his designated representative during the various types of energy crises. It constitutes a series of sequential steps to coordinate crisis management operation and includes both priority activities relating to the governmental response and to public information.

Emergency Services Actions. The Emergency Services Actions for various specified types of energy crises are concerned with the emergency operations of the fire, police, medical, public works, and voluntary agencies usually directly involved with them. To be fully effective in your community, the Emergency Services Actions guidance should be made compatible with existing police, fire, and other established operating procedures.

Suggested Citizen Instructions. Instructions for the various types of energy crises should be developed separately to expedite public information measures. These contain general emergency information and basic instructions that should be adapted to the needs of your community. Consideration should be given to pre-positioning selected instructions for such emergencies as electrical outages at local radio and TV stations, for immediate use if the need arises.

Supporting Information

The basic operations plan should also be supported by appropriate materials. Five types of supporting material are recommended as a minimum:

Maps. County and town roadmaps (as well as other maps) with the location of electric, gas, water and other lines marked on them. The map should also take note of distribution centers, petroleum stockpiles, and the location of repair and related equipment.

Procedures. Simple organizational charts can be useful before and during crisis operations. The most effective charts are those not cluttered with detail and notations. Usually the names, titles, addresses, and telephone numbers of key personnel will be sufficient. Brief instructions on emergency purchasing and billing procedures should be included.

Listings of Resources. Every major source of local manpower, equipment, and supplies should be considered in preparing resources data. The telephone directory is a good starting point for obtaining information on those available. The resources data should not contain such details as specifications on the resource items themselves, since these will change frequently. The person responsible for custody of the items and the procedures for obtaining them should be listed.

Disaster Assistance. Officials may need information on how to request state and federal assistance. In a disaster situation the state office of emergency services is the primary point of contact between the local government and the state. Procedures are described in "Federal Assistance Handbook for Government Officials" and "Federal Disaster Assistance Program Manual for Applicants," publications of the Office of Emergency Preparedness. A copy of these publications may be obtained through the state office of emergency services.

Executive Leadership Actions

The specific actions to be taken in a particular type of crisis are covered in checklists that we have provided following this general checklist provided by the US Defense Civil Preparedness Agency:

Priority Actions for Energy Crisis Management

1. Take charge of measures to cope with the emergency.
2. Alert key staff (civil defense, police, fire, medical, public works, energy technicians, emergency welfare, public information) and set shifts for twenty-four-hour coverage, if required; test communications with emergency services, voluntary services (Red Cross, church groups, etc.); start activity logs.
3. If the immediate situation indicates it is necessary, give orders for warning the public, with instructions to stay tuned to local radio and TV stations (identify each station) for further information and advice.

4. Notify the governor's office and the state office of emergency services. Include the following information: (a) type and cause of crisis, (b) when it occurred or threatens to occur, (c) actions already taken, (d) areas and number of people involved, (e) estimate of damage expected, and (f) type and amount of assistance required.

5. Mobilize emergency services in accordance with checklist of Emergency Services Actions for the particular crisis.

6. Alert voluntary agencies as appropriate; initiate a system for assigning and using volunteers rather than having them looking for work to do.

7. Brief the staff on the situation; review appropriate checklists of Emergency Services Actions.

8. Seek additional information; determine critical problem areas; watch for sudden or unusual side effects.

9. If there is a focal point of the crisis, e.g., a ruptured utility line, designate someone to be in charge of all operations at the scene; decide on general strategy to be used. (For example, crowd and traffic control; citizens' self-help instructions; shutdown of utilities; etc.).

10. Mobilize additional local manpower and other resources to extent required to supplement emergency services; ascertain whether additional assistance is needed; as necessary, request aid, according to established procedures; make specific requests, such as number of men for security, rescue, etc., or specific equipment, such as pumpers, etc.; request military assistance only through state and only if there are insufficient civilian resources (local military commanders are authorized to act independently only if the threat to life and property is too urgent to wait for official authorization).

11. If required, ask the governor to issue declaration of emergency and invoke extraordinary powers.

12. Obtain periodic situation reports, and direct the staff to maintain accurate logs of: emergency service activities, estimates of damage, manpower and equipment utilized, mutual aid or assistance requested provided, financial expenditures, and other items as required.

13. Provide continuing direction and coordination of operations.

14. When the situation indicates, return to normal routine.

15. Prepare reports for official record.

*Priority Public Information Actions During
an Energy Crisis*

1. Provide essential information to the public, emphasizing the immediate actions being taken by local government.

2. Authenticate all sources of information being received (verify spe-

cific information with appropriate emergency service concerned; e.g. highway movement restrictions that police are enforcing).

3. Coordinate information with the staff before releasing it to the news media.

4. Issue instructions and advice to the public on what they should or should not do. Instructions and advice should be clear and simple, such as:

a. *Avoid use of telephone except for emergency requests and reports.*
b. *Monitor local radio or TV for continuing information and instructions.*
c. *Stay away from disaster areas—Sightseers interfere and can be hurt.*

5. Based on official decisions, issue additional information and instructions to the public (evacuation of dangerous areas, restrictions on highway use, location of refugee care centers, etc.).

6. Prepare information and materials needed to handle individual responses to public requests.

Appendix 10A: Shortages of Natural Gas

General Information

The nation's supply of natural gas is dangerously short. Roughly 5 percent of US natural gas is imported from Canada, and recent Canadian policy imposing higher prices and other limitations can be expected to exacerbate the situation. In the long term (ten years or more away), however, synthetic pipeline quality gases produced from coal and possibly other minerals are expected to ameliorate the situation.

For the short run, natural gas curtailments should be expected. A natural gas shortage could also result from strikes, natural disasters, or government regulation. Because natural gas supplies are inadequate to meet firm contracts nationwide, government regulation of natural gas might be imposed to distribute supplies equitably. FEA contingency plans include a mandatory reallocation program similar to that for petroleum. The Federal Power Commission, which exercises regulatory authority over interstate gas commerce, has already begun some reallocation of natural gas on the basis of end use. Their reallocation priorities are discussed in chapter 4.

In principle, federal policy may create a natural gas shortage in any area not now experiencing difficulties by causing regional distributors to reduce deliveries in their service areas and resell the surplus to achieve equity on a national basis.

A strike might result in curtailment of deliveries, but the possibility is slim, because of the civil and criminal liability of the utility and its employees that nonperformance may incur.

An accident or natural disaster resulting in a production shutdown at the well or a rupture along the pipeline is perhaps a likelier possibility. Because it is likely to be localized, such an accident is often easily isolated.

Local officials may want to adopt a contingency plan for natural gas shortages similar to the one suggested below.

Actions Beforehand

1. The best approach to avoiding a disaster when a service interruption occurs is to have the capability in critical areas to substitute other fuels. Encourage diversity in residential heating design to include some oil, some gas, and some electric heat. Individuals with fireplaces or coal- and wood-burning stoves as well should be encouraged to keep at least a moderate fuel supply on hand all winter.

2. Be prepared to forecast the acuteness of the shortage. Government agencies, especially the FEA, will give warning of approaching problems via the mass media or official communiques to the governor's office. Local governments should be prepared to seek out specific details concerning the shortage impact in their area. Maintain a list of persons to phone to find out such information. Such a list should include the various labor unions, national and local, as well as government agencies, energy suppliers and others, as well as the FEA's National Energy Information Center in Washington. From talking with these contacts local officials should be able to get a clear picture of the shortage and how it will affect their area.

3. If a crisis is expected local government should encourage local distributors to stockpile alternative fuels in larger quantities than ordinarily required for operating stocks. Also, consider adopting the "Energy Stockpiling Ordinance" in chapter 7 of this handbook. During periods of natural gas shortage affecting residential space heating expect bizarre consequences as individuals seek to make up for the loss by substitution. Thus, look for runs on local stocks of small gasoline, propane and electric heaters, warm clothing and underwear. Look also for increased fire, suffocation and hypothermia dangers as infrequently used and poorly repaired heaters are brought on line or people try to heat their homes with their kitchen range and oven or overly large fires in their fireplaces, and so forth.

4. A hierarchy of command should be established before a shortage to prevent unnecessary confusion during the shortage itself. Since gas service is often provided by a private company, be sure to include them in the planning and coordination scheme.

Procedures During a Shortage

Begin Executive Leadership Actions outlined in chapter 10.

Alternate Fuels. Some industries, schools, hospitals, etc. are equipped to run on alternate fuels (usually both gas and fuel oil). Make sure they do switch. Most organizations will switch over automatically and thus put sudden demand on locally held petroleum stocks. Make sure that priority needs are met first.

Priority Users. A list of priority users should be developed so the essential services and functions in the community will be able to function, even at the expense of those not so essential functions.

Information Gathering. Develop a plan for gathering all the information necessary for effectively dealing with the shortage. Local officials may need to know such things as the total available fuel supply (of all types) in their jurisdiction (whether publicly or privately held), outstanding needs, minimal requirements for maintaining health and safety and protecting property, the conditions of the poorest groups, etc.

Information Dispensing. Contact local newspapers, radio and TV stations and arrange for releasing information on the shortage.

Develop a Conservation Plan. Give the local residents suggestions on how to conserve the available energy, thereby limiting the shortage's influence.

Special Considerations. Contact the Federal Power Commission for assistance. Use peak-shaving supplies of liquefied gases for shortage make up.

Appendix 10B: Shortages of Coal

Actions Beforehand

1. Efforts should be made to keep abreast of strike possibilities. Possibilities of nationwide strikes are usually well publicized, as are some local and regional strike possibilities. Specific information can often be obtained from the FEA's National Energy Information Center, local news personnel or through labor union locals, the governor's office, the trade associations, and the Department of Labor both locally and in Washington, D.C.

2. Among the best strategies of preparation for a coal shortage is stockpiling. Coal requires almost no special facilities for storage (fenced enclosure will do). Local officials may encourage local coal distributors to stockpile coal and its alternatives in larger quantities than they would ordinarily use. Also consider passing a stockpiling ordinance which would allow the city to stockpile reserves for emergencies (see chapter 7).

3. Make sure the city has the capability in critical areas to substitute other fuels. FEA has made arrangements to allocate additional petroleum supplies to crisis-threatened coal users.

4. Be prepared to forecast the acuteness of the shortage. Government agencies will give warning of approaching problems via the mass media or through official communiques. Local governments should be prepared to seek out specific details concerning the shortage impact in their area. Maintain a list of persons to phone to find out such information. Such a list should include the various labor unions—national and local—as well as government agencies, particularly the FEA, energy suppliers and others. Compile a census of coal users and uses in the jurisdiction.

5. Expect bizarre consequences as individuals seek to make up for the loss by ad hoc substitution. Look for runs on local stocks of small gasoline, propane and electric heaters, warm clothing and underwear. Look also for increased fire, suffocation, and hypothermia dangers as infrequently used and poorly repaired pieces of equipment are brought on line or people try to heat their homes with their kitchen range and oven or overly large fires in their fireplaces, and so forth.

6. A chain of command should be established before a shortage to prevent unnecessary confusion during the shortage itself.

Procedures During a Shortage

Begin Executive Leadership Actions outlined in chapter 10.

Alternate Fuels. Some industries, schools, hospitals, etc. are equipped to run on alternate fuels. Most organizations will switch over automatically and thus put sudden demand on other locally held stocks. Make sure that priority needs are met first. FEA has made arrangements to provide additional allocations of petroleum to shortage-impacted users.

Priority Users. A list of priority users should be developed so the essential services and functions in the community will be able to function, even at the expense of those not-so-essential functions.

Information Gathering. Develop a plan for gathering all the information necessary for effectively dealing with the shortage. Local officials may need to know such things as the totally available fuel supply (of all types) in their jurisdiction (whether publicly or privately held), outstanding needs, minimal requirements for maintaining health and safety and protecting property, the condition of the poorest groups, etc.

Information Dispensing. Contact local newspapers, radio and TV stations and arrange for releasing information on the shortage and what is being done about it.

Develop a Conservation Plan. Give the local residents suggestions on how to conserve the available coal thereby limiting the shortages influence.

Special Considerations. Many residential and small commercial coal-burning boilers can burn wood or other solid fuels more easily than petroleum or gas. Call the FEA liaison officer in the state for additional help.

Appendix 10C: Shortages of Petroleum Products

General Information

The energy crisis of 1974 was largely a petroleum crisis, although there was some secondary impact on other fuels as well. The Arab oil embargo put a gasoline and heating fuel squeeze on many parts of the United States and, as a result, the Mandatory Petroleum Allocation Program was instituted. A number of service stations closed, heating oil was short in many places, and everyone felt the impact of a quantum leap in prices. Local petroleum shortages can be caused by strikes, shortfalls in crude oil and refinery feedstocks, insufficient refinery capacity, local aberrations of various types, and government regulation.

Actions Beforehand

1. The best approach to avoiding a disaster when a shortage occurs or threatens is to have the capability in critical areas to substitute other fuels. Encourage diversity in heating design. Individuals with fireplaces or coal- and wood-burning stoves as well should be encouraged to keep at least a moderate fuel supply on hand all winter. Hospitals, nursing homes and other large critical facilities should have the capability to burn two or more different fuels.

2. Be prepared to forecast the acuteness of the shortage. Government agencies will give warning of approaching problems via the mass media or official communiques. Local governments should be prepared to seek out specific details concerning the shortage impact in their area. Maintain a list of persons to phone to find out such information. Such a list should include the FEA, the various labor unions—national and local—as well as government agencies, energy suppliers and others.

3. If a crisis is expected, the city should encourage local distributors to stockpile alternative fuels in larger quantities than they would ordinarily. Also consider adopting the "Energy Stockpiling Ordinance" in chapter 7 of this handbook. During periods of shortage effecting residential space heating expect bizarre consequences as individuals seek to make up for the loss by substitution. Thus, look for runs on local stocks of small potrtable heaters, warm clothing and underwear. Look also for increased fire, suffocation, and hypothermia dangers as infrequently used and poorly repaired heaters are brought on line or people try to heat their

211

homes with their kitchen range and oven or overly large fires in their fireplaces, and so forth.

4. A hierarchy of command should be established before a shortage to prevent unnecessary confusion during the shortage itself.

Procedures During a Shortage

Begin Executive Leadership Actions outlined in chapter 10.

Alternate Fuels. Some industries, schools, hospitals, etc. are equipped to run on alternate fuels. Most organizations will switch over automatically and thus put sudden demand on other locally held stocks. Make sure that priority demands on these stocks are met first.

Priority Users. A list of priority users should be developed so the essential services and functions in the community will be able to function, even at the expense of those not-so-essential functions.

Information Gathering. Develop a plan for gathering all the information necessary for effectively dealing with the shortage. Local officials may need to know such things as the totally available fuel supply (of all types) in their jurisdiction (whether publicly or privately held), outstanding needs, minimal requirements for maintaining health and safety and protecting property, the condition of the poorest groups, etc.

Information Dispensing. Contact local newspapers, radio and T.V. stations and arrange for releasing information on the shortage.

Develop a Conservation Plan. Give the local residents suggestions on how to conserve the available energy, thereby limiting the shortage's influence.

Special Considerations. Call the state office of petroleum allocation for emergency hardship assistance. Call the FEA liaison offices in your state for additional help.

Appendix 10D: Electrical Outages

General Information

Local governments receive their electrical supplies from one of three sources: municipally owned and operated systems, public utilities or other private companies, or a federal agency (the Bureau of Reclamation, the TVA, etc.).

Of the nation's installed capacity, less than 4 percent is operated by hydropower, about the same percentage is nuclear powered, and all the rest is fossil fuel. In 1971 the utility industry used 7.4 quads of coal, 4.1 quads of natural gas, and 2.5 quads of petroleum. Thus, electric utilities are very sensitive to fossil fuel shortages.

Electrical outages are also likely to result from strikes, accidents, or natural disasters. Natural disasters such as storms, which knock down lines, are temporary problems that can be corrected as soon as the effects of the disaster have been overcome, although some weather-related blackouts have lasted a week or longer. Strikes, particularly of coal miners, refinery workers, linemen, and others closely associated with electrical production could result in longer outages or curtailments.

Jurisdictions that maintain their own generating equipment have these worries as well as concern about the adequacy of supply. Officials say that locally owned and operated plants are in danger without a six-month supply of fuel on hand. Some areas derive their base-line supply from a reliable source, but operate their own facilities for peak shaving; they face other, potentially less serious threats but need to develop alternative peak-shaving methods.

In a period of electrical shortage, local government should examine proposals by suppliers to distribute the shortage by means of rolling blackouts, brownouts, shut down of low priority users, or other conservation practices to determine if such proposals are acceptable. Watch for health and safety problems from water or sewer failure, traffic and street lighting shutdown, etc.

Actions Beforehand

1. It is not generally feasible to substitute for electricity. It is needed, for example, to operate the control systems of most coal, oil, and gas space heating furnaces. It is required to operate refrigeration and air-conditioning equipment, lighting, and most appliances. The best approach to avoid-

213

ing a disaster when a service interruption occurs or threatens is to have the capability in critical areas to substitute electrical power from other sources, e.g., portable generators, where possible and substitute for the electricity dependent system where it is not, e.g., using fireplaces or relocating some people to structures that are supplied. Develop a contingency plan to accomplish these ends.

2. Be prepared to forecast the acuteness of the outage. Maintain a list of persons to phone to find out such information. Such a list should include the various labor unions—national and local—as well as government agencies, energy suppliers, and others. The FPC has the power to regulate electricity, but the FEA regulates most of the fuels used to produce it. The new Nuclear Regulatory Agency regulates the nuclear fuel cycle, while hydropower is the responsibility of the Department of the Interior and various power administrations (see chapter 3).

3. If a crisis is expected, the city should encourage local distributors to stockpile alternative fuels in larger quantities than they would ordinarily. Secure portable equipment (or contingency agreements to have portable equipment supplied) for critical uses: medical facilities, local radio stations, etc. Also consider adopting the "Energy Stockpiling Ordinance" in chapter 7 of this handbook. Expect bizarre consequences as individuals seek to make up for the loss by substitution. Thus, look for runs on local stocks of small gasoline, propane, and other portable heaters, warm clothing, and underwear. Look also for an increased fire, suffocation and hypothermia dangers as infrequently used and poorly repaired heaters are brought on line or people try to heat their homes with overly large fires in their fireplaces, and so forth.

4. A hierarchy of command should be established beforehand to prevent unnecessary confusion during the shortage itself. Be sure to include an electric supplier's representative in the planning and coordination scheme.

Procedures During an Outage

Begin Executive Leadership Actions outlined in chapter 10.

Alternate Fuels. Some industries, schools, hospitals, and so forth are equipped to run on alternate equipment. Most organizations will switch over automatically and thus put sudden demand on other locally held fuel stocks. Make sure that priority needs are met first. Consider making use of these facilities for temporary shelters.

Priority Users. A list of priority needs should be developed so the portable equipment available can be assigned to the essential services and community services will be able to function, even at the expense of not-so-essential functions.

Information Gathering. Develop a plan for gathering all the information necessary for effectively dealing with the outage. Local officials may need to know such things as the totally available fuel supply (of all types) in their jurisdiction (whether publicly or privately held), outstanding needs, minimal requirements for maintaining health and safety and protecting property, the condition of the poorest groups, and so forth.

Information Dispensing. Contact local newspapers, radio and TV stations and arrange for releasing information on the outage. Make sure at least one station can maintain broadcasting operations even during an outage.

Special Consideration. The FPC has procedures that allow tie-ins with other systems in the event of an emergency (even if the owners of that system object); contact them.

Appendix 10E: Shortages of Propane and Butane

General Information

Propane and butane are by-products of other energy industries. They are manufactured either by stripping natural gas in a cracking unit or as a by-product of the gasoline-refining process. Thus, the adequacy of the supply of these gases is indirectly dependent on the oil and gas industry. Propane and butane are a primary source of heat for mobile homes, trailers, rural houses, and other remote installations in the United States. They are also widely used in industry and agriculture.

Propane and butane fall under the Mandatory Propane Allocation Regulations, which are similar to the Petroleum Allocation Regulations. The propane regulations specify that home heating needs have the highest priority, so, except for price fluctuations, the propane home heating sector should have few problems. The industrial sector will feel the greatest pinch if there is a shortage. Affected industry must apply for a priority user status on a hardship basis through the FEA.

Propane shortages could be caused by several factors; strikes, petroleum and natural gas shortages, or government regulation. Petroleum and natural gas shortages, because of their indirect relationship to propane outlets, give little recourse to local governments other than "belt tightening" procedures. Shortages derived from government reallocation programs require red tape handling through the state office of petroleum allocation and the FEA.

Actions Beforehand

1. The best approach to avoiding a disaster when a shortage occurs or threatens is to have the capability in critical areas to substitute other fuels. Encourage diversity in residential heating design to include some oil, some gas, and some electric heat. Individuals with fireplaces or coal- and wood-burning stoves as well should be encouraged to keep at least a moderate fuel supply on hand all winter. Encourage agricultural and industrial users to look at alternative processes that use less propane or butane, e.g., chemical crop drying, etc.

2. Be prepared to forecast the acuteness of the shortage. Government agencies will give warning of approaching problems via the mass media or official communiques. Local governments should be prepared to seek out specific details concerning the shortage impact in their area. Maintain a

list of persons to phone to find out such information. Such a list should include the FEA as well as the various labor unions—national and local —as well as government agencies, energy suppliers, and others.

3. If a crisis is expected, the city should encourage local distributors to stockpile alternative fuels, chemicals, and related supplies in larger quantities than they would ordinarily. Also consider adopting the "Energy Stockpiling Ordinance" in chapter 7 of this handbook. During periods of shortage affecting residential space heating expect bizarre consequences as individuals seek to make up for the loss by substitution. Thus, look for runs on local stocks of small gasoline, electric and other portable heaters, warm clothing and underwear. Look also for an increased fire, suffocation, and hypothermia dangers as infrequently used and poorly repaired heaters are brought on line or people try to heat their homes with their kitchen range and oven or overly large fires in their fireplaces, and so forth.

4. A hierarchy of command should be established before a shortage to prevent unnecessary confusion during the shortage itself. Be sure to include the local propane and butane suppliers in the planning and coordination scheme.

Procedures During a Shortage

Begin Executive Leadership Actions outlined in chapter 10.

Priority Users. A list of priority users should be developed so the essential services and functions in the community will be able to function, even at the expense of those not-so-essential functions.

Information Gathering. Develop a plan for gathering all the information necessary for effectively dealing with the shortage. Local officials may need to know such things as the totally available fuel supply (of all types) in their jurisdiction (whether publicly or privately held), outstanding needs, minimal requirements for maintaining health and safety and protecting property, the condition of agriculture, industry, of the poorest groups, etc.

Information Dispensing. Contact local newspapers, radio and TV stations and arrange for releasing information on the shortage.

Develop a Conservation Plan. Give the local residents suggestions on how to conserve the available energy, thereby limiting the shortages influence.

Special Considerations. Many agricultural crops normally dried with butane or propane heaters can be dried wholly or partially with chemicals.

Notes

Chapter 2
How to Use This Handbook

1. *56 American Jurisprudence 2d. Municipal Corporations* (Rochester, N.Y.: The Lawyers Co-operative Publishing Co., 1971), section 16, p. 81-82.

2. Reprinted with permission from Ballinger Publishing Company, *A Time to Choose: America's Energy Future,* © 1974, The Ford Foundation. (Cambridge, Mass.: Ballinger Publishing Co., 1974).

3. Paul Averit, "Coal," U.S. Geological Survey Professional Paper 820, 1973.

4. Committee on Interior and Insular Affairs, U.S. Congress, Senate, *U.S. Energy Resources, A Review as of 1973,* Serial No. 93-40 (92-75) (Washington: United States Government Printing Office, 1974).

5. Committee on Interior and Insular Affairs, U.S. Congress, Senate, *Department of the Treasury Staff Analysis of the Preliminary Federal Trade Commission Staff Report on Its Investigation of the Petroleum Industry, July 2, 1973,* Serial No. 93-18 (92-53) (Washington: United States Government Printing Office, 1973).

6. Ibid.

Chapter 3
Energy Administration in the United States

1. Committee on Interior and Insular Affairs, U.S. Congress, Senate. *Federal Energy Organization.* Serial No. 93-6 (92-41). Washington: United States Government Printing Office.

Chapter 4
Federal Energy Policy Administration

1. Energy Reorganization Act of 1974 (PL93-438), Sec. 108.

2. Ibid., Sec. 109.

3. Federal Energy Administration Act of 1974 (PL93-275), Section 2.

4. Federal Energy Administration. "Proposed Regulations: Priority Delivery of Coal—Department of Defense Contracts," paragraph 12,532 in *Federal Energy Guidelines.* Commerce Clearing House, Inc., 1974.

5. 49 Stat. 849: 16 U.S.C. 824a (c).

6. Ibid., 824a (d).

7. Federal Power Commission. "Statement of Policy." FPC Order No. 467 (as amended) in Docket No. R-469.

8. Ibid.

Chapter 5
The State's Role in Emergency Policy Administration

1. Office of Energy Conservation. Interior Department news release, 20 November 1973.

Chapter 7
Policy Alternatives

1. *56 American Jurisprudence 2d. Municipal Corporations* (Rochester, N.Y.: The Lawyers Co-operative Publishing Co., 1971), Section 212, p. 272-73.

2. Charles E. Denton, personal letter, 10 September 1974.

3. Federal Energy Administration Regulations, Section 211.13 (f), paragraph 13,613.30 in *Federal Energy Guidelines* (Commerce Clearing House, 1974).

4. Federal Administration Regulations, Section 211.13 (b.ix), paragraph 13,613.10 (ix) in *Federal Energy Guidelines* (Commerce Clearing House, 1974).

5. William J. Allen, personal letter, 22 October 1974.

6. Office of the White House Press Secretary, "Energy Policy Office Proposed Program for Crude Oil, Refined Petroleum Products and Liquefied Petroleum Gas Mandatory Allocation," 9 August 1973.

Chapter 8
The Energy Budget Report

1. National Energy Information Center, Federal Energy Administration, *Monthly Energy Review,* October 1974, p. i.

Chapter 9
Conservation Programs

1. Hittman Associates. *Residential Energy Conservation* (Columbia, Md.: July 1974), p. 4.

2. National Bureau of Standards, U.S. Department of Commerce. *Energy Conservation Program Guide for Industry and Commerce,* NBS, Handbook 115 (Washington: United States Government Printing Office, 1974), p. 1-1.

3. Ibid., p. 2-1 through 2-3.

4. City and County of Denver news release. December 12, 1973.

5. Office of Government Preparedness, General Services Administration. "Guidance on Fuel and Energy Shortages for State and Local Officials." Unpublished memorandum, dated August 8, 1973.

Chapter 10
Managing an Energy Crisis

1. Defense Civil Preparedness Agency. *Disaster Operations: a Handbook for Local Governments.* DCPA, July 1972.

2. Maine Revised Statutes Title 37-A, Sections 53, 57, 58, 67, as amended by Laws of 1974, Chapter 757, effective March 26, 1974.

Encyclopedic Index

The following "Encyclopedic Index" combines an index to this book and a glossary of energy policy terms. The glossary is a partial compilation of terms commonly found in energy policy publications. Many very technical terms confined in usage to small segments of the industry are excluded because of their apparent absence from use in policy discussions. On the other hand, many terms which may seem to have obvious meanings are included because some regulatory agency has given them a specific legal definition.

Air Quality Standards. Limits set by government on the amounts of pollutants that may be released into the air; principal pollutants covered are: a) carbon monoxide, nitrogen oxides, and hydrocarbons from automobiles, and b) sulfur oxides, hydrogen sulfides, nitrogen oxides, hydrocarbons, and particulates from furnaces and boilers. Variances from, 65, 112.

Allocation. A voluntary or mandatory plan of sharing in time of short supply; to spread the shortage equitably throughout the economy; distinguished from a rationing system by which quantitative limitations are placed on endusers (46-54, 116-117 and citations under specific fuels). *Allocable Supply.* Under FEA regulations the total supply of allocated substance of any supplier. *Allocated Products.* Under FEA regulations, residual fuel, oil and refined petroleum products.

Alternate Energy Sources. Energy sources that could replace those now in use including gasified and liquefied coal, energy from the sun, from fusion, and so on.

Anthracite or Hard Coal. Coal containing less than 10 percent volatile matter (*see* coal).

Atomic Energy Commission. See Nuclear Regulatory Commission.

Atomic or Nuclear Energy. Energy released by changes in the nucleus (protons and neutrons) of an atom, either by the splitting of a large nucleus (fission of uranium, plutonium, and so on) or by the joining of smaller nuclei (fusion, usually of one of the hydrogen isotopes such as deuterium or tritium).

Barrel or Bbl. Standard unit of measure in the oil industry (42 U.S. gallons).

Bituminous or Soft Coal. Coal of rank between lignite and anthracite, containing 15 to 20 percent volatile matter (*see* coal).

Blackout. A condition in which customers of an electrical utility are temporarily without electricity. See Brownout. *Rolling Blackout.* A strategy to conserve electricity by intentionally shutting off sections of a service area on a revolving basis for short periods. Emergency responses to, 213. *See* Electricity; Shortage; Federal Power Commission.

Bonded Fuels. Fuels produced outside the United States, held in bond under continuous custody of the U.S. Customs and destined for use outside of the United States.

Branded Independent Marketer. Under FEA regulations, a firm engaged in the distribution of petroleum products under a franchise with a refiner (usually a "major").

Breeder Reactor. A nuclear reactor that converts one reactor fuel, usually Uranium, into another, usually Plutonium, while it releases energy. The resulting fuel can be used in other nuclear reactors (*see also* burner reactor, converter reactor). *Liquid-metal Fast Breeder Reactor (LMFBR).* A breeder reactor which is cooled by a liquid metal such as liquid sodium.

Brownout. A condition in which an electrical utility reduces the voltage to its customers as a means of reducing peak demands. *See* Blackout; Conservation; Electricity.

BTU. A British thermal unit, the amount of heat necessary to raise the temperature of one pound of water 1°F., is a standard measure of energy:

> Bituminous coal....................26.2 million Btu/metric ton
> Natural gas........................1,032 Btu/cubic foot
> Crude oil.......................... 5.615 million Btu/barrel
> Motor gasoline.....................5.253 million Btu/barrel
> Distillate fuel oil.................. 5.825 million Btu/barrel
> Residual fuel oil...................6.287 million Btu/barrel

Bulk Plant or Bulk Terminal. A facility consisting of a number of tanks from which oil products are distributed to retail outlets or to consumers. *Bulk Purchaser.* The operator of a bulk plant.

Butane. A colorless flammable gas, easily liquefied, often mixed with propane and sold as LPG (liquid petroleum gas). Allocation of, 49; emergency responses to shortages of, 217. *See* Conservation; Emergency; Shortage.

Coal. A naturally occurring black, combustible, solid fuel. Coal is classified by rank (the percentage of fixed carbon and heat content) and by grade (the content of ash, sulfur and other impurities). Ranks include anthracite, bituminous, subbituminous, and lignite (in descending order of heat content). Estimates of coal production, reserves and other coal statistics are available from the FEA, the FPC, and the Bureau of Mines, 14; industry structure, 14-16; allocation of, 16, 50; emergency responses to shortages of, 200; price of, 16. *See* Shortage; Substitution; Conservation; Storage; Stockpiles; Emergency; Air Quality. *Coal Conversion.* The conversion of coal into refined, gaseous or liquid fuels.

Coking. A process that converts residual oils into distillates and coke, a solid material. *Coker Feedstock.* Any crude or unfinished oil.

Combined Cycle Plant. A generating plant that combines features of gas and steam turbine power plants, as when hot gas turbine exhaust provides heat to a conventional steam turbine generator and power is derived from both gas and steam turbines.

Condensate. Some gas and oil wells produce condensate, a mixture of liquid hydrocarbons condensed from underground vapors.

Congressional Committees on Energy. See 38.

Corps of Engineers, U.S. Army. See 37.

Covered Products. Products covered by the Mandatory Petroleum Allocation Program: crude oil, residual fuel oil, and refined petroleum products.

Crises. See 103, 195-218. *See also* Emergency.

Actions required, emergency services, 200
Actions required, executive, 201-203
Coal, 209-210
Communications during, 195
Conservation, 195
Defense Civil Preparedness Agency, 195
Developing plans, 196-200
    for alternative fuel use, 198
    for management, 198
    for priorities, 199
    for voluntary conservation, 198
Electrical outages, 213-215
Instructions to citizens, 200, 202-203
Management of, 195-203
Natural gas, 205-207
Petroleum products, 211-212
Planning for, 195-201
Propane and butane, 217-218
Specific crisis instructions, 205
Supporting information required, 200-201.

Crude oil. Petroleum as it comes from the ground before being refined into various products for consumers; synthetic crude (or syncrude) also exists, e.g. from oil shale coal and bituminous sands. *Crude Oil Domestic Production.* In FEA statistics, the volume of crude oil flowing out of the ground measured at the wellhead; includes condensate. *Crude Oil Imports.* In FEA statistics, the volume of imported crude oil reported by the refineries. *Crude Oil Runs to Stills.* In FEA statistics, the volume of crude oil piped to distillation units. *Crude Oil Stocks.* In FEA statistics, the crudes held at refineries and in pipelines but excluding stocks held in storage facilities adjacent to the wells. *Sweet and Sour Crude.* Sweet crude has less than 1% sulphur content, sour has more. *See* Petroleum Allocation, 46-49; Industry Structure, 16-17.

Crygenic Gas. Natural or synthetic gas condensed to liquid form by reducing its temperature (less than 200 degrees below zero Fahrenheit). *Crygenic Tankers.* Any tanker equipped to transport crygenic gases.

Dealer Tankwagon (DTW) Price. The price at which a retail dealer purchases gasoline from a distributor or a jobber.

Degree Day. Definition of, 129-130.

Demand. U.S. statistics, 11-13. *See* Consumption; Energy Budget Report

Denver. See 110-111.

Depletion Allowance. A provision of the U.S. income tax law applying to 75 minerals, including oil and gas that allows a producer a "percentage depletion" deduction against gross income. The amount of the deduction varies for different minerals reflecting such factors as the relative scarcity of the mineral and the risks in exploring for new reserves.

Deuterium. One of the two heavy isotopes of hydrogen that occurs naturally (the other is tritium); nuclear *fusion* fuel.

Diesel Fuel. The distillate petroleum fraction used as fuel in diesel engines. *See* Petroleum.

Distillates and distillate fuel oil. The liquid petroleum products condensed from vapors during distillation, e.g., jet fuel, kerosene, diesel and heating fuels; distinguished from residual oils. In some uses the condensate from natural gas wells.

Domestic Noncontrolled Crude Oil. In FEA regulations, that portion of domestic crude oil production which may be sold at a price exceeding the ceiling price; also "new," "released" and "stripper" oil.

the United States has an adequate supply of electric power and of natural gas available at the most economical price possible. *See* 37, 50-53.

Feedstock. The raw processed material in a refinery or chemical plant.

Finance, Energy and. Bibliography on, 26.

Financial assistance for energy bills. See 90.

Fission. The process in which atoms (usually of uranium or plutonium) release energy when struck by a neutron. It is the process harnessed by today's nuclear reactors.

Ford Foundation. Energy Policy Project, 7

Forecasting. See 126-140. *See also* Energy Budget Report
    of demand, 127-131
    of supply, 131-136
    survey forms, 137-140.

Foreign Equity Crude Oil. In FEA statistics, crude oil produced and owned in a foreign country.

Foreign Posted Price. In FEA statistics, the reference price for crude oil upon which taxes and royalties are based.

Fossil Fuel. Any fuel such as coal, oil, and natural gas, thought to derive from once-living organisms; sometimes called "conventional" distinguished from the less conventional energy sources of nuclear power, geothermal and solar energy.

Fuel Oil. The residue from the distillation of crude oil. Various grades are compounded by blending residue with distillate. Fuel oils are identified according to use; loaded into ships' bunkers it is called bunker fuel; used for heating boilers it is called boiler fuel; and when employed in industry, industrial fuels. *See* Petroleum.

Fuels, Primary and Secondary. See 11.

Fusion. Sometimes thermonuclear fusion. A reaction in which very high temperatures bring about the fusion of two atomic nuclei to form the nucleus of a heavier atom, releasing a large amount of energy. Workable fusion reactors have not yet been built but may become commercially available within 50 years.

Gaseous Fuels. See natural gas, ethane, liquefied petroleum gas, and so on.

Gasification of Coal. A process by which coal is converted into a mixture of gases. Several gasification pilot plants are now in operation.

Gas Oil. A brownish distillate similar to kerosene.

Gasoline. Volatile fuel used in automobile and other engines. *Motor gasoline production.* In FEA statistics, total production of gasoline by refineries. Relatively small quantities of motor gasoline are produced at natural gas processing plants, but are not included in most statistical reports. *Motor gasoline stocks.* In FEA statistics, primary motor gasoline held by gasoline producers; does not include stocks at natural gas processing plants, at service stations or in stockpiles. *See* Petroleum.

Gas Processing Plant. A facility which recovers ethane, propane, butane, and/or other products from natural gas.

Geological Survey, U.S. See 36.

Geothermal Energy. Energy derived from heat found under the earth's surface. Within the earth, there are vast deposits of molten rock. Underground aquafiers in or near these deposits generate steam and hot water which can be used to generate electric power, directly in space heating, or for process heat.

Half-life. The length of time it takes half of a given quantity of radioactive material to decay (become inactive).

Heat Content. The amount of heat that can be produced by a specific quantity of fuel. *See* BTU.

Heating Oil. A general term covering many different oil products including both distillates and residuals used to heat homes, offices, and plants. Emergency problems, 89-90, 211-212. *See* Conservation; Emergency; Petroleum; Shortage; Stockpile.

Hydrocarbon. Any one of several organic compounds composed of carbon and hydrogen and occurring in petroleum, natural gas, coal, and bitumens.

Import Quotas. Quotas limiting the volume of oil imports; the current quota system is intended to stimulate domestic production of petroleum.

Independent. Any petroleum firm which operates one or more but not all of the following: a production facility, a refining facility, a marketing facility, and so on. Distinguished from a "major" which operates all such facilities. Most independents operate refineries, some operate marketing outlets.

Industry, U.S. Energy. See 11; Bibliography on, 27.

Integrated Oil Company. Any company that performs all the principal functions of the industry: exploration, production, refining, transportation, and marketing.

Interior and Insular Affairs, Committee on. National Fuels & Energy Policy Study, 29.

International Energy Program. See 116.

Jobber. In FEA statistics, a petroleum distributor who purchases refined product for the purpose of reselling. *Jobber margin.* In FEA statistics, the difference between the price at which a jobber purchases and the price at which the jobber sells to retail outlets. *Jobber price.* In FEA statistics, the price at which a petroleum jobber purchases refined product.

Kerosene. A colorless liquid, more viscous than gasoline, widely used as a jet fuel. *See* Petroleum.

Kilowatt-hour (kwh). A unit of work or energy, one thousand watts in one hour (equivalent to 3,412 Btu's). Most statistical summaries of demand for electricity are quoted in kilowatt hours or megawatt hours (a thousand kilowatt hours). See Electricity; Load.

Landed Cost. In FEA statistics, the cost of imported crude oil on arrival (includes transportation cost).

Land Management, Bureau of. See 36.

Lease Sale. An auction where bidders seek the right to explore for oil or other minerals, usually on federal or state-owned lands; the rights are granted by Lease contracts providing for an annual cash rental as well as a royalty.

Lignite. Low rank coal. *See* Coal.

Liquefication of Coal. The conversion of coal into a liquid fuel, usually clean burning and usable in transportation.

Liquefied Natural Gas (LNG). Natural gas that has been changed into a liquid by cooling about −260°F. LNG is the form used to transport natural gas when pipelines are not available.

Liquefied Petroleum Gas (LPG). Propane, butane, or mixtures liquefied by compression and refrigeration. LPG is common in applications to farm and home heating and other appliances. *See* Butane.

Load. The demand or use of energy is often called the load, particularly in the electrical and gas utility industry. *Base load:* minimum demand for energy. *Peak load:* maximum demand for energy. *Load factor:* the ratio of the average load to the peak load. *Margin:* excess of capacity maintained above the peak load to allow for unanticipated demand. *Peak shaving:* a process by which peak load is reduced either by increasing delivery capacity (e.g., bringing backup generating capacity on live) or reducing demand as with brownout programs; in natural gas utilities, peak shaving is often accomplished by introducing propane or butane into the system to supplement pipeline gas.

Local government.

Major. In common usage, any of the several dozen of the largest petroleum companies (e.g., Exxon, Shell, and so on) which maintain production, refining, transporting, and marketing facilities. Sometimes called integrated companies; distinguished from "independents."

Mandatory Petroleum Allocation. See 46-49. *See also* Petroleum Allocation.

Maximum Efficient Rate (MER) of Production. The highest rate of production that can be sustained by a petroleum or natural gas field without jeopardizing recovery.

Metallurgical Quality Coal. Coal with strong or moderately strong coking properties. *See* Coal.

Methane. A flammable gaseous hydrocarbon; a product of decomposition of organic matter or of the carbonization of coal; the basic constituent of natural gas.

Middle Distillates. Petroleum products (including kerosene, home heating oil, range oil, stove oil, and diesel fuel) which are heavier than gasoline but lighter than residual fuel.

Mines, Bureau of. An agency of the Department of the Interior responsible for overseeing the production of minerals and some fuels in the United States, enforcing health and safety rules in mining, studying and controlling the effect of mining on the environment and researching and developing mineral resources.

MMBD. One million barrels (42 gallons each) per day. A common unit of measure for petroleum consumption.

Monthly Energy Review. See 126, 136, 141-142.

Natural Gas. A gaseous hydrocarbon found in nature composed largely of methane. Most oil wells produce gas together with the crude oil ("wet" gas); some wells produce only wet gas, while others yield gas without the hydrocarbons that make it wet ("dry" gas). Wet gas is processed to recover its liquefiable hydrocarbons, leaving dry gas. *Natural Gas Liquids.* In FEA statistics, the residuals from drying wet gas; included are ethane, liquefied petroleum (LP) gases, natural gasoline, plant condensate, and minor quantities of finished products such as gasoline, special naphthas, jet fuel, kerosene, and distillate fuel oil. *Natural Gas Marketed Production.* In FEA statistics, the gross withdrawals from the ground, less gas used for repressuring and quantities vented and flared; gas volumes are reported at a base pressure of 14.73 pounds per square inch absolute at 60°F.

Allocation, 52-53
Industry structure, 17-19
Shortages of, 205-208
Statistics, 19
See Conservation; Emergency; Shortage; Stockpile.

Natural Resources, Department of. See 55-57.

Natural Resources and Energy Office of Department of Treasury. See 37.

New Crude Petroleum or New Oil. In FEA regulations, the volume of domestic crude petroleum produced which exceeds the base production control level for well.

Nuclear Electric Powerplant. One in which heat for raising steam is provided by nuclear fission rather than combustion of fossil fuels. *See* Atomic Power.

Nuclear Regulatory Commission. See 37, 53-54.

Oil Policy Committee. See 37.

Oil Shale. A rock containing kerogen, a mixture of solid hydrocarbons and other organic substances. Kerogen can be extracted in liquid form by heating the shale. Yields vary from 15 to 50 gallons of oil per ton of shale. Further refining can then convert the kerogen to gasoline and other fuels. Large oil shale deposits have been discovered in the U.S.

Old Oil or Old Crude Petroleum. See Controlled Crude Oil.

OPEC. The Organization of Petroleum Exporting Countries is an association of the world's largest oil producing and exporting countries. There are 12 full members: Abu Dhabi, Algeria, Ecuador, Indonesia, Iran, Iraq, Kuwait, Libya, Nigeria, Qatar, Saudi Arabia, and Venezuela. Gabon is an associate member. OPEC was formed in 1959 to protect and promote the members' economic and social interests.

Peak Shaving. See Load.

Petroleum. A class of naturally occurring materials (gaseous, liquid, or solid) composed of carbon and hydrogen and refined into fuels and petrochemicals.

Petroleum Allocation.

problems of, 89

State Office of, 63

See Allocation.

Petroleum Allocation Regulations. See 46-49

Adjustments, 48

Aviation, 48

Enforcement, 64

FEA/State Liaison Office, 47, 69

Retail Gasoline Stations, 49

Space Heating, 48

State Setaside, 47-48, 63, 69, 71-72

Supplier's Sources, 49

Supply, Requests for additional, 49, 71-72

Utilities, 48

Petroleum Coke. A solid residue of cracking, consisting mainly of carbon; used for production of carbon or graphite electrodes, structural graphite, motor brushes, dry cells, and so on. *Refined Petroleum Products.* Gasoline, kerosene, middle distillate (including Number 2 fuel oil), LPG, refined lubricating oils, diesel fuel, and so on

Allocation. *See* Petroleum Allocation

Industry structure, 16-17

Shortages, 211-212

Statistics, 16

See Conservation; Emergency; Shortage; Stockpile.

Plant Protection Fuel. In FEA regulations, the use of propane or butane in the minimum volume required (usually for space heating) to prevent physical harm to plant facilities or danger to plant personnel but not to maintain plant production.

Plutonium. A radioactive metallic element chemically similar to uranium found in pitchblend, useful as a fuel for nuclear reactors.

Power. The rate at which energy is made available or work is done. The faster work is done or the greater amount of work done in given time the greater the power. Measures of power include kilowatt hour, horsepower hour, Btu per hour, and so on.

Prices, Energy

Bibliography on, 26

Federal regulation of, 54

See under specific fuel.

Primary Sources. See Fuels, Primary and Secondary.

Primary Stocks. Stocks held at refineries, bulk terminals, in pipelines, and so on—not including secondary storage such as stocks held by jobbers, dealers, independent marketers, and consumers.

Prime Supplier. In FEA regulations, the supplier who makes the first sale of any allocated product subject to the state setaside.

Priority of Use. See Allocation.

Private Brander. A small oil company that markets petroleum products under its own brand; often products refined by others.

Production
  Bibliography on, 24
  Statistics, 11.

Project Independence. See 29, 39-43.

Propane. See Butane.

Quadrillion Btu or 1 Quad. 1 Quad-10^{15} (thousand trillion) Btu's.

Quintillion Btu or 1 Q. 1Q-10^{18} (million trillion) Btu's.

Rationing. See Allocation.

Reallocation. See Allocation; Energy Policy.

Reclamation, Bureau of. See 36.

Refined Products. In general usage, any refined petroleum products including motor gasoline, naphtha-type and kerosene-type jet fuel, liquefied petroleum gases, kerosene, distillate fuel oil, residual fuel oil, petrochemical feedstocks, special naphthas, lubricants, waxes, and asphalt. *Refined Products Domestic Demand.* In FEA statistics, the total domestic demand for refined petroleum products. *Refiner.* In FEA regulations, a firm which refines or substantially changes covered products. Also included are owners of covered products who contract to have them refined for sale. *Refinery.* In FEA regulations, those industrial plants, regardless of capacity, processing crude oil feedstock and manufacturing refined petroleum products, except petrochemical plants. *Refinery Gas.* In FEA regulations, a gas normally produced in the refining of crude oil, predominantly used for refinery fuel. *Refinery Switchover.* The change a refinery makes in product mix to help meet seasonal changes in demand for oil products.

Regulatory Policy, Energy. Bibliography on, 26.

Released Oil. In FEA regulations, oil from which price controls have been lifted.

Reseller. In FEA regulations, a wholesaler. *Reseller-retailer.* In FEA regulations, a wholesaler/retailer.

Reserves. The amount of energy resources expected to be recovered. *Reserve-Product Ratio.* The number of years it will take to use up known reserves at current production and consumption levels. *Dedicated-Reserves.* Reserves committed by their owner to a buyer through a long-term contract. *Prospective-Reserves.* Reserves from existing deposits that can reasonably be counted on to be available in the future. *Proved-Reserves.* Already-located reserves known to be recoverable with existing facilities, present technology, and at current cost and price levels. They are calculated anew each year. Proved reserves can be decreased by production abandonments, poor performance or price declines. Bibliography on, 23. *See* Supply. *See also* under specific fuels.

Residual Fuel Oil. The heavier higher heat content oils that remain after the distillate fuel oils and lighter hydrocarbons are boiled off in refinery operations.

Included are Nos. 5 and 6 oil, heavy diesel oil, Navy Special Oil, Bunker C oil, and acid sludge and pitch used as refiner fuels.

Resources. See Reserves

Retort. A vessel in which ore, coal or other substances are heated to extract gas, oil or other semi-refined fuels. *In Situ Retorting.* A process by which energy minerals (usually coal or oil shale) are fractured and retorted in place underground.

Royalty. Payment made to the mineral-rights owner for the right to produce. Payment is usually a percentage, often one-sixth to one-eighth of the actual production. In modern practice, the landowner almost always sells his royalty share to the producing company. However, he often retains the right to sell it separately if he can get a better price than offered by that company.

Scf (Standard cubic foot). A common measure of natural and synthetic gas (1 Scf = 28.3 liters).

Secondary Sources. See Fuels, Primary and Secondary sources.

Secondary Recovery. See Recovery.

Self Sufficiency, Energy. See Project Independence.

Severance Tax. A business tax paid to states by energy resource developers for producing energy minerals.

Shortage. A condition in which supply falls below demand. Discriminatory practices during, 88; effects of, 87-90; gasoline problems, 89; government action during, 88; impact on low income groups, 87-89; migrant problems, 89. *See* Demand; Stockpile; Supply.

SOPA. See Petroleum Allocation, State Office of.

State Setaside. An amount of fuel (currently 3 percent of the national petroleum supply) set aside by the Mandatory Petroleum Allocation Program for administration by the State Office of Petroleum Allocation. *See* Energy Policy, State.

Statistics, Energy. See 11; Bibliography on, 27.

Steam Coal. Coal that is suitable for generating steam as distinguished from that used for metallurgical processes.

Stockpiles. Stockpiles are inventories of energy, fuels, and so on used to maintain energy flows, to shave peaks or as a hedge against disruption of supply. *See* 107-108; conflicts with FEA regulations, 110-111. *Stockpiling.* Financial risks of, 42,108; Legal aspects of, 108-111; Model ordinance, 119-123. *See* Energy Policy, Local.

Storage. See Stockpile.

Stripper Well. A property whose average production does not exceed 10 barrels per day.

Subbituminous Coal. Coal of a rank intermediate between lignite and bituminous. *See* Coal.

Substitution. See 111-112; Conservation. *Substitute or Synthetic Natural Gas (SNG).* A substitute for natural gas generally produced from coal or oil.

Substitute Oil (SO). Syncrude: a substitute for petroleum derived from coal or oil shale.

Supply. Bibliography of projections, 22. *See* Energy Budget Report.

Syncrude. Any synthetic replacement for crude petroleum.
Synthoil. A clean synthetic oil derived from coal.

Tankwagon Price. See Dealer Tankwagon Price.
Tar Sand. Rock impregnated with bitumen or other heavy petroleum material that cannot be recovered by conventional petroleum recovery methods.
Taxes, Energy and. Bibliography on, 26.
Therm. 100,000 Btu's. *See* BTU.
Thermal Pollution. Pollution from adding heat to a natural water body or air shed often rendering that body unfit to maintain life in or near it and inducing climatic changes in the air shed.
Toll Enrichment. A proposed arrangement whereby privately owned uranium could be enriched in uranium-235 in government facilities upon payment of a service charge by the owners.
Total Energy System. A total energy system is a system for supplying the total energy needs (light, heat, electricity, mechanical, process heat, and so on) of a given user from a single source usually a small plant on the users' grounds.
Transportation. Bibliography on, 24.

Watt. A unit of electric power, equal to one ampere at one volt. Kilowatt— 1,000 watts. Megawatt—one million watts.
Weather. Weekly Weather and Crop Bulletin, 130-131. *See* Degree Day formulas.
Wellhead Price. Crude oil, natural gas, and condensate are priced as they come from the well; this is the "wellhead price" or the "field price," and is the price at which these fuels are valued for tax purposes.
Wildcat. A well drilled in a locality that has not previously produced crude oil or gas.
Winterization. See 90.

ZEG (Zero Energy Growth). See 9.

About the Author

Edward H. Allen received his education at Stanford University, Swathmore College, and the University of Pennsylvania. He held a post at the Foreign Policy Research Institute of Philadelphia, Pennsylvania before joining the faculty of Utah State University where he directs an energy policy research and consulting group.